Kate

The Swim Coaching Bible

Dick Hannula

Nort Thornton

Editors

Human Kinetics

Library of Congress Cataloging-in-Publication Data

The swim coaching bible / Dick Hannula, Nort Thornton, editors.
    p. cm.
  Includes bibliographical references.
  ISBN 0-7360-3646-6
  1. Swimming--Coaching. I. Hannula, Dick, 1928- II. Thornton, Nort, 1933-

GV837.65.S95 2001
797.2'1--dc21

00-054241

ISBN: 0-7360-3646-6

Developmental Editor: Julie Rhoda; **Assistant Editor and Copyeditor:** Carla Zych; **Proofreader:** Bob Replinger; **Graphic Designer:** Robert Reuther; **Graphic Artists:** Kimberly Maxey and Brian McElwain; **Photo Manipulation;** Brian McElwain; **Photo Manager:** Clark Brooks; **Cover Designer**: Keith Blomberg; **Photographer (cover):** ©SportsChrome East/West; **Photographer (interior):** Please see page viii for credits; **Art Manager:** Craig Newsom; **Illustrator:** Roberto Sabas; **Printer:** United Graphics

Human Kinetics books are available at special discounts for bulk purchase. Special editions or book excerpts can also be created to specification. For details, contact the Special Sales Manager at Human Kinetics.

Printed in the United States of America

10 9 8 7 6 5 4

Human Kinetics
Web site: www.HumanKinetics.com

United States: Human Kinetics
P.O. Box 5076
Champaign, IL 61825-5076
800-747-4457
e-mail: humank@hkusa.com

Canada: Human Kinetics
475 Devonshire Road, Unit 100
Windsor, ON N8Y 2L5
800-465-7301 (in Canada only)
e-mail: orders@hkcanada.com

Europe: Human Kinetics
107 Bradford Road
Stanningley
Leeds LS28 6AT, United Kingdom
+44 (0)113 255 5665
e-mail: hk@hkeurope.com

Australia: Human Kinetics
57A Price Avenue
Lower Mitcham, South Australia 5062
08 8277 1555
e-mail: liaw@hkaustralia.com

New Zealand: Human Kinetics
Division of Sports Distributors NZ Ltd.
P.O. Box 300 226 Albany
North Shore City, Auckland
0064 9 448 1207
e-mail: blairc@hknewz.com

THE SWIM COACHING BIBLE

Dick Hannula and Nort Thornton, Editors

Endorsed by the World Swimming Coaches Association

CONTENTS

ACKNOWLEDGMENTS

Dick Hannula and Nort Thornton would like to acknowledge and thank all the chapter authors of *The Swim Coaching Bible* for contributing their great knowledge and experience. All of them were willing to share their talents and to give back to the entire swimming community. Their time and effort made this book a success.

PHOTO CREDITS

INTRODUCTION

Dick Hannula and Nort Thornton

What has brought the greatest change in swim coaching over the past 50 years or so? It would have to be the increase in knowledge made available through various reference sources for swim coaches.

We can remember being fascinated, as young swimmers and then as young coaches, by what the more famous American swimming coaches—Bob Kiphuth of Yale, Matt Mann of Michigan, Mike Peppe of Ohio State, and many others—had to say about swimming and training. We would read and listen to everything we could find about the training philosophies of the great coaches—George Haines, Peter Daland, Don Gambril, and Doc Counsilman—and could hardly wait for *Swimming World* magazine to arrive each month so we could read the "How They Train" columns. One of us even corresponded with the great Australian coach Forbes Carlile at his Ryde Club in Australia, in an effort to soak up every bit of swimming knowledge possible.

Books, clinics, and magazine articles have always been great sources for cutting-edge coaching information. In swimming, there is a great willingness on the part of coaches to share information. Coaches in all the leading swimming nations have the attitude that as each swimmer gets faster the expectation level of all swimmers is raised, that in this way all of swimming will get faster. This attitude was apparent when we approached potential contributors to this book and asked each to write a specific chapter. Every coach accepted on the first request. The advancement of the quality of coaching was their primary consideration.

When we began to talk about the possibility of putting this book together, we were very excited at the prospect of having the top coaches of today write a chapter on the topic that they are best known for. Each of the coaches who contributed to this book is tremendously successful in his or her own right; each does many things well and could easily put out an entire book filled with knowledge gained from his or her experiences. The beauty of this book is that it features an all-star cast—a smorgasbord of superstars.

INTRODUCTION

The Swim Coaching Bible is a compilation of the best written material of some of the world's most successful swim coaches into a one-source reference book. We have gathered the best available writing on topics of importance to produce a work that we hope will serve as a guidepost for swim coaches around the world as well as an invaluable source for swimmers and parents who want to know more about competitive swimming.

The coach-contributors were given free rein within their assigned topics. They were free to develop that topic in whatever way they felt necessary to attain the best results. The overlap of some of the contributors' information was considered a necessary consequence of allowing many coaches to share their roads to success. There is a tremendous amount of individual and collective knowledge in this book. If you use this book as a reference, we are certain that you will find what you are looking for today and will revisit the book many times in the future for information and opinions on totally different topics.

The contributors we've selected offer a diverse assortment of views, experiences, and nationalities. Most of the chapter authors coach in the United States. Three contributors—Bill Sweetenham (chapter 7), Bruce Mason (chapter 9), and Doug Frost (chapter 17)—hail from Australia. Deryk Snelling (chapter 10) has coaching roots in both Canada and Great Britain.

The wisdom and experience of the contributors has been proven by the success of their swimmers. Almost all the authors have either coached Olympic gold medalists or have acquired gold medals themselves as swimmers. Richard Quick, Mike Bottom, Doug Frost, and Jon Urbanchek have coached individual Olympic champions as recently as the Sydney Olympics.

We've organized *The Swim Coaching Bible* into five sections. Part I establishes priorities and principles necessary for the foundation of any swimming program. Richard Quick leads off in chapter 1 with "Believing in Belief." One of the most successful coaches in the world, the Stanford University women's coach and many time US Olympic coach gives his distinct insight on the necessity of belief in order to succeed. We've watched Richard work his coaching magic as a manager of an Olympic team and as a Pan-Pacific assistant coach. This is a must-read chapter for every coach and swimmer.

Jean Freeman, the women's coach at the University of Minnesota, is one of the most successful coaches in the Big Ten Conference. She is well known for her ability to make the swimming experience fun and to instill a lifelong love of the sport in her swimmers. Her philosophy and methods are the subject of chapter 2.

Peter Daland, retired coach of the University of Southern California and two-time US Olympic head coach, is one of the most respected men in swimming. Dick Hannula knows this firsthand, as two of his sons swam for Peter at USC. He is well qualified to speak on coaching with integrity, and his work on the drug committee of the World Swim Coaches' Association has contributed greatly to the control of performance-enhancing drugs in swimming.

Part II includes five chapters about directing a program to its full potential. In chapter 4 John Leonard, swim coach and executive director of the American Swim Coaches' Association, discusses how to adapt your coaching approach to meet the needs of the entire spectrum of swimmers. He specifically addresses differences in age, ability, and gender as well as the particular concerns of high school and college teams.

Jack Bauerle coaches at the University of Georgia and was a US Olympic team coach in 2000. He provides many insights into administering and marketing a successful program in chapter 5.

Chapter 6 deals with developing a successful team. Skip Kenney, coach at Stanford University and US Olympic head coach in 1996, gets to the very heart of this subject. Skip's college teams have won the NCAA Championship title many times. His Pac 10 Championship meet titles extend over 20 consecutive years, surpassing John Wooden's consecutive Pac 10 Championship record in basketball at UCLA. This is one of the most phenomenal records in collegiate swimming.

Chapter 7 is written by legendary Australian swim coach Bill Sweetenham. Having served many times as the Australian Olympic coach and having spent the past several years as the National Youth Development Coach in Australia, he is now taking over the position of National Team Coach for Great Britain. Bill's experience and knowledge of swimming is unsurpassed, and he covers the subject of maximizing swim talent clearly and specifically in his chapter.

Creating an effective practice session and season is the subject of part III, and the three related chapters cover this topic comprehensively. Jill Sterkel covers long- and short-range planning in chapter 8. As a former world-record holder, four-time Olympic swimmer, and the current women's coach at the University of Texas, Jill brings great experience to her chapter.

In chapter 9, Dr. Bruce Mason discusses putting science—biomechanics, physiotherapy, altitude training, and more—into practice. He is one of the most qualified swimming biomechanists in the world and serves the Australian Institute of Sport, the Australian Olympic team, and (as a director) the International Society of Biomechanics in Sports.

Deryk Snelling writes on the art of coaching in chapter 10. He has coached successfully internationally for decades. Dick first knew Deryk as the coach of the Vancouver Canadian Dolphins; Deryk had then, as he does now, an uncanny ability to get more out of his swimmers than their obvious talent might indicate. His insights on the art of coaching are highly valued.

Part IV concentrates on teaching stroke technique, including starts, turns, and finishes. Each chapter in this section is written by coaches who have brought something unique and special to the teaching of technique. Rick Demont, former world-record holder in the 400 meter and 1,500-meter freestyle, covers two different freestyle techniques in chapter 11.

Dick Hannula discusses the finer points of backstroke technique in chapter 12. Dick focuses on the 3 R's of backstroke and looks closely at the unique style of Lenny Krayzelburg.

Pablo Morales is a former world-record holder and gold medalist in the 100-meter butterfly who now coaches at San Jose State. He has written clearly and with great feeling about sharpening technique for better butterfly in chapter 13.

Dave Salo has had phenomenal success with breaststrokers as a club coach and was an assistant coach for the United States at the Sydney Olympics. His greatest breaststroke success thus far has been Amanda Beard's performance at the Atlanta Olympics. At the Northwest Swim Coaches' Clinic a few years ago Dave gave an exceptionally comprehensive and understandable presentation on breaststroke technique. His chapter 14 covers the same topic in similar fashion.

John Trembley has continued the tradition of great racing starts and turns that the University of Tennessee is know for. He is unquestionably the best clinic speaker and writer on the technical aspects of starts and turns in swimming today. He was a natural choice to write chapter 15 on starts, turns, and finishes.

The final section, part V, covers the training necessary to achieve optimal performance. The list of coach-contributors is once again most impressive in terms of the success they've had with their swimmers. Mike Bottom, who swam at USC and now coaches with Nort Thornton at the University of California at Berkeley, specializes in sprint training (chapter 16). Mike's training program for sprinters is highly specific and very unique. His unconventional program has been very successful, producing NCAA champions and three of the five fastest swimmers in the world in 2000—including the two 50-meter freestyle gold medalists in Sydney, Gary Hall Jr. and Anthony Ervin.

Doug Frost coaches the great Ian Thorpe of Australia. In chapter 17, on middle-distance training, Doug details his philosophy and training methods. We are very proud to have him as one of the contributors to this book.

Dick Jochums is an innovator as well as a practical coach who has always believed in specificity over yardage. His swimmers have achieved great success, including Olympic gold. He shares his philosophy on freestyle distance training in chapter 18.

Eddie Reese, who wrote chapter 19 on backstroke and butterfly sprint training, is one of the great communicators in coaching. Eddie has that rare ability to make a difference. A great storyteller and a great leader, he continues to stay at or near the top of the collegiate championship scene.

Bill Rose has coached in both Canada and the United States, and is presently coaching the Mission Viejo Swim Club. Author of chapter 20 on backstroke and butterfly 200-meter training, he has coached top-ranked back and butterfly swimmers in the 200 event for many years. He continues to be one of the more successful elite coaches in the United States today.

Jon Urbanchek is known for his down-to-earth style and his ability to identify with his swimmers. His program at the University of Michigan is responsible for a steady stream of Olympic champions, including world-record holder Mike Barrowman in the 200-meter breaststroke. While he writes about breaststroke training in chapter 21, he could have also written on the 200 butterfly, the event his athlete Tom Malchow won in Sydney; the 400 IM, the event in which Tom Dolan, a former University of Michigan swimmer, has twice been Olympic champion; or distance freestyle, in which another of his athletes, Chris Thompson, won the bronze medal in the 1,500 meters at Sydney. We are very pleased that Jon has provided this excellent chapter on training for the breaststroke.

Dick Shoulberg is a walking bundle of enthusiasm. He loves swimming and the swimmers who are willing to do the work to be successful. After 31 years at the Germantown Academy, Dick continues to turn out Olympians. In chapter 22, he writes about individual medley training, a topic with which he is quite familiar. His successes in the IM include a world-record holder as well as several Olympians and medal winners.

David Marsh has been quite successful at Auburn University, having won national championship titles in both men's and women's swimming. He served as an assistant coach for the 2000 US Olympic team.

His Auburn relay teams have been awesome, and he was a great choice for chapter 23 on relay training.

One of the great innovators in swimming, Randy Reese has always been willing to try new approaches. His unique ideas of developing strength and power while in the water have been most successful. When Randy speaks, as he does in chapter 24 on power training, smart coaches listen.

Our final chapter (25) on preparing to excel in competitions is written by legendary coach Don Gambril. Don coached five US Olympic teams and produced world-record holders almost from the start of his career. He is one of the most successful swimming coaches ever; he knows what it takes to excel and can talk effectively and convincingly to swimmers. As a coach, he could tell swimmers what the world record was, what it would take to break that record, and that he believed that the swimmer could do it. We think you'll find that Don closes this book on a positive, inspiring note.

As we put this material together, we found it fascinating reading and could not wait to use the information in our coaching. We believe this is exactly the way you will feel when you delve into the chapters we have collected here. Whether you are actively coaching or swimming, or are simply taken with the sport of swimming, you have many hours of interesting reading ahead. We urge coaches and swimmers to read *The Swim Coaching Bible* and then to keep it handy for future reference and motivation.

PART
I

Establishing Priorities and Principles

CHAPTER ONE

Believing in Belief

Richard Quick

How could Dara Torres—at age 33 and having been out of swimming for seven years—return to the sport in 2000 after only 14 months of training and swim significantly faster than ever before in each of her events, setting two American records and taking five Olympic medals (two of them gold on world-record relays)?

How could American 200-meter butterflyer Misty Hyman drop from 2:09.2 (her lifetime best) at the 2000 Olympic trials to 2:05.88 just 30 days later to beat world-record holder and defending Olympic champion Susie O'Neill, breaking O'Neill's six-year winning streak in the 200 butterfly?

How do several women, and thousands of men and boys, now swim the 200-meter freestyle faster than Don Schollander ever did? Recognized as one of the most talented swimmers ever to put on a Speedo, Don was the first man to break 2:00 in the 200-meter freestyle. He had a perfect stroke and swam in the best swimming environment possible in the 1960s, the Santa Clara Swim Club. He was coached by the greatest coach of all time, George Haines, who coached more Olympians, more gold medalists, and more world-record holders than any coach in history. How is it that today, swimming in less than perfect environments, guided by coaches less proficient than Haines, so many swimmers can achieve faster times than Don Schollander did?

The common denominator among Dara Torres, Misty Hyman, and all the swimmers who swim faster than Don Schollander is a deep core *belief* that they can accomplish what at one time appeared to most people to be impossible.

Belief Makes the Extraordinary Ordinary

Have you ever noticed that once something extraordinary is accomplished it becomes more ordinary? Why is that? When one human being, believing that he or she will be successful, prepares to achieve and then accomplishes the extraordinary, it seems to give the rest of us permission to believe we might be able to accomplish (or surpass) the same goal. The feat becomes feasible, attainable, and therefore more ordinary. Our belief system is expanded beyond the previous limits we may have placed on it.

Thirteen months before Misty Hyman's extraordinary upset of Susie O'Neill in the 2000 Olympic 200-meter butterfly event, Misty finished a very disappointing third in the 200 fly at the Pan-Pacific Championships in the Olympic pool in Sydney. Susie O'Neill dominated that race, nearly breaking Mary T. Meagher's long-standing world record, and beating Misty by at least four seconds. Misty was discouraged and began to doubt that she had what it takes to be successful.

I met Misty in the long hallway on the way to the warm-down pool. (This is the same place I would meet her to celebrate her great Olympic victory 13 months later.) I put my arm around her, and as we walked to the warm-down pool I told her she was the only swimmer in the world who could beat Susie in the 200 fly in the Olympic Games. I said that although it might seem impossible after such a poor performance I believed she could win the Olympic gold medal in 2000. Then I told Misty that it didn't matter what I believed she could do if she did not believe she could do it. At that moment Misty began to believe. She began to believe that if she swam the ideal race at the ideal time, she'd have a chance.

Over the next 12 months as she prepared for the Olympic trials, did doubts ever creep in? Absolutely, but she knew that her belief in her ability and in the possibility of putting together the ideal race at the ideal time could lead to the extraordinary. Did she have setbacks? Absolutely; she was beaten in the NCAA Championships in the 200 fly, she suffered continuously from allergies that resulted in a chronic lack of energy, and she dealt with a few illnesses that year. But Misty's belief system kept giving her hope. Believe in belief. Belief in yourself and in your goals is the basis for extraordinary performance.

Belief Brings Commitment

Belief in yourself and in your goals facilitates the attitude that you will do whatever it takes. Belief allows you to commit to your goal as if you cannot fail. Dara Torres had a belief that she could make the Olympic team as an alternate on the 400 freestyle relay when she called me to ask if I would be willing to coach her. My first question to her was, "Will you do whatever it takes to be successful?" Her answer was yes. From that moment on, Dara's belief in herself and in her goals encouraged her to pack three years of training into 13 months. Her training included up to eight hours a day of water training, weight training, spinning, running, Tae Bo, resistive stretching, dryland exercises, cutting edge nutrition and supplementation, deep-tissue massage, and becoming familiar with "awareness thinking." Dara's belief system allowed her to train and to commit to her goals as if she could not fail.

Believe in belief. Belief in yourself and in your goals allows you to set new goals as you approach or accomplish your previous goals. At first Dara believed that she could only make the relay; as she improved she began to believe that she could make it in an individual event, then in more than one individual event. Eventually she began to believe that she could win an individual Olympic medal. Finally she came to believe that she could win an individual gold medal. Dara's growing belief in herself led to five medals in the 2000 Olympic Games, more than any other swimmer. She won three bronze medals, the first individual Olympic medals in her storied, four-time U.S. Olympic team member career. Believe in yourself and in your goals; grow and act as if you cannot fail.

True goals are products of an individual's belief system. A true goal can only exist if an individual believes it is possible. A true goal is something that you absolutely believe you can and will accomplish. It is more than something you write down, something you *hope* you can reach, or something a coach or a parent wants you to do. A true goal is something you know you will accomplish.

A true goal is so much a part of your core belief system that it affects every activity you do that is even remotely related to that goal. It keeps you from doing anything that might hinder your success. It allows you to act, to train, and to compete as if you cannot fail. Your belief system cannot conceive of failure; it will not let you fall short of your goal. A true goal is not just a wish or a hope. A true goal will be accomplished. Believe in belief.

Most people sell themselves short. Most people need permission to accomplish something. Most of the swimmers who now swim faster than Don Schollander swam in the 1960s are not considered the most talented swimmers around, and most are not as well trained or as well coached as Don was. Most of these swimmers would not have been able to swim that fast in the 1960s even if they'd had the expert coaching and the modern, scientific training available today. Why? They would not have believed it was possible. Until Don Schollander broke the barrier, no one thought a human could swim that fast.

Belief Gives Permission Beyond Limits

Most of us have to wait for someone else to prove to us that something can be accomplished. We need permission. The greatest athletes, and for that matter, the greatest innovators in any field, say, "This will surely be done in the future; why can't I be the one to do it now?" They do not need permission to accomplish feats that others think are unbelievable or impossible. Their belief systems are so strong that what seems extraordinary to most people seems attainable to them.

By far, the most important thing to believe in is yourself. True belief in yourself allows you to act as if you cannot fail. However, sometimes circumstances beyond your control will prevent you from accomplishing your goals, no matter how much you believe in them. This is disappointing, but not devastating. True belief in yourself means that your self-worth is not dependent upon your accomplishments or your possessions.

Jenny Thompson is one of the greatest swimmers in the world. She broke the world record in the 100-meter freestyle in 1992 and in the 100-meter butterfly in 1999. Throughout her career, she has won many world championships, national championships, and Olympic medals, including eight gold medals in relays. In fact, Jenny has more gold medals than any other female swimmer in history, but none of her golds are in individual events. Jenny's goal was to win an individual gold medal in her final Olympic Games appearance in Sydney. She did not accomplish that goal. Certainly she was disappointed, but her belief in herself does not allow her to measure herself by whether or not she received an individual gold medal in the Olympic Games. While Jenny celebrates her accomplishments in swimming, her many awards, her degree from Stanford, and her acceptance to Columbia University Medical School, her self-worth is not measured by those things either. Jenny has a deeply rooted belief in herself as a human being that transcends what she has or has not done and what she does or does not have.

Belief in yourself and in the possibility of success is the most important requirement for living an extraordinary life. Believe in belief. Believe in yourself and the best of the world will come to you—and like Dara, Misty, and Jenny, you will be prepared to receive it. Don't sell yourself short. You do not require permission to do the extraordinary.

Summary

- Extraordinary swimmers have a core belief that they can accomplish what others believe to be impossible.
- Belief will carry you through difficulties and setbacks.
- Belief allows you to commit to your goals.
- Act as if you cannot fail.

CHAPTER TWO

Putting Fun Into the Swimming Experience

Jean Freeman

Remember why you joined your first swim team? Most likely you enjoyed being in the water and thought swimming was a fun way to be with friends. I began swimming because the kids in my neighborhood were swimmers and said it was fun. I joined my first team at age eight and have been involved with competitive swimming ever since—for over 40 years. I am still enjoying the sport, possibly more now than ever. Many things have made the sport fun for me. I hope that as I share some of my ideas on swimming you will discover some ways to add fun and enthusiasm for the sport to your coaching and your program

As I look back on what led me to become a swim coach, I realize that I have wanted to teach ever since I was a young child. Teaching and coaching have much in common; in many ways coaches are teachers, too. In the course of my development as a coach, I have watched teachers interact with their classes and have tried to understand how they achieve rapport with their students. I have found that the best teacher-student relationships come from an understanding based on trust and respect, an understanding that takes time and consistency to build. The same is true of coach-athlete relationships. The best coaches nurture small successes every day and celebrate them along the way. This positive reinforcement goes a long way toward building trust and respect; other swimmers on the team notice that attention and encouragement are given to those who strive to improve and to do well. Success may be built on good attendance, learning key technique or competition concepts from a disappointment, making a new friend, or swimming faster. Coaches must be aware of the physical, mental, and emotional development level of each age group they work with, as well as any pertinent economic factors affecting their swimmers, so that they can tailor their approach accordingly.

The swim coach is in a great situation. Most people who join teams expect the coach to be in charge. They expect the coach to help them become better swimmers. The key is to figure out how to get swimmers from where they are to the next level of development—in technique, conditioning, discipline, social skills—as well as teaching them appropriate competitive attitudes, how to deal with failures, how to strive for success, and how to celebrate. I am thankful for my education major in college because of what it taught me about planning. It was drilled into me that each session should have a clear purpose and a clear plan. The importance of continually evaluating and attempting to improve the purpose and plan was also emphasized.

Another important concept that I learned through my training as an educator is the necessity of establishing clear communication. Communication among coaches, swimmers, and parents is critical for any swim coach. Whether it is accomplished through monthly newsletters, web pages, e-mail, or seasonal parent meetings, this communication not only serves to keep everyone involved in the program informed, it also helps coaches find out what their swimmers think is fun and what they are passionate about. This kind of communication helps swimmers *want* to come to practice rather than feeling they *have* to come to practice.

The following are some observations I have made that I apply to my everyday coaching to ensure that my athletes have a fun, rewarding swimming experience that allows them to continue to grow. These observations relate to five basic responsibilities of a coach: building confidence, nurturing self-esteem, learning from competition, developing team leaders, and planning for growth. Throughout this chapter I will expand on each of these responsibilities and offer ways to approach them.

Make Swimming Fun!

- Fun is necessary in all worthwhile activities.
- Swimmers will stay in the sport if they continue to have fun.
- Athletes perform their best when they are having fun.
- Champions go fast because they are having fun.
- Self-esteem and self-confidence are the two most important gifts we can nurture in others and ourselves.
- Welcome everyone to your program, wherever they are in life's journey.
- Help your swimmers discover their passion and "go for it."
- Enthusiasm is important on a daily basis.
- Maintain a positive attitude toward everything you do.
- Forgiveness is necessary everyday.
- Listen to swimmers, to staff, and to parents.
- Fear of failure is natural. Learn from it and move on.
- Celebrate success and give thanks for it along the way.

In order to reach your goals, you must begin with the end in mind.

Building Confidence Through Fun

What is fun? How do we know what will be fun for the swimmers we are working with? Fun is often age specific, but it is important for coaches to remember that adults as well as children need to "play" and to have fun. Practice activities should focus on developmental concepts and on incorporating fun into these concepts. As you move from group to group within a team, respect where each group is developmentally and the skills and techniques they have already learned. Here are some concepts I think need to be emphasized for particular age groups:

- Age 6 to 8: Having fun, building confidence, and stroke technique
- Age 9 to 10: Learning what a team is, learning teamwork, and swimming relays.
- Age 11 to 12: Understanding conditioning, beginning goals, self-esteem, and cooperation skills
- Age 13 to 14: Improving social skills, acceptance of others, and coordination of high school activities
- Age 15 to 16: Specializing in events, swim training, and dryland training
- Age 17 to 20: Balancing college or career goals with team and individual pursuits
- Age 21 and up: Balancing swimming with career and life goals

All ages should keep reinforcing the skills they've already learned. I've seen coaches move swimmers up a group level and not keep any of the stroke drills from the swimmer's previous group level. This can cause the swimmer to become uncomfortable, lose confidence, and drop out of the sport. Instead, when moving swimmers up into a higher group, coaches should retain some of the swimmer's old routine and introduce a few new skills at a time.

Younger swimmers need to have fun and to gain confidence in themselves and in their swimming skills. From there, they can branch out and realize the benefits of being on a team. Small rewards can help inspire teamwork along the way. For example, I like to give swimmers in the lane that starts practice on time a special reward, such as being captains of the relays for that day or deciding what stroke the next set will be. I also like to reward younger swimmers as a group for working well together. Create small groups by stroke, by car pool, or by age to get them working together. Today's more mobile society doesn't provide children with the same opportunities children of the past had to develop loyalty toward one another. So it is especially important to create practice groups that encourage cooperation and loyalty.

As the swimmers get older and more skilled, turn their conditioning workouts into a game. See who can control pulse rate or stroke rate most consistently during specific sets. Have swimmers guess their times prior to particular sets and see who is the best in each lane at calculating the margin of error. I have my swimmers swim a 6 × 100 set this way. First the swimmers guess the time they will meet, then they swim the 100 trying to match their goal time. Once they touch the wall, they tell the coach their goal time, and the coach tells them their actual time. Then they calculate the margin of error (the first one is a "gimme" and doesn't count toward the margin of error). After 3 × 100, we compare margin of error for athletes in each lane in order to enhance competition. After 6 × 100, we see who the lane winner is and who is the best overall that day. The winner can choose what stroke the next set will be or be a captain of the relays. During taper we use this set and let the swimmers go any speed they wish. They generally get caught up in the game, and it becomes a good way to get some yardage in without the athletes' being too nervous.

Another fun exercise I use at the beginning of the season, usually during the first week of practice, is a set I call "social kicking." This set consists of 25s or 50s of kicking with a board. Swimmers are put into groups of two to kick together while talking to each other about their summer; each swimmer changes partners every 25 or 50. The purpose is to make sure each swimmer talks with each of their teammates and doesn't exclude anyone. This helps the shy team members to talk with more people. It's far different than kicking for conditioning, but it works well as a warm-up and helps to break down any cliques that otherwise might not talk with swimmers outside their group.

There are many other ways to ensure fun during practice. Some coaches are very creative in their workouts. I try to stay up on new ideas by attending at least one coaching clinic a year. I have attended several of Debbie Potts' talks at American Swimming Coaches Association (ASCA) conferences and highly recommend her book *Drills & Games: A Fun Way to Run a Practice* (ASCA: 800-356-2722). She provides many creative ideas. Here are some ideas for coaches of all levels:

- Add one new thing to your pool each season, be it a record board, a bulletin board, or backstroke flags. Don't get pool blindness; jazz it up!
- Celebrate birthdays and holidays at the pool. Incorporate the celebration into your workouts. If it is Suzie's birthday and she is 10, do 10 repeats of Suzie's favorite stroke.
- Set up a system whereby swimmers can earn a letter jacket, or T-shirt to enhance team spirit. Establish guidelines and a progression of clearly defined steps for team members to follow.
- Encourage swimmers to wear team caps, jackets and other items to

workouts as well as meets. Team apparel helps develop team pride and respect.

- Create an annual picnic or awards ceremony to celebrate individual progress; recognize each swimmer in a positive way. Meet away from the pool for some special fun activity—biking, rides at an amusement park, whatever your swimmers would enjoy.

- Take one team bus trip a year. Friendships are made, and independence from family blossoms, during travel. Set up activities to prevent swimmers from getting into trouble. Recruit volunteer chaperones for these trips. Be sure to rotate parent chaperones from year to year so that all the kids have a chance to gain independence.

I have coached college for the last 27 years, so my idea of fun has been shaped by my work with this age group. I believe in games and play, but I focus more on helping student-athletes feel good about themselves and about our team process. Here is a list of items we have added to our program to keep everyone challenged and to keep the fun alive:

- Welcome picnics when the swimmers move into campus—We invite the men's and women's teams, and student-athletes invite whoever helped them move. It's a fun, social way to get the year started.

- A Big Sister program run by our captains—This program begins the summer before the new team members arrive. It includes letters, e-mails, and phone calls to help them get acquainted before they arrive and to questions about what students will need while they're at college.

- Bike rides to get to know the area—We give swimmers a tour of the Twin Cities, the lakes, and the bike paths. Student-athletes are more likely to enjoy their new environment if they know how to get around.

- All-sports pentathlons—We encourage our team council to have social, athletic events that include all the sports teams. It can be a lot fun.

- An athletic booth at our state fair—We invite children up to the stage to meet our athletes. The athletes talk about themselves and their sports over a microphone. They show Olympic medals, awards, or take pictures. It is a great role-modeling experience. Each day one sport volunteers and is featured.

- Inner Circle breakfast or dinner—Each month our women's athletic department hosts a breakfast or dinner at which the athletic director gives a five minute report, a head coach and a student-athlete or two are interviewed, and an alum talks about what he or she has gained from his or her experience at the University of Minnesota.

The event ends with "Brag-a-Buck," where attendees can contribute a buck and say whatever they want. It's a great time for thankyous. A local media person always emcees it, which helps encourage media interest in our program.

- 3.0 cookouts or dinners—We celebrate all swimmers whose grade point averages are above a 3.0 and give the 4.0 students some special recognition, such as being served first.
- A wall of fame—Started by the swimmers and divers in their locker room to celebrate individual success in all areas of life, this creation can be used for new internships, dean's list, or anything.
- Team movies—We get together to watch sport-related, inspirational movies—*Fire on the Track: The Steve Prefontaine Story, Without Limits, The Mighty Ducks*, and so on.

One of the most rewarding events of each season is our end-of-the-year awards banquet. Our captains are in charge of music, a slide show, funny awards, and introducing our guest and the head table. Our assistant coach, Terry Nieszner, is in charge of reserving the restaurant and related details, but her real talents lie in being able to make the nicest, most meaningful comments about each student-athlete at the banquet. By turns, we have each swimmer stand and face his or her peers, family and friends. Being honored in this way gives the swimmers a great feeling to take into their next season or into their years as faithful alums.

Every year we celebrate our alums at homecoming by having an alumni swim meet. It is a co-ed meet with mostly 25s, 50s, and 100s. Many alums come back, and we try to make sure that they have a good time and feel welcome. We arrange events for their families, picnics, relay races in the park, and so on. We have nametags at the meets so people can find one another. Our team knows that this is an important weekend. We tell stories about our alums the week before to get them in the mood. We introduce our current team members to the alums, and we encourage them to mingle and join in the fun. This gives our swimmers the message that they will be welcomed back in the future. People want to feel needed, wanted, and respected.

Nurturing Self-Esteem

I believe self-esteem is the single most powerful force in our lives. The way we feel about ourselves affects every aspect of who we are and the kind of relationships we have. Coaches must look in the mirror and make sure they are happy with who they are. The happier and healthier the coach, the better the coach. The best gift coaches can give athletes is the ability to nurture their own self-esteem, but coaches must have it themselves before they can give it.

I try to make sure that everyone on our staff is on the same page in this area. I encourage them to use at least one of the following self-esteem builders every day.

- Use body language that is inviting and pleasant; a smile goes a long way. Be on deck when swimmers arrive; smile and say hello to them by name. Interacting positively during practice is critical. Sometimes this can nip poor behavior in the bud.

- Give a personalized comment such as, "You looked good yesterday in practice," or celebrate a swimmer's good set in front of other team members.

- Show enthusiasm for each person on the team. We all want to feel needed, wanted, and appreciated, no matter what age we are.

- If you need to change a swimmer's behavior, give the correction along with a compliment on something that the swimmer is doing well. The earlier in practice the correction is made, the better.

- Encourage swimmers to aim higher or to move to the next level. Let them know they are ready.

- Use a respectful tone of voice.

- Give compliments daily, not just during taper.

- Let team members know they make a difference. The team is better because of each one of them.

- Encourage group work and teamwork.

- Encourage swimmers to thank others for racing them in workout.

- Encourage swimmers to cheer others on daily.

- Learn to forgive mistakes and move on. Don't dwell on a poor performance or bad behavior.

- Teach swimmers to learn what they can from mistakes or problems and to expect better in the future. For example, if a swimmer has a bad turn, point out how he or she can do it better by building speed into the wall.

- Acknowledge risk-taking, as individuals and as a team, and celebrate it.

- Have a five-minute meeting each day to acknowledge some successes of the day before. Ask others to share their dreams or successes. This can be done during stretching.

- Assess the goals and accomplishments of your swimmers weekly. Use bulletin boards, web pages, and pictures. Celebrate good attendance and promptness, new skills learned, sharing, volunteerism, races won, and improved times at practices and meets.
- Set up practices so each person can experience success.

Another important way to nurture self-esteem in your swimmers is to have them face their fears. Fear is a natural response that will never go away as long as an athlete continues to stretch and grow. But if the fear isn't faced, it can become a strong demotivator. It drains energy. Procrastinating in facing it can be paralyzing and can cause a swimmer to miss out on potential growth and improvement. The most effective way to deal with fear is to tackle it head on. Go out and do what you are afraid to do; then you have taken care of that fear.

One way to help a team face their fears is to talk about fear with them and to have them share stories of their own fears. I may plant a seed by telling a story about a fear I've overcome or by leading off with someone else who will talk positively about fear. Pushing through fear is less frightening than living with fear. Swimmers can help one another understand this.

Another good way to have swimmers face their fear is to include a set of intervals that they have never done and to have them set up goal times that they have to achieve in this set. Tell them a day in advance so that they have time to get a bit anxious, and then hold them accountable for their results. Conclude the sets by talking about what the swimmers learned from doing them. I use these sets every so often to help our team handle challenges.

One set we do every three weeks or so is a set of goal 50s. The athletes first warm up for about an hour, then do three sets of 10×50 on 1:30 with an easy 200 after each set of 10. We use goal times for each athlete starting with the time of their second, third, and fourth 50 of a 200 from a meet. If the athletes make their goal times for all 30, they can cool down and go home. If not, they stay until they make 30. They can also use one or more teammates to help them make up the number they missed. If a swimmer uses teammates, each one needs to make their own goal times for it to count for the person who missed. So if someone misses six, he or she could get two teammates and each of the three could swim 2×50. If all three swimmers make their own goals, that would equal six 50s and they could all cool down. The group effort is helpful in reinforcing the concept that swimmers can count on their teammates for support and encouragement.

Revise the goal times right after practice. I try to set the time faster every three weeks unless the swimmer has missed some. I like to see them make 30 of 30, but it's important to tighten up the goals for the more experienced swimmers. Remember, you can learn a lot from failing. Our staff will generally drop goals 0.2 or 0.5 seconds every three weeks. We ask swimmers during their easy 200 how many they have made, to help them with accountability and to foster communication between coach and swimmer. Some individuals love the goal 50s; others fear them. It has become one of my favorite ways to help swimmers learn how to deal with fear and anxiety and to encourage teamwork.

A final note about nurturing self-esteem involves welcoming everyone to the team, no matter where they are in life's journey. There is a place for almost anyone on our team. If a student-athlete has not had year-round swimming experience and wants to come out for the team, I let them try. That person might make it as an athlete, become a good manager, or turn into a valued volunteer at practices and meets. Keep an open mind! As long as an individual can fill a role that supports the swim program in some way, welcome him or her to the team. While our program is evaluated on graduation rates and how well we do at Big Tens and NCAAs, of course, there are other things we want to do well—helping our students become good citizens, get into the majors of their choice, make great friends, get good jobs, and so forth. I feel there is a place for many different types of people in a program. If we keep a welcoming environment and find out where everyone's passions are, we can all work together to accomplish great things.

Encouraging Competition as Learning

I have noticed that swimmers seem to come into a program knowing more about healthy competition if they happen to come from a large family. Having experienced constant competition with their siblings from day one for toys, attention, and so forth, these athletes know how to take advantage of and to learn from competition. As coaches, we want to encourage competition, to welcome it, and to celebrate it as a way for our swimmers to learn. Swimmers need not avoid competition to avoid the bad feelings that can accompany failure. Coaches can help by emphasizing *winning and learning* versus winning and losing.

Coaches must communicate clearly to help swimmers see the learning benefits of an experience they might otherwise perceive as a loss. Coaches should also help swimmers understand that they can gain much through healthy competition within practices; they can help each other achieve their best efforts. Teach the swimmers to thank those in their lane for helping them become better. I expect to hear swimmers say, "Thanks for racing; it was fun!" even at the college level. Create lane assignments so that racing is more likely to occur. Thank individuals for working hard or learning a new skill; it will help them and the team become better. Encourage swimmers to pair up with training partners, or pair up individual swimmers yourself such that the more negative swimmers are paired with more positive teammates.

Because competition can be a good motivator, I encourage coaches to schedule a light competition schedule in the off season. Some teams have maintenance programs for high school swimmers in the off season, but I think it is important for coaches to do more than "maintain"; they should continue to evaluate and to challenge swimmers by encouraging competition in the off season. Design an off-season practice schedule that allows balance for the younger swimmers as well as time for the older swimmers to have meets. Swimmers who do a maintenance program in the summer that does not include some competitions are often not motivated enough to gain many benefits. Swim meets are checkpoints for conditioning as well as race awareness. Create a meet schedule even for summer maintenance swimmers. Celebrate every good race, whether it takes place in workout or at a meet.

The following are some brief tips to help you encourage healthy competition among your swimmers:

- Help swimmers view failure as an opportunity to learn about themselves.
- Talk to those who experience a setback as soon as possible to encourage them to see what can be learned from the experience and then move on.
- Make each practice enjoyable, and summarize what was learned or accomplished.

Developing Team Leaders

I still remember my age-group coach stopping practice to talk about life lessons, the importance of fair play, and developing a good work ethic. He created an environment where even as 10-year-olds we would try to stop other swimmers from being disruptive, by standing on the bottom, for example, because we knew we would all have to stop and listen to this talk again. We wanted to swim, so we helped other kids make better choices. The coach who leads sets the stage for developing leaders.

By putting each of your athletes in a leadership role, you encourage good leadership from everyone and thus good team work. One of the most effective ways to encourage leadership from each athlete is to seek out and place value on skills found in different swimmers. For example, sculling often brings to the front of the group swimmers who may not necessarily be the fastest in other strokes; see who can create whirl-pools just by sculling. Kicking without a board and balance drills are other good ways to help vary who the "best" is. Find swimmers who are good at a particular drill and have them demonstrate their skill to the group. Try not to always use the fastest swimmers; encourage leadership in every member of the team.

The following are some other ways to develop team leaders:

- Encourage the older swimmers to include the younger ones in some relays or to mentor activities. Have 15- to 16-year-olds talk to younger swimmers about a race or fun season they may have just had.

- Create opportunities for members to give back to the program. This is a win-win situation. It gives the younger swimmers role models to look up to and helps the older swimmers celebrate their success. It helps foster self-esteem all the way around.

- Use lane leaders, age-group leaders, captains, and stroke leaders to help encourage, cheer for, and celebrate success daily. Allow them to lead stretching or warm-ups, choose the drill to use that day, or be captains of relays.

- Create an environment in which athletes begin on time and work hard, and thank those who lead the way in these areas.

Planning for Growth

Swimmers like patterns to their training. Have a daily, a weekly, and a season plan. Explain it to all team members and to parents of a club team. Respect the beginning and ending time of practices. Use the last five minutes to celebrate what has been learned or accomplished and to cool down.

As I plan each season I look at what I want to have happen at the end of the season, and then go back and set it up from the beginning. Begin with the end in mind. I think about the types of things we want to say at our end-of-the-season banquet, at NCAAs, at the Big Ten Championships, at dual meets, at the training trip, and so on. I encourage our staff and our student-athletes to do the same. This helps to make each season fresh and acts as a stepping-stone to a solid season.

I hope you can take an idea or two from this chapter to help your experience and your team members experience with the sport as enjoyable for you as it has been for me. Enjoy the rest of the journey!

Summary

- Fun is one of the most important reasons that young swimmers first join a swim team.
- Fun, enthusiasm, attitude, and self-esteem are interrelated.
- Communication is critical at all levels—coach, swimmer, and parents.
- Create opportunities to help define the passions of your swimmers and to keep your program challenging and fun.
- Each practice should have a clear purpose and plan that is evaluated continually so the next day is even better.
- Coaches must be aware of the developmental issues facing each age group and must understand that fun is age specific.
- Create rewards appropriate to the age group.
- As the swimmers get older and better, turn the training into a game.
- Emphasize winning and learning, as opposed to winning and losing.
- Fear is natural and must be met head on.
- Set the stage for developing leaders.
- Show enthusiasm for each person on the team.
- Be in the present to prepare for a better future.

CHAPTER THREE

Coaching With Integrity

Peter Daland

One of several definitions of *integrity* by Webster (*Merriam-Webster's Collegiate Dictionary,* 10th edition) is "firm adherence to a code . . . of moral . . . values." For this chapter I make use of this definition since it fits in well with the role of the swim coach.

We live in a world of declining moral values. People today no longer hold the high standards of personal and group behavior that guided past generations. This would appear to be especially true in the United States. Although it can be observed in most aspects of life, nowhere is this decline more evident than in the world of sport, even in swimming. However, coaches in our sport are in a position to take action to counteract this decline by showing integrity in all that they say and do.

Since the Viet Nam War and the student unrest of the 1960s, there have been major changes in popular behavior and lifestyles, in America and in other western countries, that discourage personal and group discipline. This has made the relationships of individuals and teams in sport more difficult. In an activity such as competitive swimming that requires hard training, commitment, and a strong work ethic, the attempts of youth to challenge or disregard adult authority create tension and conflict. This could well be one of several reasons for the decline over the last two decades in both the numbers and the quality of swimmers who stay committed to the sport.

Building Coaching Relationships

Coaching is a profession of relationship building. Successful relationships depend heavily on the integrity of the involved parties: the coaching staff, the athletes, the athletes' parents, the officials, and at times, the coaching staff of other teams. The individual integrity of each of these parties forms the basis of their ability to work together. If the connections among any of those involved fail, the whole structure may collapse. The work of a coach is full of relationship pitfalls that must be avoided if the team is to have success.

A coach's high personal moral standards are absolutely essential in building a team operation that can achieve long-term success. Without strong personal integrity, the coach cannot gain the respect of the swimmers and the team supporters necessary for putting together the strong relationships that lead to team success.

The cornerstone of a strong swim program is a coach with integrity. The coach, in turn, must appoint staff and find athletes who possess this same quality. If this process is carried out successfully, a fine team will develop. Moral fiber and a strong work ethic probably have more to do with success in swimming than does pure talent.

Wholly Coached

Shane Gould

The coaches I had as a teenage swimming champion nearly 30 years ago are rarely surprised when I tell them how much of an influence they had on my life. The time they spent with me at the pool during training and swim meets, the hours they took to discuss my technique, my motivation for swimming, and my goal-setting strategies, and the life instruction they offered made them nearly as influential as my parents. The coaches who guided me as a young swimmer taught me that being involved in swimming was an asset I'd benefit from for life.

The legendary Forbes Carlile was my main coach as a teenage swimmer. He was a superb role model. An expert in the ability to physiologically train swimmers to swim fast, he served as a communicator, a mentor, and a teacher to his swimmers. The way he coached not only developed strong swimmers, it made well-rounded individuals of these swimmers.

If I had the chance to choose a swim coach now, knowing what I do as an Olympic athlete, a mother of four grown children, and a swim coach, I would look for a coach with many of the same qualities that I experienced in my coaches.

My ideal coach would be knowledgeable about how to train swimmers to swim fast.

■ He would be able to make a realistic evaluation of his swimmers' potential.

■ He would help his swimmers take responsibility for their training by expecting them to be ready on time for practices and competitions and to be independent enough to train without him for a period of time.

■ He would keep records of swimmers practices, including heart rates, lactic acid levels, and intervals done and would design a suitable program for each swimmer. He would eventually have swimmers take responsibility for some of their own record-keeping.

■ He would arrange time for his swimmers to do cross training and other activities to further develop their core strength outside of the pool and to maintain variety in their workouts.

My ideal coach would serve as a mentor to her swimmers.

■ She would be a role model for lifelong fitness and good health and would swim herself for the sheer love of it.

■ She would take an interest in her swimmers' lives outside of swimming. She would ask her swimmers how they were doing at school and encourage them to put effort into their studies and brainwork.

■ She would support her swimmers' interest and involvement in other activities as well, especially those activities that help a swimmer develop the skills and confidence to take initiative, be creative, and discover new things—opportunities elite athletes miss out on when their lives are ordered and directed solely by training and competing.

(continued)

My ideal coach would be a teacher to his swimmers.

■ He would give feedback appropriate to each swimmer's age and ability. He wouldn't tell a 10-year-old after she'd won at a local meet that she could be a gold medal Olympian one day. He would, however, get her interested in the Olympics by encouraging her to watch the performances of the Olympians and would point out the great commitment they'd made to attain the highest level of competition.

■ He would praise his swimmers when they clocked a personal best time and analyze with them what they did right to achieve the personal best.

■ He would also take time to discuss with his swimmers a race in which they didn't swim their best, so that they could learn from mistakes and continue to improve. But he would never throw away a 12-year-old's silver medal because he wanted gold.

■ He would arrange for his swimmers to practice receiving medals graciously and giving speeches. He would also have a lending library of motivational and relaxation tapes.

She would initiate open communication with swimmers and parents.

■ She would make it easy for her swimmers to accept criticism by always referring to the swimming rather than the swimmer. ("Your kicking needs some extra work, Shane," *not,* "Shane you're still a hopeless kicker.")

■ She would set up a good relationship with the parents of the swimmers and would never make a decision about a swimmer's future without talking it over with the parents first.

■ When a swimmer was old enough and competing at the national or international level she would recommend a good manager who would instruct the swimmer in financial management of prize money and sponsorships earnings. She would assist the club swimmer with college scholarship opportunities.

My ideal coach would emphasize teamwork and would look for ways to build team unity.

■ He would encourage his swimmers to enjoy the delights of swimming. He would ask how each swimmer felt in the water and give swimmers the goal of getting into the zone. He would allow them to joke and laugh and enjoy the other swimmers' companionship, but expect them to listen when he gave instruction. He would create some of the fun and have a good sense of humor.

■ He would develop a good team ethic with the ethos of competing for the good of the team rather than just as individuals.

■ He would have the swimmers help out at club meets with timing or putting equipment away, having older swimmers help coordinate the younger ones. Because elite sport requires a certain degree of selfishness to meet individual training and competition goals, doing things for others helps swimmers keep a better balance between giving and taking.

The best coaches aspire to fulfill all of these roles and duties. Although they may never completely achieve this goal—perfection is as elusive to coaches as it is swimmers—they never cease striving to do so. This is the kind of coach I gained the most from, the kind of coach I want to be, and the kind of coach I challenge you to be—for your athletes and yourself.

Appearance helps to convey this integrity. Therefore, the coach must dress for the role and the situation. Sloppy, inappropriate attire can damage a coach's image with his or her pupils as well as with others. For example, a professional coaching conference is not the place to wear pool-deck attire. It will likely damage your image as a professional and invite disrespect.

The Coach–Swimmer Relationship

In order for coaches to lead swimmers to higher levels of performance, the team must become a solid unit under the leadership and guidance of the coaching staff. The swimmers and the coach must adopt a strong work ethic. The coach must become a role model, admired and respected by the swimmers. He or she must always be well prepared at team meetings and practices. Even though the best coaches are close to their squad members, they remain a step ahead of them. Where there is responsible and caring leadership, there will likely be a happy and successful team.

There are some difficult hurdles along the way to higher performance. However, if the coach displays integrity, intelligence, and patience solutions can be found. It is the work of the coach to lead his or her pupils along a high moral path and to help them to sort out the many conflicting elements in their lives. The coach must teach that sport should be part of life but should not be life itself. Studies, family, sports, and a social life must all find their proper place and priority in the life of the swimmer. During the student years, studies must come first. The coach must also emphasize the value of the team experience and encourage giving to others in order to build a strong team unit.

A lack of self-confidence is a common problem in young swimmers. With the cooperation of the parents and some individual attention from the coach, this condition can often be corrected. One of the best ways a coach can help is to keep affected athletes busy with other activities at meets, such as taking splits or leading cheers, so that they aren't left alone to think too much about the competition. A coach might also consider shortening the taper of these athletes to keep them more optimistic about their chances for success. Swimmers who lack self-confidence sometimes believe that they are getting out of shape during an extended taper period.

Some coaches find it challenging to treat all athletes on a team—faster *and* slower swimmers—equally, but a coach with integrity must accord slower swimmers the same status as the top performers and must give all swimmers the same amount of attention. This is necessary so that every swimmer feels like a part of the team. Otherwise the team is reduced to being a club for a few exceptional swimmers, and the slower athletes feel excluded from the team experience. More often than not, the less talented swimmers will gain more from being on the team than the others.

Drug and alcohol use is a problem that sometimes affects young adult swimmers. These substances pose a challenge for a coaching staff to address. In this area as in others, coaches must be role models and leaders for their swimmers. Coaches of high integrity cannot ignore habits of self-destruction in their athletes. They must establish and enforce a strong drug and alcohol use policy; otherwise whatever integrity the team may have possessed will be lost.

The Coach-Parent Relationship

In any successful club operation, there must be a strong and positive connection between the coach and the team parents. In order to gain the cooperation and support of the parents, a coach must make it clear that he or she will be a positive moral influence on the children. The coach must sell the parents on the many benefits that the program will bring to their children, in and out of the pool; however, he or she must demonstrate personal integrity in order to make the sale. If parents can see that their children will grow in a positive manner through working with the coach, then they will strongly support the club program.

A common problem for many coaches is what to do about overeager team parents who push their children too hard and too frequently. In most cases swimmers with such parents will drop out of the sport unless prompt action is taken by the coach to correct the situation. In trying to alter a family connection, a coach must proceed with caution. A simple and often effective solution is to find a job for overeager parents that will benefit the team, such as newsletter editor, fund-raising chair, or meet official—timer, deck official, starter, referee. This kind of job enables the parent to see the larger team view and should therefore ease the pressure on his or her own child. Some years ago, a very fine university and national team masseur was developed from an overeager club team parent.

Another parent-coach problem that can arise concerns the running of the swim club. Very few parent-run clubs have ever been successful in top-level competition. Such clubs are usually handicapped by numerous firings and resignations of coaches. Too-frequent coaching changes damage the team, causing many swimmers to transfer to other clubs with more stable coaching leadership.

If the coach wisely steers team parents away from the technical end of swimming and toward the business end of the club, the club will benefit greatly. It is the obligation of the coach to handle technical issues and to represent the club in federation meetings. This should not be handed over to team parents who lack the knowledge to decide what is best for the club and the sport. The integrity, knowledge, and wisdom of the coach must be utilized in order for the club to succeed.

The Coach-Official Relationship

In working with meet or governing-body officials, the coach must act with strong integrity. Remember that officials are present at competition to ensure that the events are conducted in a fair and equitable manner for all competitors. A coach's reactions to decisions that are favorable or unfavorable to his or her team are observed by other coaches, team members, team supporters and parents, the officials, and others. The coach's integrity is on public display at such moments. A coach must be aware of this, react carefully, and avoid unsporting behavior. If it appears that a wrong ruling was made by an official, then the written protest procedure should be followed with as little fuss as possible.

Coaches should do their best to see that team members and supporters treat officials appropriately. The coach should educate team members and parents on the basic rules of competition so that they can better understand the sport and can avoid unnecessary disqualifications. Some team followers and parents may even decide to become officials to better serve the club and the sport.

The Coach-Coach Relationship

One of a coach's most important connections is with other coaches. Integrity is absolutely essential in dealing with one's peers. The most permanent people in swimming are the coaches. Swimmers and officials come and go, but the coaches remain because it is their profession. What your fellow coaches think of you will have an important impact on your professional life.

Coaches should help their fellow coaches whenever possible. They should assist in the training and education of younger, developing coaches. Mentor programs can and should be of great benefit to all involved.

It is vital for coaches to be gracious in victory and dignified in defeat. Win or lose, be tactful and compassionate. Compliment other coaches on their victories and make no excuses for your losses. In and out of competition, always be courteous and friendly to rival coaches.

Recruiting With Integrity

Recruiting swimmers from other teams is almost always a source of trouble for all concerned. The exception to this is, of course, a college or university coach recruiting a high school senior or a junior college student. The accepted, normal procedure for moving to the next level in sport is seldom problematic. Other situations are rarely simple and often not correct.

An athlete's changing from one high school to another should not be complicated, because place of residence usually determines which school a student attends. However, if coaches encourage a change of residence, they are not showing integrity even though they may be within the rules. If they use swimmers or team parents to do this work for them, they are just as guilty.

Encouraging a transfer from one university or college to another for other than academic reasons is uncommon because of the NCAA transfer rule, which requires a transferring student-athlete to sit out a year before competing unless the coach of the original institution signs a release. Such transfers still reflect low integrity if the coach of the receiving institution is involved in the athlete's decision to transfer.

At the club level, USA Swimming has instituted the 120-day transfer rule, which prevents an athlete from participating immediately after a transfer, but the time period specified is really too short to serve as a deterrent. Only coaches with strong integrity will be able to keep their fingers out of this pie.

Serving as a Coach-Administrator

Part of the work of the best swim coaches today involves playing a part in the administration of swimming. As with all other aspects of coaching, this side of the profession requires people of high integrity. It means going to meetings and serving on working committees at the club, high school, or university level. The work calls for an additional time commitment to the sport and is often unpaid. It requires knowledge of and concern for the sport. If swimming is going to be well run, then the leading coaches must play a key role in its administration.

One of the main frustrations encountered by coaches in swimming administration is the lack of technical knowledge and understanding on the part of the noncoach administrators. In such cases coaches must be patient and helpful. This too is a part of coaching with integrity.

Summary

- Coaching depends on integrity in relationships among coaches, athletes, parents, and officials.
- A coach provides leadership to the team through his or her integrity.
- A coach's personal integrity gains the respect of swimmers and team supporters.
- A coach must help swimmers prioritize their activities.
- A coach should accord every team member the same status.
- A coach cannot ignore any team member's use of drugs or alcohol; he or she must establish and adhere to a strong policy regarding use of these substances.
- There must be a strong and positive connection between a coach and the team parents.
- A coach must maintain integrity in dealing with other coaches and in recruiting swimmers.
- A coach with integrity must assume a role in the administration of swimming.

PART

II

Directing a Program to Its Full Potential

CHAPTER FOUR

Tailoring Your Approach to Specific Competition Levels

John Leonard

Legendary swimming coach James "Doc" Counsilman providing poolside instruction.

As we look across the broad landscape of world swimming, it is clear that the most successful swimming coaches share the skill of being able to tailor their program to the level of the athletes' development and to the level of competition that they will face in their present team and positions. Coaches who work with multiple skill, interest, and ability levels are adept at changing their style and approach to fit the situation, in some cases, hour by hour. This flexible mental approach comes from the ability to create true empathy with the athletes in the group. This empathy, in turn, comes from the coaches' honest desire to serve the needs of their athletes.

In this chapter, we look at several variations on this same theme. First, we look at communication issues in coaching and how coaches necessarily adapt and change to suit the different groups or competition levels with whom they are working. Next, we discuss the changes in the physical demands coaches make on their teams at various levels of the sport, based on some of the characteristics of various competition levels within swimming. Finally, we paint a complete picture of highly successful coaching behaviors at each level of the competition pyramid (see figure 4.1).

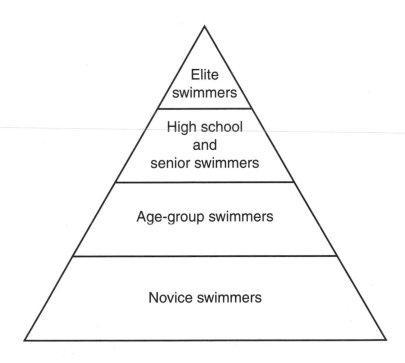

Figure 4.1 Each level of the competition pyramid presents its own set of coaching challenges.

One of the most memorable examples of this "shifting" coaching behavior that I have seen was the great Doc Counsilman of Indiana University. In the summer, Doc had a busy and varied schedule. At 5:30 AM, he was dealing with Olympic-level athletes preparing for the most prestigious of world events in late summer. By 9 AM, he was working with high school-age swimmers attending his swim camps, and by 11 AM, he was often working with the littlest swimmers, the 8-, 9- and 10-year-olds, who attended the camp. Clearly each group had different expectations of the great man, as they met with him in turn, and different needs.

Doc never missed a beat, going from a congenial, collegiate coach in the early morning, acting in concert with his senior swimmers (and, it must be said, occasionally throwing a small bit of the dictator into the mix for seasoning!) to a strict disciplinarian with the highest expectations with the high school-age group, to a fun-loving, grandfatherly character with the young children. Doc could play all the roles and he moved seamlessly between them. He was also brilliant enough to occasionally allow brief glimpses of who he was with the "group above" to the "group below" so that when the group below moved up, they were not totally shocked to discover another side of the Doc.

Communicating in Coaching

It has been wisely stated that coaching is largely a job of selling: selling your ideas to your athletes and to others, selling belief in yourself and your system of preparation, and selling the value of our sport and the hard work that goes into it. Selling, sales professionals are told, is a transfer of emotion that moves a person to act. It is further stated that people "buy" based on emotion, and then must justify their emotional choice with objective reasoning.

The job of the salesman, therefore, is to create the emotion to move people to action and to provide them with the objective data to justify their choice and action to themselves, their parents, their friends, and so on.

Everyone must justify their purchases or decisions to someone. Therefore, if one is to sell an idea to an athlete, one must communicate with that athlete. Communication, as everyone knows, takes many forms, oral (both face-to-face and over the telephone), body language, and written. Coaches must become highly skilled communicators in whichever forms they use.

Doc Counsilman once asked a large group of coaches who would win a swim meet if four coaches were given identical teams: a physiologist, a biomechanist, a nutritionist, or a psychologist? His answer, of course, was the psychologist, because the psychologist could best communicate with the team.

The most famous communicator in modern coaching is perhaps the fabled coach of the Santa Clara Swim Club during the 1960s and 1970s and later of the Stanford University swim team, George Haines. George was skilled enough to convince two or more swimmers in the same event, on his team, that each could win, and that each could set world records. Each swimmer believed that "secretly" George was pulling for him or her more than the others, though George would continually declare his total impartiality. It was said that George could convince anyone of anything, and amazing stories are told of his ability to do this at the highest level of competition, the Olympic Games. This ability made him a coach to be feared in world competitions.

Listen

One of the most important "secrets of success" in Stephen Covey's *The 7 Habits of Highly Effective People* is "seek first to understand, then later to be understood." In coaching communication, this simple phrase offers deep meaning.

The first critical skill in communication that every coach at every level must learn is to listen to the athlete. Coaches must listen with the ear, the mind, and the heart. They must listen for words but also listen for intent, for meaning, and for the emotions behind the words. Repeating back to the athlete what you have heard—"may I repeat what you just told me to be sure I have it right?"—is a good way for a coach to let an athlete know that you have been listening and want to understand. A final, "Is that right?" is vital to emphasize your desire to know the athlete's true point of view.

Listening to an 8-year-old is different, in terms of the content, meaning, and emotion involved, than listening to a 25-year-old, and there are gradations throughout the spectrum. Adjust accordingly. Listening to the little people is best done by physically getting down to an eye-to-eye level with them, not expecting to get a "clear picture" right away, and allowing time for these generally less expressive communicators to find a way to tell their story.

I work to keep communication open with my swimmers every day, rather than simply waiting for them to come to me with a problem or issue. "What's your story today?" is one of favorite greetings to young people as they enter the pool. At first, they look at me blankly and say, "What?" or tilt their heads in bemusement, but later, as I explain that everyone has a "story of the day" (or two or three!), they open up and disclose what is important to them on that day. This usually gives great clues about how to conduct practice effectively for a particular person on a particular day. While the language may change, the impact of such a short discussion on all ages is profound. This type of exchange demonstrates concretely your interest in their lives, and if you take the time to really listen, gives you real insight into their lives.

Coaches must modify verbal communication in content, complexity, length, and emotion depending on the age group they are working with. They must also adjust according to the specific situation. Some coaches think that they should never display real emotion, even when an athlete's behavior is inappropriate and out of line. In my view, a coach has a deep responsibility to "set the lines" within which the team will operate. Young people of all ages expect and want those lines; and if they aren't sure, they will push until they find out the hard way how far out the boundaries are. There is nothing wrong with an occasional loud, attention-getting, strongly-worded comment; in fact, such comments can be very beneficial. Your team needs to know that you care. People who care get angry once in a while—once in a while, not everyday. Use your emotions, both the joyful and the unhappy ones, sparingly. They have more effect if not overworked and overdisplayed.

Be Aware of Body Language

Body language is another major component of communication. It is critical that you know what you look like when you are coaching. One of the best ways to do this is to have a friend secretly videotape you at practices and meets, then let you review the tape in private. Most assuredly, you will find flaws as well as good things in your physical presentation. There is a place for active, aggressive body language with certain teams or individuals at certain times, as well as a place for the opposite kind of behavior. With younger, less experienced children, a calm, peaceful atmosphere and calm, peaceful body language generally provide the best learning environment. But that calm learning environment is not what most athletes need when the state finals come up in the 50 free in high school competition. Now is the time for arousal! Neither limp relaxation, nor extreme tenseness will help athletes in this situation. But the presence of an eager, involved, focused, and slightly tense coach can be a real motivator.

Send the Right Message

In the beginning levels of competition, communication must focus on the process, such that swimmers hear, "Here is what you need to do (or remember or learn) in order to improve. Concentrate on doing these things." Clarity, simplicity, and a cheerful, upbeat nature are assets when communicating with beginning swimmers. As you climb the competitive pyramid, the intensity level typically builds, though you must gauge what approach is best for each individual athlete in preparation for top competition. Some need high arousal levels; others need to stay calm. The ability to provide different things to different athletes at high-stakes competitions is one mark of a first-rate coach.

The great Australian coach Laurie Lawrence is a poet, a writer, a professional speaker, and one of the greatest on-deck swim meet coaches in history. He is legendary for finding the right motivational "pitch" and tone for each of his athletes at the Olympic Games. He used an upbeat, "Go get 'em; you're the best, the very best!" approach with Jonno Sieben in Los Angeles in 1984 before he upset Michael Gross to win the 200 butterfly gold medal, and at the same Olympics used quiet reassurance for some of his female stars who responded better to that approach.

Great coaches not only know their athletes and what they need but also how to deliver their message in the form and the terms that are most meaningful to the athletes. Delivering a verbal message to an athlete who responds to tactile communication may not be terribly effective, but a hug and a squeeze might get the point across.

Having established that communication is the key to coaching effectively at different levels, let's look at how coaches individualize the physical demands of training to accommodate the different developmental and competition levels of their athletes.

Differentiating Physical Training

An important job of any coach is to develop training programs that are appropriate to the fitness and skill level of the athlete. Novice swimmers, age-group swimmers, high school and senior swimmers, and elite swimmers have different needs and characteristics.

Novice Swimmers

At the base of the competition pyramid, a coach may be working with a novice team, perhaps in a YMCA setting, a park district summer club setting, or a country club swim club setting. These athletes are typically youngsters right out of the learn-to-swim program, with half-formed stroke skills, a great deal of enthusiasm, and absolutely no training background whatsoever. Working at this level of swimming, the coach concentrates on teaching skills and stroke techniques. There is little of the real training that athletes will do later in their swimming careers.

The coach of the novice swimmer presents, teaches, and repeats many drills to hone skills and technique, working in repeats of 12½ or 25 yards or meters or even shorter lengths for more complicated strokes such as butterfly. The simple repetition of these skills and drills by themselves not only improves stroke technique but also helps establish an athlete's base conditioning.

At this stage, the coach emphasizes good training skills and habits as well as how to properly swim a practice. This work may not seem very sophisticated, but it is truly vital for launching successful swim careers. Novice coaches are the unsung heroes of American swimming, often underpaid and underappreciated.

Bonnie Brown, a coach with 30 years of novice coaching experience in Syracuse, New York, has seen her "graduates" go on to age-group top-16 rankings, Junior and Senior National time standards, and in one case, an Olympic berth. She puts it this way, "My job is to set the foundation. I love the fact that I get to start them on the right path. If I do my job, the job of every coach who will follow me will be so much easier and more enjoyable. When I teach them something correctly, and it sticks, they will never swim a length of the pool incorrectly and establish bad habits that may never be broken. I *know* I do a critical job in developing athletes for our team!"

Characteristics of Novice Swimmers

- Novice swimmers join to be with friends, to have fun, because their parents bring them, and/or to learn something new (develop mastery).
- Parents may have either no expectations or unrealistic expectations.
- Parents and athletes are likely to be unversed in youth sports and swimming in particular.
- Education of parents is crucial to the success of the program.
- Typically, the athletes have low physical capacities. Some may be frighteningly short on endurance.
- Athletes will communicate in a very literal way, not knowing the jargon of swimming, so the coach has to be very careful to be clear. For example, you wouldn't say, "You died on that last 25," without explaining the exaggerated swimming slang.
- These swimmers will consider fun to be "laughs and giggles," *not* achievement and hard work.

- Enthusiasm will be high. Excitement will be high. They will be rather easily motivated.
- External motivators such as ribbons and awards are highly sought-after; their use is necessary to help develop inner drive.
- Practices need to be short and fast-paced, with no one activity too long or "boring." Creativity counts.
- Attention spans are limited. Teach to the point, one point at a time.
- Repeat key points each day.

Age-Group Swimmers

After coaching novice swimmers, a coach's next assignment might be an age-group or intermediate swim team, with members ranging from C- and B- level swimmers to highly skilled triple A qualifiers who are competitive nationally in their age group.

Coaches of age-group swimmers must shift their approach to include a bit more on the conditioning side of training, constantly doing daily stroke instruction and correction, while simultaneously challenging the group with more demanding workouts.

Gradually, progressively, increasing the physical load on the athletes can be done in many ways. A few are listed below:

- Increase the *frequency* of workouts, that is, the number of days the athlete practices each week and month.
- Increase the *duration,* or amount of time, in each workout.
- Increase the amount of *volume,* or distance covered, in each workout.
- Increase the *density* of work in the time allotted, that is, more swimming, less rest built into the program, (measured by yards or meters per hour being swum).
- Gradually increase the *intensity,* or speed, of the workouts done.

The toughest coaching issue with age-group teams is that the level of swimmer in one workout will vary a great deal. Each group must be developed to have athletes of similar capabilities training together, in the same lanes, so they can challenge and support each other's efforts, and can all rise together to the challenges presented by the coach. Coach Kathy McKee of Mecklenburg Aquatic Club in Charlotte, North Carolina, is a master at providing group differentiation for her swimmers. While she currently coaches in an 8-lane pool, she has worked in a 10-lane pool in the past, which allowed her to have as many as six slightly different workouts going in those 10 lanes. She prefers to have assistant coaches with her to help with the different workouts but sometimes works with each of the different groups herself. This group differentiation allows her to very gradually turn up the physical demands and to maintain positive training progress for each group without overwhelming any one swimmer.

One of the adaptations that age-group coaches introduce to their swimmers is the concept of dryland training, usually starting with body weight exercises. The coach's role in this age group is especially focused on teaching the swimmers how to do exercises correctly with good form.

Characteristics of Age-Group Swimmers

- Teams may have a large swimmer-to-coach ratio.
- Teams and swimmers may show a diversity of skill levels. Even within an individual, skills may vary; a child may have a proficient freestyle but a nonexistent breaststroke.
- "Fairness" is a major issue in swimmers at this age. Explore and explain the decisions you make and the rationales you use daily.
- This group needs to understand the "why" of all things.
- Physical development is better than at the novice level but must be addressed systematically to nurture improvement. Coaches need a planned program of increasing stress at specific times for each individual.
- Swim meets can be emotional times. Athletes must understand the appropriate time, place, and manner for handling their emotions.
- Team aspects of swim meets are important to the athletes.
- Swimmers may start shifting their focus from their most significant other, friends, or family to the coach. Swimmers find that good coaches make loyal friends
- Real awareness of training and competition times emerges at this level, and many youngsters will take ownership of the sport for themselves for the first time.
- Muscular and endurance development will be rapid if children consistently come to practice. If they don't, they will likely still improve, just on natural growth cycles.
- Adolescent hormones may create first awareness of the opposite sex, sometimes with very distracting results.
- By the time swimmers are 8 to 10 years old, they are ready to begin to consider the mental side of peak performance.

High School and Senior Swimmers

Next in the pyramid is presenior or high school swim training. Coaching high school swimming is perhaps the greatest challenge in all of American swimming because the coach works with the greatest range of swimmer ability, from beginners just out of learning-to-swim classes through All-American caliber swimmers.

Coaches at this level will increase work on all aspects emphasized in previous levels and add a strong dryland training component as well. This may also be the time to include some basic sport psychology in the form of self-directed skills. Training becomes complex, with a fair amount of work done beyond the aerobic type of training that dominates age-group swimming. Mature body chemistry demands more complex physical training for peak competitive performance. A complete review of this sort of physiology is far beyond the scope of this chapter, but suffice it to say that the coach must become more aware of the scientific aspects of physical training, including training specificity, periodization, and stroke mechanics.

Characteristics of High School and Senior Swimmers

- Larger bodies mean fewer swimmers per lane than with younger teams; more safety care is needed.
- Endurance needs are primary. Strength and speed needs are secondary.
- Swimmers at this age begin to choose what they want to eat. Nutrition plays a big role in their success.
- This group feels a tremendous pressure to fit in and be part of the group. Peer pressure is enormous. Good friends are critical; friends who lead in the wrong direction are mortally dangerous.
- Athletes are generally ready for more in-depth discussion of the mental aspects of the sport.
- Stroke-specific and event- or distance-specific training in the pool needs to be more carefully geared toward the needs of each athlete.
- Discipline is needed. Female athletes tend to like parameters and feel safe within them, while many males put on a rebellious facade, secretly hoping to be "reined in."
- A swimmer's ability to work can rise to world-class levels as early as ages 11 to 12 in women and 14 to 16 in men. This is the exception, however.

- Friends, peers, and confidants are very important to swimmers at this age. The coach may take a secondary role to peers as the most valued resource and influence.

- Competition can be at all levels from the most ordinary, mundane event to national and world-class groups in training. Take care to reinforce team unity.

- This age group really wants to be treated as adults, and deserves to be, within the boundaries of common sense and good taste. Reward success with small praise; deal with failures by pointing out what can be learned from them, rather than punishing athletes in any way.

- Introduce additional dryland strength and flexibility training as well as mental training. Include such training in practice on a regular basis to fill the needs of swimmers at this level of competition.

Elite Swimmers

At the peak levels of competition—collegiate, national-, and international-level swimming—the demands on the coach change again. Effective coaching now depends on individualizing training to be maximally effective within the team concept. At the truly elite World-Championship and Olympic levels, coaches must be prepared to shift their approach to something close to one-on-one coaching. Although they may coach 10 to 20 athletes all together, they will have a one-to-one plan for coaching each swimmer. Clearly, coaching at this level is sophisticated and demanding.

Characteristics of Elite Swimmers

- Training plans must be individualized (to a great degree).
- Swimmers must participate in the planning of their training.
- Swimmers must be treated as adults who are making a choice to participate in a very demanding activity.
- The role of the coach is as a mentor or partner with the athlete; both parties are seeking high-level performance.
- Physical and mental demands are great on the athlete. More rest may be needed as the athlete gets older.
- Competitions serve as motivators. Mastery is assumed; now it's time to race and reward.
- Each athlete may need something different from the coach, and may need different things at different times.

- An athlete at this level is often on the border between perfect condition for racing and physical illness. The margin is thin.
- Illness equals nontraining, which equals suppressed performance levels, which equals no reward, which equals lessened enthusiasm, which can equal illness. Watch out for this downward spiral.
- Elite athletes consume a huge chunk of pool space and time, coach's time, team money, and so on. If they don't "give back" to the program, others may feel resentful.
- Fun is largely replaced by satisfaction in work well done.
- Paralysis by analysis is a danger. These athletes know about the sport; sometimes they think they know too much.

Next, let's look at the characteristics of successful coaches working with athletes at each level.

Characteristics of Successful Coaches

Coaches at different levels of the sport of swimming face radically different situations. Thus, their skills and abilities, as well as their knowledge base and behavior, must also be different in order to produce success.

Indeed, success itself will be defined differently at different levels. For novice swimmers, enjoying the sport, learning new skills, and wanting to continue mean success. At the age-group level, the mastery of skills, learning the culture of swimming, and learning to compete are critical success factors. At the high school and senior swimming level, competitive victories and improvements in times and skills are success measures. For elite athletes, success is lifetime-best times and performing well in major competitions.

Coaches of Novice Swimmers

The coach of novice-level swimmers is most successful if he or she is able to attract and retain the interest of young children. This "Pied Piper" quality is easy to spot in a coach; children will gravitate toward such a coach and literally follow him or her around, seeking attention and approval.

These coaches are able to communicate in words and gestures that are meaningful to new swimmers who are not familiar with swimming jargon. They are friendly and open with all children, regardless of whether the children have a background in the sport. They provide leadership to the group. These coaches communicate with parents in an easy, friendly manner, without being dominated by them or swayed by their possibly uninformed and unrealistic aspirations for their children. The coach educates parents as well as athletes in the sport.

Successful coaches of novice swimmers possess the ability to be *teachers*; they provide lessons in short, meaningful interludes and present material in small, logical, progressions. Knowledgeable novice coaches provide a physical development program, including both dryland and in-the-water training, that progressively increases in challenge so that physical conditioning improves. These coaches recognize the importance of letting each child find and demonstrate mastery in some part of the swimming experience, in or out of the water. Such coaches provide a competitive experience that focuses on learning and feedback, and keeps the "fierce competition" aspects of sport in the background.

Successful coaches of novice swimmers emphasize that working together in a supportive team environment is the best way for a group to improve; they stress that the improvement of other swimmers benefits each individual and helps each individual improve. Moreover, this supportive team environment teaches children that improvement comes from hard work, attention to detail, and enthusiasm for the task at hand. These lessons constitute the real value of the sport experience. Satisfaction in effort and in results is a mature form of fun that novice swimmers must learn.

Successful coaches provide suitable opportunities for their novice swimmers to learn and grow in both directed and more free-form activities in the sport. Most practice time is devoted to structured lessons, but time is also allowed to explore the water in a less structured manner through games or activities with no measurement.

Finally, the best coaches of novices always demonstrate their enthusiasm for the sport of swimming.

Coaches of Age-Group Swimmers

In addition to implementing the basic tactics of successful coaches of novice swimmers, successful age-group coaches further develop their swimmers by providing a well-planned progression of physical training covering weeks, months, and years that will prepare age-group athletes for senior swimming. These coaches educate athletes and parents on the need for an ever-increasing commitment to training and competition in order to be optimally successful in the sport. They emphasize that the senior level is best reached with an approach that expands the aerobic training base through the age-group years. They reinforce that the fastest way to improvement in swimming is through attention to technique.

Successful coaches of this competitive level must be able to organize and effectively manage a large group of athletes. They recognize that this is the time to develop quality feelings about the team aspect of the sport within youngsters. These coaches allow age-group athletes some social time and some time for peer friendships in the team environment—to athletes at this stage the team means more than "just swimming."

Coaches of age-group athletes can be a friend to each athlete while remaining an authority figure. They explain the logic and the "why" behind their decisions and the work being done so that athletes become intellectually involved in their own training to some extent. This lays the groundwork for athletes to develop the beginnings of a peak-performance mental process.

Coaches of High School and Senior Swimmers

The role of the coach changes a bit in coaching swimmers in their teenage years. At this age swimmers' friends are their peers, and the coach becomes more of a mentor. For this reason it's important that the coach act as a quality role model in all things. The most successful coaches at this competitive level are able to subtly develop a group of positive peers who role model for other swimmers. Being able to shape the team environment is a great skill for coaches to develop. A coach can then affect the culture of the group and help define what is considered "cool," as well as provide a vision of what is possible for the group.

The effective high school coach develops cooperative working relationships with each athlete and with the team as a whole, recognizing the swimmers' need to be treated as adults. These coaches become skilled at helping teenagers set goals in swimming and in life, and then at helping them move from achievement-oriented goals to process-oriented "task recognition." They are aware of safety issues, as the teen years are accident years, for many reasons. They become capable of recognizing which teen problems they are competent to address and which ones need referral to appropriate professionals.

Successful high school coaches devise training programs that can be individually modified for optimum training. They emphasize to their athletes the critical importance of consistent training and of "hidden" training—what a swimmer does away from the pool dramatically affects what he or she achieves in the pool. Many coaches also provide mental training opportunities for athletes to learn focus, concentration, peak-performance skills, and life skills that will extend far beyond swimming.

Effective coaches of this level provide a disciplined, stable environment for training. They offer competitive opportunities, and they make sure that each athlete understands how to maximize those opportunities for themselves. They help each athlete ask and answer questions such as "Where does this meet fit into the plan for my improvement?" and "What do I focus on and achieve here?" These coaches create chances for athletes to demonstrate their increasing self-reliance; their goal is to develop independent athletes, not athletes who are dependent on the coach.

Coaches of Elite Swimmers

The coaches of experienced swimmers competing at the national and international levels are masters in the planning of training and have developed their technical knowledge of swimming to the highest possible level. These coaches are "consultants" for their athletes rather than minute-to-minute "directors." They are willing to bring in any and all resources necessary to help an athlete improve. The support of others is likely to be a critical success factor in any elite athlete's success; thus the coach of this competitive level needs to provide only as much as the individual athlete needs. The elite coach will be a different coach to different athletes.

In addition to being masters of swim training, the most successful elite coaches are aware of the need for planning the "detraining" of their athletes at the end of their swimming careers. They provide guidance for the athletes as to what comes next.

Most coaches will coach many different levels of swimming and should recognize that they will be asked to provide different skills and abilities at each level. At some point in their careers, many coaches will do more than one level of coaching simultaneously. Great coaches perform many roles for their athletes, and they do so with grace and with a seamless transition. We can all aspire and continuously work to reach that level of coaching performance.

Summary

- The most successful coaches tailor their programs to the level of the athlete they are working with and to the level of the competition their athletes will face.
- Successful coaches are adept at changing their approach and their style to fit the situation.
- Coaching is selling; selling depends on effective communication, both verbal and nonverbal.

- Seek first to understand, by listening to your athletes, then to be understood.
- Communication must be modified to fit the age group of the audience.
- Differentiate training according to the level of your athletes.
- Teaching skills effectively is critical for the coach at the beginning levels.
- The novice coach must be able to attract young children to swimming and to maintain their interest in the sport.
- As the coach moves up the developmental ladder, he or she must focus more on the training side.
- The age-group coach must develop a long-range training plan and maintain attention on technique.
- High school swimming usually presents the greatest range of athletes.
- At peak levels of competition, the coach must employ a one-to-one approach with each athlete.

CHAPTER FIVE

Administering and Marketing a Winning Program

Jack Bauerle

When I was asked to write a chapter for this book concerning administering and marketing a winning swim program, I was surprised and very flattered. Our program at the University of Georgia has been fortunate enough to win two NCAA Championships, and of this I am very proud. However, I also feel that our program still has a long way to go. Maybe it's because we put ourselves up against some of the best programs in the world, those run by Richard Quick (Stanford), Mark Schubert (USC), and Eddie Reese (Texas), to name a few. When I compare our program with programs such as these, I feel that we still have much work to do. But we have come a long way in achieving the goals that we set out for ourselves in 1978, when I took over the swimming program. I don't think many people in the swimming world would have given us a snowball's chance in Hades of winning an NCAA Championship when we started out.

My first victory as a swim coach—and the first time I got thrown in the pool by the team—was against Brenau Women's College in Gainesville, Georgia. It took an SEC Championship some 17 years later to get me to take another dip! I'm not sure we had championship-level success in mind when we started, but being surrounded by very successful programs, we knew what we wanted to achieve. It has been a challenge, but there is nothing more satisfying than working hard and achieving your goals.

I honestly believe that if we were able to win a championship with the humble program we started with—a horrendous facility and very little financial support—any program in the country can win a championship. That first year, my father funded the year-end dinner for my women's team because there was not enough money in the budget to finish the year. We slept three, four, or whatever was necessary to a room on the road to make ends meet. Though I fought for a better budget every year, I honestly felt that we were not going to receive *anything* until we began to win—which proved to be the case. The University of Georgia is and always has been a very conservative and fiscally responsible school. The unwritten word was work hard, keep your nose clean, and the better you do, the more the department will help you out.

It was a difficult process. Many relationships had to be fostered around the school, among the faculty, and among the athletic board to enable us to arrive where we are today. Certainly as we finally walked into our new facility in 1995 we felt a different kind of pressure to win than we had known before. We stood up and did just that. I couldn't be more proud of our performances.

But programs should not be judged on winning national championships alone. Some of the best coaches and some of the best programs around have never won a championship; some of them may never reach that goal. What is important is to offer athletes the best program possible. I think that it is feasible to win with above-average athletes who work extremely hard. Having a champion or two doesn't hurt, but at the same time there is too much emphasis on getting the best athletes available. Some of my best swimmers were not heavily recruited. We are fortunate to be in a sport, unlike basketball and football, where above-average athletes can become NCAA and USS champions. I believe that our program is still a work in progress because I believe that it is still not as good as it can, and I hope will, be.

Before I address how we have administered and marketed our program for the past 21 years, I would like to mention that almost every aspect of this program, outside of our basic hard work and tears, has been begged, borrowed, or stolen from other programs. I am not an original thinker; many of my so-called ideas have been taken from successful coaches who run successful programs and lives. Three people that come to mind immediately are Dick Shoulberg at Foxcatcher and Germantown Academy, who was instrumental in steering me in the right direction and getting me started in coaching, and Jon Urbanchek at Michigan and Eddie Reese at Texas, who acted as mentors. Year-in and year-out, they not only produce great swimmers but great kids. More important, these coaches are willing to share their ideas whenever they have the opportunity to do so. Don Gambril's advice has also been instrumental in some decision making along the way, even while we were competing against one other.

Administering and marketing a winning program implies that coaches do an awful lot besides coaching. Nothing could be more true. With any successful team, every aspect of the program must be administered to and meticulously checked on a day-to-day basis. Because of NCAA legislation and some of the preposterous constraints it places on our sport, the demands on our time have become even greater, and the time that we can spend with our athletes has become even shorter. However, it is important to remember that athletes are our first responsibility. Our commitment to them is our first priority. Every decision made in our program is designed to enhance the performance of the athletes in the pool and in the classroom, and more important, to make them more well-rounded people by the time they leave the confines of the university.

A few key administrative and marketing related tasks that the head coach of any program should attend to include selecting the coaching and support staff, delegating effectively, establishing means of financial support other than the university (such as booster clubs and endowment scholarships), planning the structure of the season, maximizing the use of the facility, and developing lifelong swimmers.

Assemble the Best Staff

The first responsibility of the head coach in administering a successful swim program is to assemble the best staff—assistant coaches and support personnel—possible. Most head coaches agree that we are only as good as our help.

Collegiate coaches' lives have become more cluttered and complicated with the intrusion of the NCAA into our sport; therefore, we have had to become even more organized than ever before. Assistant coaches have become even more important in assisting the organization so that head coaches are as accessible as possible to their athletes. This is no small feat in this day and age; any swim coach at the NCAA level will tell you that the job has changed dramatically in the last five to six years.

It is most important to pick assistant coaches that you believe will be loyal to your program. I believe loyalty is much more important in a coach than ability. You can teach certain aspects of coaching to an individual, but it is impossible to teach loyalty. Loyalty is innate. By selecting people you like who are also loyal to the program, you will receive an extra bonus of longevity. You don't need to look far to find some ultrasuccessful head coach–assistant coach teams whose success has fed their longevity and whose longevity has no doubt been a big part of their success. The first couple of examples that come to mind are Eddie Reese and Kris Kubik, who have been together at Texas since 1986 (and before that from 1978 to 1981); and Mark Schubert and Larry Liebowitz, who have been at USC since 1992. At Georgia, I have been fortunate enough to have Harvey Humphries with me since 1982, and diving coach Dan Laak since 1987; I had another assistant coach with me for 12 years. It makes me feel really good about our program to know that my staff members have been taken care of by the program, that they have been treated fairly, and that they have had enough responsibility to feel that they are an integral part of the success of the program. Obviously it is important that assistant coaches be compatible and that they reflect the values of the head coach, both at the pool and away from the pool.

Coaching staff selections also have to meet the program's needs. You need expertise in sprinting, distance, and middle distance. For our program, I don't care if this expertise comes from a woman or a man; my desire is to find the best possible person who is available for the job. There is no doubt that if you coach a women's or a combined program it is important, if at all possible, to have a woman coach on staff. At the same time, some coaches hurt their programs by hiring coaches based more on their gender than on the expertise they can provide. Many times our best coaches are right under our noses—our own swimmers who become grad assistants and perhaps move on to become full-time assistants. If you make the experience in the pool fun while coaching your athletes, you will find that more than a few pupils will go on to be coaches.

Meet With Staff Away From the Pool

As you work with your staff, plan some social time with them. We try to get together as a staff, at football games or dinners or similar events, during the course of the year. We plan some outings just so that we have a chance to talk away from the office and pool. This brings the staff closer and provides a chance to discuss a lot of things that would not be addressed at the pool.

Fight for Your Coaches' Salaries

Coaching, and swim coaching in particular, has never been the most highly paid of professions, though certainly it is among the hardest work in sports. If we sit back and accept the salaries that are given to us year after year, it is our own fault that we labor in poverty. None of us became a coach to get wealthy, but we should fight to receive what we deserve. Any type of success, athletic or academic, warrants asking for more money. The more coaches fight for good salaries, the better. The higher the salaries go for a few coaches, the higher they will go for others.

Coaches must remember that their swimmers are, for the most part, terrific student-athletes, which makes them great ambassadors for the school and its athletic department. This point is one that coaches can emphasize to their athletic directors. I remember going into Coach Dooley and asking for a raise not too many years ago. He told me about his first year back in 1963, when he was hired as the head football coach at Georgia for $12,000. I didn't want to remind him that that was 30 some years ago, nor did I want to remind him that they gave him a 6,000-square-foot house for $1, so I accepted what he had to offer. I do believe, however, that if I had not gone in every few years to ask for a raise, I would not have received more than I was first offered. If you feel that you have done a good job, ask for what you deserve.

Fight for your assistant coaches' salaries as well. These are the people who are going to make or break your program. If the assistant coaches' salaries are fair, it will have a significant effect on the overall stability of your program. Moreover, the fact that you are in there fighting for them will mean an awful lot to your assistant coaches; it will encourage them to do their best and to remain loyal to the program.

Delegate Effectively

Obviously it is necessary to delegate some coaching responsibilities to your staff. As you do so, make sure that staff members take full responsibility for one area of the program. Delegating in this manner allows your members to use their expertise and to know that they are important to the program, and it allows you to focus more specifically on the areas you need to take care of. The following section explains how we divide the coaching responsibilities at Georgia.

Assistant Coach Harvey Humphries has been with me for 18 years. His main responsibility is recruiting. All the coaches assist in recruiting—making calls, conducting campus visits, and so forth—but Harvey coordinates the recruiting effort and plans all the official recruiting visits. Harvey is also in charge of our USS club, the Athens Bulldogs, and all the responsibilities that go along with it—managing club training, practices, travel, pool time, and so forth. Carol Capitani is in charge of team travel and budget issues with the program. Morgan Bailey is in charge of the weight training program, the orientation session, and handling the video equipment for taping meets and practices. Finally, Whitney Hite, a graduate assistant, is an assistant to all three assistants; he is more or less available to do whatever is necessary to help them. Assistant coaches must also delegate, or they will be inundated with mountains of paperwork and other duties that take them away from coaching athletes.

Dan Laak is our head diving coach. His first responsibility is, of course, to have a successful diving program. However, because diving coaches have fewer athletes than other head coaches, they often assume other responsibilities. Because swimming and diving programs spend so much time together, it is important that the programs work together. Dan sees his responsibilities as lying not only with his divers but with the program as a whole. I have been fortunate to have in Dan not only a well-respected diving coach who does a great job with our athletes but also one of the best organizers in the college ranks. Dan was the meet director for the NCAA Championships. He is in charge of meet management, works closely with me in scheduling meets, and acts as a liaison between me and the people in charge of the aquatic facility

Although the strength and conditioning coaches are not my direct assistants, they are integral to the overall success of the program. It is very important that great communication be established between the strength coaches and the rest of the program.

Every program has some coaches who are better communicators and some who are more technically oriented. It is imperative that each coach find a place within the program where he or she feels comfortable. At the same time, young coaches need to learn a little bit about all aspects of the program, so we make sure that all coaches visit and assist with every area of the program, including distance, middle distance, IM, and the sprint group.

One thing I demand from our staff is that they not go home immediately following the conclusion of a home swim meet. We sit down together after every home meet and discuss how it went. We go over all the races and talk about how each swimmer performed. We try to get a general feel of where we are at that point in the season and what things we need to address at the next practice and during the next week in training. This discussion is crucial, because it puts everyone on the same page. It gives everyone a clear idea of where the team is headed and how each coach feels about the performance of particular athletes and the team in general. More often than not, we all go out somewhere after the meet or grab a meal. This is invaluable time, as it gives us a chance to discuss our athletes in a relaxed environment away from the office, without interruption and without being rushed.

Considering all the people within the university environment that are there to help, coaches would be remiss not to take full advantage of their support. Here at the University of Georgia, after a 16-year battle, we have finally received our own secretary for swimming. This allows me the opportunity to stay on top of many jobs that I might otherwise let go, such as communication with recruits, boosters, and parents. Good sport information personnel are invaluable as well; they can organize publicity meetings, newspaper and television interviews, and write a large portion of the material that goes directly to the media. This position has been a bone of contention for me for many years, as there seems to be a terrific turnover from one year to the next and we are in a continual process of educating the latest person assigned to our program. The more successful a program becomes, the more important it is to have competent sport information personnel. Bring a sport information contact along on as many away meets as possible so that they are familiar with the athletes as well as the coaches. Include them in year-end banquets and see that they receive any year-end awards other program members receive so that they know they are appreciated. They will work that much harder for you the next year.

I put other people to work for our program, including athletes who are on fifth-year scholarship aid. Athletes who are finishing a degree are allowed by NCAA rules to receive the same percentage of scholarship they were awarded during the course of their eligibility, in some cases more if they performed at a very high level. We use our fifth-year people to help out in every way we can think of; they film meets, help out at home meets, and coach a masters/faculty team during the lunch hour. Athletes who receive an athletic scholarship for their fifth year should earn it by contributing as much as they can to the program.

Another very important contributor to our success as a program is our academic counseling department. It is imperative that competent people are in place in this department. I am careful to listen to the athletes regarding their academic counseling and tutoring, and have come to realize that if they are not comfortable with certain academic counselors, I need to address the situation promptly. Academic counselors work very closely with our athletes. They help with scheduling conflicts, tutoring, and monitoring grades throughout the semester. Most important, they keep us informed of the progress—or the lack of progress—of each athlete over the course of the year.

Last but not least, the promotions department contributes by drumming up public support for the program. The University of Georgia's promotions department does a great job in promoting our team, putting up swimming and diving posters around town, posting flyers, distributing schedule magnets, and introducing the team to the crowd at events such as home basketball games.

Establish Other Means of Support

I am sure there isn't a program in the country that is completely satisfied with the budget it receives. There are many ways to bolster the financial standing of a program. Booster clubs can do wonders in easing some of the financial burdens on a team. Since swim programs don't have the same resources as, for example, football and basketball, even $1,000 can make a very big difference in providing a winning environment. Booster clubs can raise money to help pay for such things as awards banquets and equipment, and they can make athletes feel "well taken care of." If the athletes are treated in a first-class manner, they are more likely to give first-class performances in the pool.

Booster clubs are without question time consuming, but they are extremely helpful in promoting and supporting the program. They can greatly impact your ability to raise money for endowment scholarships. Our club, the UGA Swim Club, consists of alumni, alumni parents, current parents, and some friends of the program. Each year the club raises an extra $30,000 to help our program. Our booster club has become very important to us; because of its success we have increased our fan support and have found it increasingly easy to raise money every year.

This brings us to another very important aspect of sports that needs to be addressed: endowment scholarships. Head coaches must realize that part of their role is that of businessperson. It is crucial that swimming and diving programs—especially men's programs, given the recent cuts in several men's programs across the country due to Title IX compliance—are secure in the years to come. We have to work on taking the grandest burden away from overextended athletic departments, namely the money given to scholarships.

By the time this book is published, one-third of our scholarships will be endowed. This achievement is the result of many, many hours of work and is something we are quite proud of. In raising money for scholarships, it is important to pinpoint your "heavy hitters"— individuals on the athletic board, successful ex-swimmers, friends of the program, and others who have an interest in swimming or in your athletic department and who also have the means to donate sizable sums of money. We have tried to be very aggressive in our efforts to secure money for endowment scholarships because these scholarships will help ensure that the swimming program here stays in good standing for a long time to come.

Plan a Structure for Your Season

The structure of each season definitely contributes to the overall success of the program. For the most part, dual meets should meet the needs of the team. As your team gets better, be sure to challenge the team with superb competition even if they think they cannot win. Eddie Reese was instrumental in the success and rise of our men's team, as he was willing to bring in his Texas team to swim us at a time when the other powerhouses would not. I am thankful to him because although we didn't offer much of a challenge those first few years, the meets with Texas brought out the very best in our kids; they were extremely excited to race swimmers of that caliber. Those better performances fueled my team's confidence and allowed us to become stronger.

There should be one meet on the schedule that you probably won't win and a few meets that you are not sure of. At the same time there should be some meets that you know you can win so you can move swimmers around to events that they wouldn't normally win or even swim. The schedule should also be different each year. Variety is good for a team, and a change of scenery doesn't hurt either.

As coach of a combined men's and women's program, I like to schedule some solo meets so that the women's team and the men's team can establish their individual identities. Solo meets also provide coaches of combined programs the chance to be with 25, rather than 50, athletes for the weekend. We also try to schedule back-to-back meets during the season to help prepare athletes to swim three-day championship meets.

In the last six weeks of training there has to be a definite separation of the women's team from the men's team. It is important to do things differently for each team. Men and women generally need different types of work going into the last few weeks. It is quite difficult to hit both groups right on with the taper. If you have the guts to do a little separating at that time, your efforts will be rewarded.

Maximize Your Facilities

Many coaches feel handcuffed by their available facilities. Certainly we were in this position at the University of Georgia until 1996. At no point in time, however, should poor facilities ever be an excuse for the performance of the team. Such facilities are certainly a detriment to recruiting, though. Once upon a time we tried valiantly to get through our recruits' official 48-hour visit without showing them the pool; now we make our new facility the first stop on the tour.

Leaving our old facility couldn't have come soon enough. It was losing water. It was somewhat tilted. It was gray and dank. But it was home and we tried to keep it up as much as possible, though no one else on campus seemed to care about it. I knew it was a bad sign that a hawk came flying in one of the end doors one afternoon, picked up a rat (we had a few of those around), and dropped it into lane three next to one of our swimmers. Thankfully this was near the end of our term and we were getting out of there in a matter of weeks. Still a pool is a pool, and if people don't believe that, they should go to Germantown Academy to see the remarkable job that Dick Shoulberg has done with a six-lane pool. With a lot of imagination and hard work, he consistently produces some of the best national-class swimmers, in a place that some people could not even imagine being able to work in.

No matter what situation you've inherited, make improvements, minor or major. It took almost 10 years of politicking and getting the right people working for us to make our new facility a reality. If indeed you find yourself in a situation where a new facility is in the works, take the time to involve yourself in as many aspects of the process as you can, so that the design—including the pool, the general look, the seating, the locker rooms, separate meeting rooms, the coaches' offices, and so forth—suits your team. It is time very well spent. I will say that it is like having another job, and the responsibility is as grand as you can imagine, as your greatest fear is someone walking into the pool 10 years from now and asking: "Who was the idiot that planned this?" I asked for as much help as possible. Go see other facilities and talk with the coaches who have been working in some of the better facilities in the country. The opportunity to help design the facility that your program will be living in for the next 20, 30, or perhaps even 50 years, must be taken advantage of. There are many stories attached to our old Stegeman pool, and it took a lot of extra work and maintenance, but here in our new pool I don't have to touch even one little gadget, except maybe the pace clocks. I do continue the tradition of having the swimmers do the lane lines, and I think I that will always be the case, to keep them a little less spoiled.

We currently have one of the top facilities in the country, and we do not take this for granted. But remember that the ability to use a facility when you want, and in the manner you want, is as important as having a nice facility. We have fought some tough battles here to get clearance to use this facility in the manner that we desire, but we have finally come out on top. If you find yourself in a situation that is incompatible with your needs, at no point in time should you settle. Fight for your athletes, if necessary, to get the pool time, to be able to host the meets you want, and to be able to access the facilities at the times that are best for your athletes. Toward this end it helps to have a good working relationship with the management. We try to include management in as many aspects of the program as we can, and we distribute T-shirts, hats, and such to let them know that we appreciate their cooperation.

Develop Lifelong Swimmers

Our USS club (the Athens Bulldogs Swim Club) has produced some great success stories, and it offers assistant coaches the opportunity to make more money and to hone their skills with athletes outside the collegiate arena. The USS club also serves as a viable program for athletes who need to remain at school and train during the summer. In the last nine years we have had an NCAA Champion, a four-time US National Champion, an NCAA All-American, and an NCAA Honorable Mention All-American—four athletes who have contributed greatly to the success of our college program—come out of our local program. The USS club also provides a solid support base of parents who are interested in swimming and willing to help financially as well as by volunteering at meets and so forth.

It is a wonderful but complicated (due in large part to the inordinate amount of restrictions imposed by the NCAA) time in collegiate swimming. We have the chance to coach young people in the best of all settings, while they are still forming their identities and building their lives. There is much satisfaction and fulfillment in coaching, but we have to be organized in order to accomplish the task at hand—to be the best possible coach for the athletes that are with us, the athletes that we recruited to our program. Organization is the key to providing the best possible environment for our athletes, and it enables us to live up to our commitment to coaching these young people well.

I hope the information in this chapter sheds a little light on the administration of a swim program. Maybe the most important item to remember is this: there are no limitations on the hours we spend coaching. We have to be willing to work as long and as hard as necessary to be successful. Swimming continues to become more competitive. There are more good coaches. There are more people willing to do the hard work. The job is not done until it is done; if *you* work hard you can demand the same level of effort and performance from your assistant coaches as well as from your athletes.

Success comes step by step. Assess after each year, figure out what can be done better, and address issues head on. But let us not forget how important it is to enjoy what we are doing and to enjoy the athletes around us on a daily basis. Keep priorities in the correct order, with athletes holding the highest place on the list. If all efforts in the program are made by putting the athletes' concerns first, the program will be successful in winning or in producing quality student-athletes—or better yet, both.

Summary

- Offer the best program possible, and winning will become possible.
- A good program is always a work in progress.
- Athletes are the first responsibility in a successful program.
- Administering a program goes beyond coaching.
- The head coach must assemble the best staff possible and select assistants who will be loyal to the program. Loyalty is more important than ability.
- Delegate responsibilities and allow your assigned staff full responsibility for their respective duties.
- Communicate with your swim staff as well as with the strength coaches, sport information personnel, and academic counselors who are vital for the success of the program.
- Evaluate all meets immediately after the competition. All staff members need to take part in the evaluation.
- Booster clubs can do wonders for your team.
- The structure of each season contributes to the success of the program.
- Each year's schedule should provide some variety.
- The facility you have available should never be an excuse for the performance of the team.
- There is no limit on the hours a coach must work in order to be successful.
- Evaluate your program at the end of the each season. See that it stays a work in progress.

Developing a Successful Team

Skip Kenney

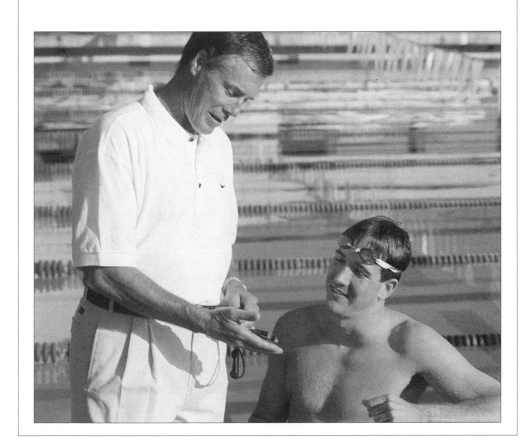

When a swimmer steps up on the blocks to compete, he or she is the ultimate master of his or her destiny. The moment of truth is revealed once the starting gun sounds, a moment when the athlete is in complete isolation from external help, relying only on strength, intellect, and desire. There are no coaches to shorten the distance of the race, no parents to mend bruised egos, and no teammates to make up for a lack of effort. The distance is constant, the time absolute. No one else can swim the race. From a performance perspective, swimming is an individual sport. Similarly, during training, nobody else can take a stroke for the individual. The pain is his or hers alone to embrace and master. However, the sport of swimming has adopted a training environment that is based on a team structure—a collection of athletes and coaches working together to optimize individual performances. Consequently, what culminates as the effort of one athlete begins with effort of many.

By training and competing within the context of an efficient team environment, individual athletes in sports such as swimming are able to perform at a higher level than if they were to train alone. Therefore, coaches and athletes alike are challenged to create and sustain the team chemistry and dynamics that will improve individual performance. By identifying the benefits of team training and competition, coaches and athletes may be better able to develop the kind of team that improves individual performance.

The Benefits of Team Training

While numerous benefits exist, the collective bond, mutual learning opportunities, and competitive challenge are three key characteristics of a positive team dynamic that can improve individual performance.

Collective Bond

When individual athletes train together for a team, a social network is created. If this social network is cultivated carefully, it can have a profound impact in assisting each athlete. By joining a team, every individual automatically has something in common with every other team member. The team itself serves as a shared identity and creates a bond among members. The standard uniform, the team colors, the mascot, and even the group slang contribute to a sense of camaraderie.

But it is the shared experience of training together, of pounding out mind-numbing yardage while enduring physical and mental anguish, that forges the real bond among swim teammates. This powerful bond motivates athletes to succeed for the sake of their teammates. Through self-sacrifice and hard work, every individual can contribute to the improvement of the team as a whole.

Coupled with team identity and culture, the team bond generated from shared experience is an extremely intense motivating factor. If an athlete were to train alone, there would be no special bond to rekindle the spirit during hard times. When workouts are difficult and a team member is having trouble succeeding, the social network of a team can provide support to help him or her push past the difficulty. Alone, the athlete might be likely to weaken and give in to the hardship. Through the collective experience of team training, an athlete is less likely to feel self-pity during intense training because others are enduring the same difficulties. The social network of a team presents each individual with the opportunity to observe and to feel connected to others.

Mutual Learning Opportunities

Both in and out of the pool, a team provides opportunities for the athletes to learn from one another. More often than not, the habits of successful athletes transcend the swimming pool and locker room; the same traits that are applied in the arena of sport are displayed in the classroom, in the office, and in the home. Time and time again, champions in the pool succeed out of the pool. Essentially, they have become 24-hour athletes, always applying winning habits to the game of life.

In a team environment, individuals are exposed to and are able to learn from the success of others. Some athletes on a team may lead by example in constantly applying an unyielding work ethic. The team structure provides an opportunity for others to model the behavior of a swimmer who consistently puts in outstanding effort, day in and day out. Other athletes may display perfect technique, or positive attitudes, or simply inspiration. Whatever it may be, each team member has something to contribute to the learning environment, directly or indirectly. Due to the competitive nature of athletics, the learning opportunities on a team also foster a healthy competitive environment. When a teammate succeeds in training, others will want to match or better his or her efforts.

Competitive Challenge

The competitive atmosphere of team training is a perfect opportunity for individual athletes to push themselves to do their best. An integral part of team training includes simulated competition, an opportunity for athletes to go head-to-head and compete with one another. While success in individual sports is often measured in seconds, meters, or points, victory is not assured without outpacing the competition.

In addition to learning how to perform, athletes must learn how to win. Competition within a team environment instills winning habits. In essence, competition within a team provides a dress rehearsal for the times when an athlete must step up to the real event. Team competition provides athletes with both physical and psychological competitive training. Considering that an athlete must be sound in both mind and body to win, approaching psychological training with the same intensity used in physical training is essential. Competition among teammates provides this intense training on a daily basis, something training in isolation simply cannot do.

The Coach's Role in Team Dynamics

While there are many more benefits to training for an individual sport within a team framework, these benefits can only be derived from a positive team environment. A negative team dynamic holds very few advantages over individual training and at times can even be detrimental to performance. The responsibility for establishing positive team dynamics and chemistry falls mostly on the shoulders of the coach. Coaches exert a profound impact on the success of a team. As an example, the recent success of the National Basketball Association champion Los Angeles Lakers is largely attributed to head coach Phil Jackson. After establishing a winning legacy with the Chicago Bulls, Jackson took over a talented but fragmented Los Angeles team in dire need of leadership and guided them to a championship in his first season there.

Because of the magnitude of influence coaches have on team chemistry and success, they must consider and bring into play several factors in building a positive team environment. Strong leadership, group communication, and individual accountability can help to build a positive team dynamic that will enhance individual performance.

Team leadership from both the coaches and team members is essential. Certainly a coach must provide leadership to his or her athletes by establishing procedures and boundaries, and by modeling the kind of behavior he or she expects from the athletes. But if a coach can identify other individuals with leadership potential and can place them in positions where they can lead their teammates, this will also help to ensure that the positive benefits of a team structure are realized. Strong leadership can grow the collective bond as well as afford increased opportunity for athletes to learn from one another.

Additionally, coaches can benefit from fostering group communication among team members. If good communication is established, individual athletes will become comfortable sharing feedback, thereby increasing learning opportunities. It does a team no good for members to have positive ideas or encouraging remarks that are inhibited or muffled by poor communication.

Because a team is made up of many individuals, it can be a real challenge to see that all members are pulling their weight. In a group environment, certain individuals assume they do not have to contribute because others will. Essentially these individuals feel little or no responsibility to the team. Coaches must ensure that all team members are accountable for their actions and feel compelled to contribute to the team. Through strong leadership on the part of the coach and through the development of a strong team bond, accountability can be instilled in every member of the team.

Although there are some standard ways to develop a strong team, a coach must understand that every team is different. From year to year, as members depart and new individuals are added, even the chemistry within a particular team changes. Despite these differences and changes, the benefits of a positive team environment remain the same. Team structure can benefit athletes at all levels, from the Olympic Trials qualifier to the up-and-coming age-grouper. In addition to being fun, when they are positive and productive, team environments can improve the individual performance of every athlete.

Summary

- Coaches and athletes work together to optimize individual performance.
- By training and competing within a positive team environment, individual athletes are able to perform at a higher level than if they trained alone.
- Three key characteristics of a positive team dynamic are the collective bond, mutual learning opportunities, and competitive challenge.
- The shared experience of training together creates a strong team bond.
- Champions in the pool often experience success out of the pool.
- In the team environment, individuals are exposed to and are able to learn from the success of others.
- Athletes must learn not only how to perform but how to win.
- Competition within a team environment instills winning habits, both physical and psychological.

- The responsibility for establishing positive team dynamics and chemistry falls largely on the coach.
- The coach must not only exhibit leadership but also identify leadership potential in others and place those individuals in positions where they can lead.
- Individual athletes must become comfortable sharing feedback and other types of communication.
- The coach must ensure that all team members are accountable for their actions.

CHAPTER SEVEN

Maximizing a Swimmer's Talent Development

Bill Sweetenham

I have coached and taught thousands of athletes over a 25-year period, yet I have never coached an untalented athlete. What is talent? Talent is a combination of physical and mental skills, some of which are trainable and some not. Each athlete is a special person possessing various levels of talent and potential in different areas. It is when the athlete has high skill levels in the untrainable skills and perhaps less talent in the trainable skills that quality coaching can make the biggest difference.

It has been my responsibility to recognize the unique talent within the individuals I've coached and to obtain the best possible swimming result from each of them at the appropriate meet or competition. The key to maximizing and sustaining talent over the long run is to plan the correct mix of training loads prior to physical maturation and to plan for continued improvement after physical maturation through technique development and proper training. This is not an easy task; there are recommended guidelines, but every swimmer is unique. The coach's ability to obtain the best result from each athlete, regardless of talent, determines the quality of the coach. Therefore, coaches should judge themselves on what is achieved by their least talented rather than their most talented swimmer.

To develop the full potential and talent of each swimmer (and thus the whole team) the coach must start with a two-to five-year plan and a swimmer development model that suits the ambition, desire, and capability of the swimmer, the coach, and the program. The club program must have a financial plan that also coincides with these goals. Over a period of time, the coach best develops the talent of his or her athletes by finding ways to expose each athlete to a wide variety of skills beyond their pool and dryland training, such as self-management and coping strategies, and nutritional education (including cooking lessons for the athlete and nutritional lectures for the parents). In this way, the athletes develop physical and mental tools that are transportable from one program to the next, from their home teams to district, provincial, and national teams. Athlete and coaches must produce the best results at the right meets under conditions they can neither predict nor control. This means they must be able to handle the unexpected effectively; they must be able to maintain their focus on the job at hand despite distractions, keep their emotions in balance, and conserve their energy for a perfect performance.

Creating the Environment

Coaching is convincing the willing and the unwilling to accept the wanted and the unwanted in order to achieve the "unattainable" and the unknown. Coaching is knowing no boundaries and disregarding what can't be or hasn't been achieved. Perhaps the coach's greatest challenge is selling these philosophies to swimmers, parents, and club officials, thus converting involvement into commitment—100 percent commitment.

The commitment of the parent to be a swim parent, of the swimmer to compete, of the coach to coach, and of the club to support the swimmers must combine to best serve and develop dedicated athletes. Most competitive clubs are an amalgamation of different levels of participation and mass mediocrity where no one swimmer aspires to be beyond average. There is no such thing as part-time commitment; social competition may provide entertainment for the participants, but it is of no value to competitors. Quality coaching begins with creating an atmosphere and environment where parents, swimmers, and officials unite with great pride and enthusiasm to recognize individual excellence and team success (see figure 7.1). The creation of a challenging but supportive club environment will greatly assist in developing and maximizing the potential of all swimmers in the program. If such an environment does not exist, then many opportunities and much talent will be lost or wasted.

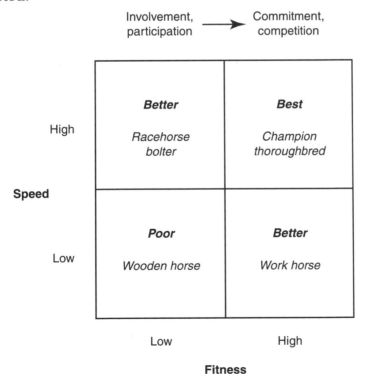

Figure 7.1 Maximizing a swimmer's talent means converting involvement and participation into commitment and competition.

To create the proper environment for developing and maximizing talent, the coach must possess a strong work ethic, a good quality control system, flexibility, consistency, and honesty. The athletes must take responsibility for their performances, be coachable, accept criticism and praise, be team players, have positive attitudes and be mentally and physically prepared for every workout and competition. The environment must allow the athlete to be physically challenged, mentally relaxed, and totally focused on the present.

Once a success-friendly environment is established within the club and the coaching program, it is wise for the coach to privately interview each swimmer and parent at the start of every training or competitive season or at the start of every year. Rather than telling the swimmers and parents what you as the coach expect of them, start by asking the swimmers what they are willing to do to achieve their maximum potential and what they expect of themselves. Next, ask what the swimmers expect of you as coach, and then confirm with the parents that they are willing to support this commitment in terms of attendance and punctuality at meets, training sessions, and so forth. Parents must provide unconditional love for their child but conditional support for their athlete; that is, the athlete must show commitment in order for parents to support his or her involvement in the sport. After talking with each swimmer and his or her parents you can decide whether the athlete will fit into your program and whether you can coach the athlete to his or her full potential.

Focus on Maximizing Each Individual

As a coach, you will eventually look back on your career and ask truthfully, "How many senior swimmers did I coach to their absolute maximum potential and did they enjoy a lifetime swimming experience?" Your answer will reveal whether you have been a great coach or just a good trainer. You will train many, but you may really coach only a few. Formula One racing cars do not come off an assembly line; they require much individual attention and refining. This same principle applies to coaches and athletes.

Coaches must frequently question if they would do the same workout if they were coaching only their most talented, fittest athlete or their weakest, least efficient athlete. By doing so, coaches can offset a middle pitch philosophy that so often persists in designing and implementing team swim workouts. A coach should feel that he or she can adapt a workout—main set, swim down, or kick set—to an individual athlete's attitude, dedication, or physical attributes. Such adaptations help the better or more focused athletes to see the positive effects of their application and help the less dedicated athletes to understand the negative effects of their application. The challenge for the coach is to have everybody in the program rise to the higher standard.

Workouts should be competition based, just as competitions should be a continuation of the training process. Athletes should be encouraged to race someone faster than themselves. Of course this can be difficult to achieve since most squads contain significantly different personalities, attitudes, and percentages of male and female athletes. It is important, though, that all workouts encourage an open attitude toward challenge and that they finish, whenever possible, on a positive note.

Along these lines, it is not wise for the coach to train or work out with his or her athletes. Besides setting an unreasonable mark for athletes to attempt to reach, doing so makes it impossible for the coach to supervise practice. It compromises the swimmers' workouts and undermines competitiveness, and it breaches the professional standing and relationship between coach and athletes.

Seek to Improve Your Coaching

Of the approximately 450 practice sessions per year that the coach must ask of each swimmer, how many achieve their particular objective? How many, or what percentage of, missed objectives or missed practices do you consider excusable? Assess whether it is the coaching, the athlete, the stimulus, or the environment that requires changing to improve this statistic for the individual and the team.

The coach's level of experience in maximizing individual talent should always be beyond that required by his or her athletes. Do not rely solely on self-evaluation of your coaching. Ask another coach, from out of town or even from another sport if necessary, to do a factual, critical, "don't spare the feelings" coaching assessment.

Provide Balance

Most of your swimmers will be combining an academic career with the demands of high-performance competitive swimming. This can require detailed planning by the coach, parents, and swimmers. Coaches should try to program recovery or adaptation weeks to coincide with return-to-school dates and exam weeks. Weekly practice sessions might vary throughout the year to accommodate school; this could mean training twice a day on weekends and once a day on weekdays for selected weeks. Appointing a team manager who is a schoolteacher is helpful if extended

Standard Coaching Strategies

You have your own coaching philosophy, but the following guidelines should fit somewhere into them, even if you make personal modifications to them. Everything you do and say at practice and meets will be dinner-table conversation in each of your swimmer's homes.

- Dress appropriately and act professionally. On the pool deck, there should be no using mobile phones, no eating or drinking, and no sitting down.
- Speak and demonstrate skills clearly and confidently. The swimmers are seeking and appreciate leadership.
- Keep your approach simple and consistent. Don't complicate things; simplicity facilitates success.
- Demand attention (both looking and listening) and do not proceed without it.
- Praise endeavors and show confidence in the ability of your swimmers to achieve the standards you set. Communicate to the swimmers that it is not what they do that matters, it is how they do it and how often they do it well.
- Review skills from the previous session. Allocate 10 to 20 percent of practice time to this purpose. Do not put skill extension ahead of skill acquisition.
- Continually and consistently reinforce expectations—equipment, punctuality, lane etiquette. Do not compromise standards.
- Plan lane organization to allow for an efficient use of space (e.g., down backstroke, return freestyle). Vary lane leadership.
- Be prepared to answer the question, "Why are we doing this?" Relate activities and drills to the outcomes you are seeking to achieve.
- Always outline for the swimmers in advance what's in it (the session, the drill) for them. Use incentives and rewards (e.g., cards, certificates, praise for each swimmer, novelties such as candy), but be sure to expect the best they can offer—no less, no more, no excuses.
- Positive, corrective feedback (from coach to swimmer to coach) should prevail. Swimmers should walk away from each session confident that they have enhanced their knowledge and skills.
- Be in control at all times; allowing swimmers to make decisions is just another way of your being in control. Keep the session moving with a minimum of talk; demonstrate and explain only as needed. Have swimmers use many and varied skills to achieve any predetermined objective.
- Don't be distracted.
- Have a theme or mantra for each session such as "100 percent right is 100 percent right; percent right is 100 percent wrong" or "Good is not good enough where better is possible."
- Use care and common sense, but don't be afraid to challenge your swimmers. Young people love to acquire new skills and to have those skills recognized. They enjoy being able to do things others cannot do.
- Do something positive and personal for every swimmer at every session, whether it's offering praise, stroke correction, a comment or joke, or having them demonstrate to the group, lead the lane, or correctly answer a question.
- Watch the strokes and skills over every athlete at every workout.

There are many other strategies and guidelines you may want to add to this list based on your own experiences.

camp periods away from school are required; he or she can advise the team as to what is required or acceptable when swimming and school conflict and can also be of assistance in an educational capacity.

Keep it Serious but Fun

A coach should establish a minimum requirement with regard to team members' training standard, competition standard, skill standard, and attendance at practice and competition. No compromises to these standards should be considered.

One good way to help younger swimmers grow and develop is to create a buddy system for athletes that pairs younger, less experienced swimmers with older, more experienced swimmers. This may make progressing from one group to the next significantly more challenging but also more rewarding. The training of the junior squads should include all four strokes and individual medley training, with the 12- to 13-year-old 200-meter individual medley race being a focal point of talent development.

Include relay swimming and skills in the squad progression and make it an expectation within the more senior groups. Make relay a priority of the training for members of the squad who are nearing the specific ages at which swimmers' performance and interest tend to wane. Vigorously promoting the team concept to an athlete and his or her parents just prior to the swimmer's last year of secondary school enhances the swimmer's enjoyment of the sport and helps prevent plateauing or losing interest in swimming and dropping out.

One objective of the coach in maximizing individual talent is to keep that talent motivated and improving within the program, at least until the swimmer reaches his or her early 20s. This means that the program must offer something new, different, fun, more challenging, and more rewarding every year. It therefore becomes very important for the program to offer social development directed toward the needs of the senior athletes. Age-group swimming is a means to an end, not an end in itself.

Develop Solid Stroke Technique

The stroke technique that enables an age-group swimmer to be successful may not be the technique that will carry a senior athlete to his or her full potential because of the changes in muscle bulk, flexibility, and mental focus that occur as a swimmer matures. It is therefore extremely important that the stroke technique that is developed at a young age be able to carry the athlete to postmaturation success. Quite often, the most limiting factor in maximizing individual talent is a swimmer's not developing his or her stroke technique correctly at a young age. A compromised technique does not allow the swimmer to improve as the body matures and develops. The young athlete also benefits from a high frequency of exposure to training; that is, it is much better to do shorter practice sessions more often (9 to 10 shorter practice sessions per week) than longer practice sessions less often.

Albert Einstein described frustration as "endlessly repeating the same process hoping for a different result." Unfortunately, we witness this process far too often with individuals in the training and competition arenas of our sport. Competitive swimming is a technique-based sport and the biomechanics of the sport and the strokes can be complicated and confusing. To simplify this, I ask athletes to remember and apply four simple rules of biomechanics to all aspects of their strokes:

1. All movements in swimming, from recovery through underwater pulling, have a slow-into-fast action.

2. If the head is elevated, the hips are down (causing maximum resistance), and if the head is down, the hips are up (causing minimum resistance).

3. You cannot learn or improve anything you cannot "feel." This includes the "feel" for water. Athletes should close their eyes and feel the water as as they complete each step in the following sequence.
   - Body position
   - Kick
   - Sculling
   - Specific sculling
   - Timing and breathing
   - Full (perfect) slow-motion technique
   - Distance per stroke
   - Turns
   - (Choice) weak or strong drill segment

4. If you put the hips in position before the arms, any application of limb force will result in forward movement.

Identifying and Improving Swimmers' Talents

One might compare the talented athlete to a high-performance bicycle. The bicycle may have the best wheels available and may be capable of traveling 100 kilometers per hour, but if the pedals break down at 50 kilometers per hour and the seat is inadequate, the 100-kilometer-per-hour wheels are of little value. Just as the bicycle is only as valuable as its weakest link, so is the swimmer. Therefore, it is the coach's responsibility to build the athlete as a total package. Elimination of weaknesses in every area, both physical and mental, in lifestyle and in training facilitates the final outcome of maximizing swimmers' talent development.

Prior to the beginning a training program, the athlete should have a physical or physiotherapy check-up for possible injury risks, muscle balance issues, and overall alignment. It is also wise for the athlete to have a full medical and blood profile at the start of each training year, at the onset of any significant increase in volume or intensity of workload, and if possible, just prior to or just after major competitions.

In identifying talent, I find it best to confirm your coach's "eye" for talent with a sport science evaluation of a particular athlete to accurately and independently measure the strengths and weaknesses of the individual. Any individual athletic qualities that can be both measured and controlled (i.e., that are trainable or changeable) should be monitored. Such qualities include range of movement, endurance, seed, distance per stroke, distance per kick, and turning time. Athletes will win or succeed due to their strengths but will fall short of their potential because of their weaknesses. To develop the maximum potential within, athletes must work on improving their strengths and lessening their weaknesses. Here are some things to look for when identifying a swimmer's talents:

- Strong "aquatic feel" (good stroke efficiency, smooth glide through the water, bouyancy)
- Long-limbed body with big hands and feet, long and lanky body, narrow hips, wide shoulders, and hand speed
- Rhythm, a relaxed quality in basic swimming skills, and recovery ability
- An ability to learn new skills to perfection quickly
- A known athletic history in a variety of sports (including parent profile)
- Good body coordination
- Parental support and commitment
- Good swimmer attitude
- Access to quality coaching

I see talent through the same eyes as Istvan Bayli, renowned author and exercise physiologist to the Canadian Ski Team. Important aspects include speed development, stroke efficiency, overall conditioning, technical skills, tactical skills and experience, and psychological strengths. Every training session must be executed according to the coach's expectations in terms of the predetermined training speed, stroke length, and heart rate. The workout must be evaluated based on the individual athlete's ability to achieve the workout's objectives. The coach must ask "Did the swimmer at every workout improve in the areas of speed, stroke efficiency, overall fitness, technical skills, tactical skills, or psychological skills?"

Speed Development

Speed is the ability of the athlete to swim fast or to perform an event at a controlled or specific speed. The ability to swim fast is often deemed less trainable than other aspects of training because it depends in part on an athlete's genetic muscle fiber make up (fast twitch to slow twitch fiber ratios). However, the ability to control and to sustain specific speeds can be influenced greatly by training and should therefore be practiced all year round at an early age. Speed training should not be practiced to fatigue, though; this defeats of the purpose of training efficiency at speed. Speed training is most effective when done in short sets over distances of no more than 30 to 40 meters, with full recovery. Athletes should not work on speed if they are in a severely fatigued state.

One good way to help develop speed is to use the following formula: Start with the swimmer's best 100-meter time minus 5 seconds. Divide this number by 4 to get 25-meter split goal times. (If the swimmer is a 200-meter specialist, take his or her best 200-meter time and subtract 10 seconds.) Using these goal times, record how many strokes it takes the swimmer to reach the distance at the goal speed. The idea is for the swimmer to swim at maximum speed with minimum effort. A talented athlete can travel at about 100 percent speed with 90 percent effort. Training speed to fatigue rather than speed for speed occurs when the athlete is traveling at 90 percent speed but 100 percent effort, and usually at a compromised stroke length and stroke rate. Thus, an important part of developing speed is recording the athlete's stroke length and rate accurately throughout his or her career. Such record-keeping can enable a swimmer to reap a long-range result from an immediate training stimulus.

Stroke Efficiency

I believe that both efficiency and quality of technique are teachable, trainable, and coachable. From the time a swimmer first learns to swim, certainly within the first three years of the athlete's career, he or she should be taught and drilled in his or her most efficient stroke. This efficiency is measured in optimal distance per stroke or distance per kick. Drilling this efficiency should first be done with minimal-effort sets to have the swimmer focus on technique rather than speed. Quality technique is vital to success; there are no successful world-class athletes with poor technique or poor efficiency.

While optimal strength and power development are also important, they are no substitute for proper technique. Yet I regularly witness swimmers who try to muscle their way through a stroke with strength and power *instead of* rather than *as well as* great efficiency. Dryland strength and power training is like medicine: it should only be included in an athlete's program when and if required to aid in efficiency. Unless athletes can swim efficiently, they will not be able to sustain speed and power. For athletes to be efficient, they must have adequate shoulder, hip- and lower-body flexibility and mobility. Flexibility and mobility are developed and maintained through a balanced dryland program that includes periodical or sustained exposure to training in core strength, general fitness, specific strength, and power conversion from land to water. Females will usually require dryland training more frequently and starting at an earlier age than males.

Overall Conditioning

A swimmer's overall fitness and conditioning enables him or her to sustain and to maintain speed and efficiency at certain levels over set distances. Fitness is the most trainable and changeable talent attribute of an athlete. However, its value depends on the athlete's ability to efficiently swim specific and variable speeds on demand. That is, fitness can only be maximized if speed and efficiency values have been addressed. Overall conditioning is the most overemphasized dimension of developing and maximizing talent because it is very trainable. But for the vast majority of athletes, it is emphasized at the expense of efficiency and speed training.

Adhering to this simple progression will ensure that athletes do not sacrifice technique, efficiency, or speed for the sake of overall conditioning.

- Quality control (swim a distance with perfect technique)
- Quality control with goals (number of strokes)
- Quality control with speed (time)
- Quality control with goals and speed
- Quality control with goals, speed, consistency, and frequency

Determining and controlling appropriate training intensity is necessary for maximizing sport performance. Applying the basic principles of sport physiology and integrating an intelligent, balanced mix of training intensities as well as a variety of training activities are essential elements of successful coaching.

Swimmers should be given a wide range of training experiences and should learn to control their training intensity; this is the basic principle of individuality. The biggest challenge is individualizing training intensity when working with a team. A training program must have a sound, long-term swimmer development model that clearly outlines volume of training, content of swimming workouts, and content of dryland workouts. This training plan should be easily understood and appreciated by club members, parents, and swimmers.

To improve overall fitness, the swimmer and coach have several choices to consider. Keeping in mind the importance of sustaining efficiency as training load increases, coaches and swimmers can improve overall fitness in a number of ways. They may decide to have the swimmer

- do more repeats at same speed and efficiency;
- do the same number of repeats faster but maintain and sustain efficiency;
- do fewer repeats with the same rest and recovery but faster and with maintained efficiency;
- do the same number of repeats at the same speed but at improved efficiency; or
- do fewer repeats with more rest and recovery but faster, at race speed, while maintaining improved efficiency.

Keep in mind that it is wisest to improve one aspect of swim performance at a time, followed by another. To attempt to improve speed, efficiency, and fitness all at once makes it very difficult to create systematic adaptation and to evaluate training effects.

The coach conducting a regular training set should follow a progressive system similar to the following:

- Exposure 1—Have the swimmer complete repeats at either a percentage of his or her maximum heart rate or at a beats below maximum (BBM) value. Record swimmer's times and heart rates as he or she maintains even split swimming and even split stroke counts and predetermined efficiency.
- Exposure 2—Have the swimmer hold the average speed of the set

from exposure 1 while maintaining efficiency and even split stroke count and speed. Record his or her improved (hopefully) heart rate.

- Exposure 3—Using the average repeat times from exposure 1 and the heart rate and lactate values from exposure 2, ask the swimmer to improve either one or both, or to improve his or her efficiency while maintaining both and continuing even split swimming and even split stroke counts.

- Exposure 4—Using the information from the first three exposures, develop a set to either challenge the weaknesses or the race-specific strengths of the athlete. The swimmer should maintain or improve efficiency.

Each of the four exposures can then be repeated at improved values in order to match the intensity to the swimmer's improving fitness. Training or competing at uncontrolled speeds and efficiency produces a chance or potluck result based on doing enough of every type of training at varying levels of fatigue. Doing so will have a detrimental effect on the long-term development of the athlete, jeopardizing the opportunity to maximize individual potential. All training repeats should be done at a predetermined speed, heart rate and lactate value, and efficiency using quality technical skills. Control the controllable, measure the measurable, and prioritize the training so that the controllable and the measurable exist.

Should a breakdown occur in a workout, as evidenced by cardiac creep, or the athlete becoming distracted, tired, or sick, or the athlete being generally unprepared due to a miscalculation of the coach, the coach and senior athlete can take action to adjust the workout in one of the following ways:

- Stop the set.
- Do nothing and hope for the best.
- Increase rest but hold heart rate and speed.
- Hold heart rate and ignore speed.
- Hold speed and ignore heart rate.
- Break repeats in half and hold both values.

Again, the most important guideline is to do what allows the athlete to maintain stroke efficiency. The adjustment you select will vary according to the time within the training cycle, the event being trained for, the physical and mental state of the athlete, and the all-important recovery ability of the athlete. The decision for a particular athlete at a particular point in time is cumulative and can determine the performance outcome. Only a thorough knowledge of the athlete and of the event will enable the coach and the senior athlete to make the correct decision.

For the age-group swimmer, it is best to keep weekly volume (total workload) as constant as possible. For senior swimmers, however, you'll want to vary the volume to assist in adaptation. A good rule of thumb is that for age-group swimmers, 80 percent of the volume of training should be at 70 percent $\dot{V}O_2$max (or maximum heart rate), which is approximately individual checking speed. For senior athletes, this may change slightly, with 70 percent of the total volume being at this speed or slower.

Develop exercises for lower-back and abdominal strength maintenance or improvement if required. I recommend gradually increasing the dryland program from age-group to senior levels. Swimmers should practice flexibility on a daily basis.

On occasion the coach should conduct one-on-one workouts with especially deserving athletes, have separate workouts for males and females, offer skill workouts for those with 100 percent attendance, and provide special recognition workouts for those above a certain point score.

Technical Skills

The technical aspects of the athletes' development and capabilities are related to their turning, starting, and finishing skills. Obviously, athletes must legally execute these skills at all training sessions so that they can perform them with the highest degree of skill, efficiency, and speed in competition. Ideally, the coach should position him- or herself on the pool deck in order to evaluate these skills and provide immediate feedback to the swimmers. When giving feedback, the coach must also seek feedback from the athletes as to how the corrected skill feels. This exchange helps athletes become more committed to perfection and to the philosophy that good is not enough when perfect is possible.

I find it beneficial to perfect five to six ways of teaching or redirecting each skill. As a rule, I do not persevere in trying to teach an athlete any one way more than six times. The athlete who executes the skill correctly on the first or second attempt will quickly lose interest and proficiency if forced to continually carry out repetitious drill. Conversely, the athlete who fails to properly execute the drill in the first three or four attempts tends to lose interest. Having several ways to achieve a quality end result and practicing each way no more than six times ensures success for all swimmers. This is called a 6 × 6 learning progression. Similarly, the mutual feedback between coach and athlete is a 12 × 12 progression. Within one hour of instruction, the coach should deliver 12 minutes of individual (as opposed to group) instruction to athletes and receive back 12 minutes of individual feedback.

Your training group must be the best relay changeover team and the best starting, turning, and finishing team in the competition. The skills involved relate to hand touch to foot touch or foot release, starting reaction times, and streamlining speed. A high standard in executing these skills can be taught and demanded at a very young age. It is of great value to have a referee attend one practice per week and to have him or her make a list of all observed faults. Athletes can then follow up by doing a workout with a skills coach (from another swim group) to correct the faults listed by the referee. A double coaching structure, in which each coach alternately coaches each squad, greatly assists in following up on skill corrections.

Swimming is a technique-driven sport. Regardless of the training intensity, the overriding principle of swimming performance is to maximize propulsive force and to minimize resistive force. Remember that high training intensity is not an excuse to compromise correct technique.

Tactical Skills

The tactical skills of swimmers are directly related to their pacing skills and their ability to swim in competition and training at their own speed rather than a speed dictated to them by their competitors. There are some standard rules such as that it is not good practice to back-end or negative heat swims, as the perceived exertion at the end of the race is not relative to the time on the scoreboard. However, the specific pacing of the race often makes the difference in the final result, and all combinations should be experienced and practiced in training.

Psychological Training

An athlete must be conditioned to perform under all conditions—even under the most stressful of race conditions. A strong mental attitude can be trained and stimulated so that the athlete becomes capable of achieving the required end result with a large amount of coaching influence for an age-grouper and with a minimum coaching influence for a senior athlete. One tool that I use to prepare athletes mentally as well as physically is to have them participate in three meets that are below their personal standard so that they are expected to win. In this situation, I have the athlete experiment with different tactical skills. Then I have them swim in two meets that are right at their standard so that they are expected to win and to perform best times in a situation that is challenging. Finally, I enter swimmers in one meet above their standard. In this case, they are placed in what is considered an "unwinnable" situation but are expected to perform best times. This is called a 3-2-1 competition strategy.

Another good tool for developing a rough and ready attitude is a cold swim in which athletes are expected, with a minimum of warm-up time and little in the way of competitive atmosphere, to perform a swim within 3 percent of their best time, under stressful situations.

Training for Progress

Athletes and coaches must be hungry for winning and for the rewards that go with it. Athlete burnout is usually the result of a lack of stimulus, an overexposure to competition pressure, or an underexposure to success. Sometimes, it stems from a combination of these conditions.

In age-group competitive swimming, it is quantity that forms the technical and aerobic background to facilitate improvement after maturation. The technical skills of the athlete are ingrained through high-volume (yardage), low-intensity, but high-quality technique work at a young age. The training progression and early stage preparation of the athlete can be explained in four simple steps:

1. Have swimmers hold quality technique over an extended period of time at low intensity with maximum distance per stroke.

2. Use repeats of race distances and longer. Swimmers should train at moderate intensities with distractions but hold quality technique and distance per stroke.

3. Repeats that are shorter than race distance should be swum at faster than race pace with varying rest intervals, but swimmers should hold quality technique and distance per stroke.

4. Repeats that are to be done at race pace and stroke rates should focus on improved technique and maintain distance per stroke.

When coaches request a maximum-effort swim, they usually mean a maximum-speed, minimum-effort swim. Swimming fast with minimal effort should be the objective of every competition and workout practice to assist in facilitating a strong back-end of a race or training repeat, such that speed is maintained without any loss of stroke length. To produce maximum potential in a swimmer of any race distance, this skill cannot be compromised in training in any way. Stroke efficiency is always the predecessor of speed. Applying the reverse strategy rarely if ever works, yet so many try. Even split repeat training swims must be evenly split in both speed and stroke length, with even split stroke length swims being developed before speed is introduced into the equation.

It is said that with low-intensity, high-concentration training, athletes will become bored before they get tired and that therefore coaches must be innovative and creative. However, as with any other type of training, coaches must have athletes rise to their level of expectation rather than simply accepting whatever the athletes are willing to give. It is not so much the work the athletes do that matters, but the degree of efficiency and the effort put forth. Quite often, the coach and the environment are responsible for the results. Varying workouts to keep them fresh can be as simple as ensuring that every warm-up be different and that it be supportive of but in contrast to the main workout.

Speed efficiency training (distance per stroke) must be incorporated into early age-group low-intensity, high-volume quality technique training on a year-round basis. Ideally, a 12-year-old swimmer can complete a 200 individual medley using 16 strokes butterfly, 24 strokes backstroke, 16 strokes breaststroke, and 24 strokes freestyle so that speed or overspeed training can occur at the start and/or finish of workouts, or can in fact be the main set. The young swimmer might sprint 8 strokes butterfly or breaststroke and try to achieve a maximum and measured distance, or might sprint 20 to 25 meters (50 for the trained or more advanced athlete) in the least number of strokes.

The overspeed component contributes to the quality-control objective of the practice segment. This type of swimming should be practiced between 80 and 100 repetitions each week for mature swimmers. While it can be practiced with varying rest periods, it should not be practiced to fatigue; the purpose is to develop speed faster than race pace at race stroke length. An athlete is capable of giving 100 percent effort at any time but may only achieve full speed if physically and mentally fresh. However, it is good for the coach to demand full speed from a physically fresh but mentally stressed athlete. Once this speed training is achieved, it can then be incorporated into a separate training goal of developing lactate production, then lactate tolerance and perhaps peak training. Throughout the increase in intensity, during practice and competition, stroke length and speed maintenance should not be compromised.

As age-group swimmers develop into open or international competitors, their training will change significantly. They will advance from a training program that includes only three training speeds to perhaps five or six training speeds. Later the reverse occurs. Age-group swimmers find that as the body matures, more recovery work is required and specific training is needed so that the multifocus workout or practice session now becomes a dual- or single-focus workout. The recovery ability of the athlete changes, and a seasonal recovery or adaptation period may be needed to support or replace the individual weekly recovery. The older or more practiced the swimmer, the quicker the response or adaptation will be to any given training stimulus.

For developing talent, I base the training speeds on percentages of race performance and speed, progressing to a beats below maximum (BBM) heart rate value after male swimmers are physically mature and during maturation for most females. I introduce lactate values for advanced athletes after they have learned, used, and mastered the speed and heart rate training. The end result is that we monitor, record, and evaluate all these values, along with perceived exertion, during advanced and periodical step tests, quality training, and competitions (see figures 7.2, a through g).

We record these on clear plastic graph paper or graph paper sealed in plastic so that each value or graph can be overlaid for comparisons of any value, any test, any workout, or speed. Each swimmer then has a portfolio of these values available at all times for comparison with other tests and performances. Checks are made frequently at workouts on all speed-related values. The swimmers are also aware of their own individual maximum heart rate in the water (not from a formula such as 220 less age), individual checking speed, recovery index, and stroke and speed efficiency indices. For at least 80 to 90 percent of the total training volume, training repeats must be executed at a predetermined, even split (speed) stroke length and stroke rate relevant to heart rate and lactate control.

Within training, the importance of test sets must be kept in perspective. Test sets provide the swimmer, personal coach, and national coach with a view of the swimmer's current state of fitness in specific areas by providing technical evaluations such as stroke length, stroke rate, streamlining speed, and turning and finishing speeds as compared to heart rate, lactate levels, and perceived exertion values. With this information, it is possible to estimate reasonably accurate percentages of the energy system being used. Values such as individual checking speed, speed and stroke efficiency, and recovery indices can be used as guides to the overall and specific physical fitness of the athlete.

It has been my experience that the emphasis applied to a given training

Current results

Swim	200m	1st 100m	2nd 100m	Ave. 100m	HR	La	SR	SC	SEI	RPE
1	2.52.6	88.3	84.3	86.3	141	1.1	25.4	32	1.81	7
2	2.40.1	79.0	81.1	80.1	150	1.7	27.9	33	1.89	10
3	2.37.1	77.9	79.2	78.6	159	2.1	28.6	34	1.87	12
4	2.34.4	77.1	77.3	77.2	166	2.7	29.7	35	1.85	14.5
5	2.28.7	73.4	75.3	74.4	172	6.3	33.6	36	1.87	16.5
6	2.24.8	71.0	73.9	72.5	180	10.1	36.5	38	1.82	18.5
7	2.20.9	69.2	70.7	70.0	182	13.9	39.2	39	1.83	20

Derived results

Swim	T. Time	c-La	c-HR	c-SR	c-SC	c-SI
1	90	0.40	131	22	30	1.85
2	86	0.80	140	24	31	1.85
3	82	1.57	150	27	33	1.85
4	78	3.10	161	30	35	1.85
5	74	6.13	172	34	37	1.85
6	70	12.12	184	24	39	1.85
7	66	23.94	196	42	41	1.85

Summary of derived results

La (mM)	V (m/s)	Time	HR	SR	SC	SEI	Aerobic	Anaerobic
1	1.23	81	147	25	33	1.85	100%	1%
2.5	1.25	80	151	26	33	1.85	96%	4%
3	1.26	79	153	27	33	1.85	94%	6%
3.5	1.27	79	154	27	34	1.85	93%	7%
4	1.28	78	155	27	34	1.85	92%	8%
5	1.29	77	158	28	34	1.85	89%	11%
8	1.35	74	165	30	35	1.85	80%	20%
10	1.38	72	170	31	36	1.85	74%	26%
max	1.45	69	180	34	38	1.85	63%	37%
3.68	1.30	76.8	164	31	35	1.85	88%	12%

		LTR_{5-10}	4.7	SEI variation	0%			

Summary of anaerobic threshold results

Date	La_{AT} (mV)	V_{AT} (m/s)	$Time_{AT}$	HR_{AT}	SR_{AT}	SC_{AT}	%SEIV	$%Aer_{AT}$	$%An_{AT}$	LTR
11 Oct 99	2.81	1.31	76.2	169	27.9	30	11%	88%	12%	8.1
25 Oct 99	3.27	1.32	75.6	165	28.3	31	11%	84%	16%	8.1
8 Nov 99	3.90	1.35	74.3	168	30.4	30	9%	85%	15%	4.6
11 Jan 00	3.71	1.33	75.1	169	31.6	33	1%	89%	11%	4.2
7 Feb 00	3.55	1.33	75.0	167	31.7	35	0%	87%	13%	4.7
30 Apr 00	3.68	1.30	76.8	164	31.4	35	0%	88%	12%	4.7

Figure 7.2a Monitor, record, and evaluate data during testing, training, and competition.

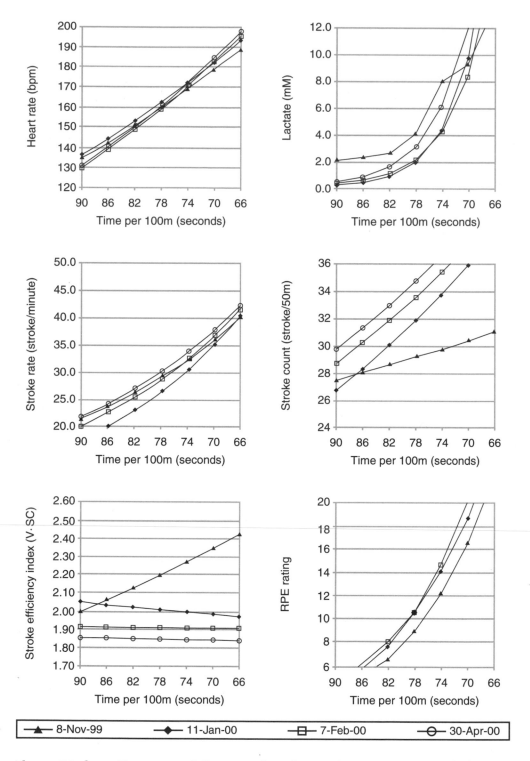

Figure 7.2, b-g Keep a portfolio on each swimmer for comparison and planning purposes.

distance is often changed significantly either by extending the distance at the same intensity or by varying the recovery of the athlete. An athlete's ability to recover is of vital importance in determining exactly how he or she might train. Quite often, the recovery ability of an athlete overrides his or her slow- or fast-twitch muscle fiber make-up as a primary concern in making training decisions.

The following are test sets that I recommend for the development of talent at the age-group and youth level:

1. Individual medley stroke-count efficiency
2. Individual checking speed tests in which the pace for the set is based on the swimmer's personal best 100-meter time + 15 seconds (+ 20 for breaststroke)
3. Maximum heart rate tests
4. Age-group and youth sprint test pacing sets
5. 7 × 200 age-group and youth test set

For further information on these test sets, refer to Bill Sweetenham's *Test Sets for Age and Youth Level Swimmers* as published in 1999 by the Australian Swimming Coaches and Teachers Association.

While there are many more tests sets, these should enable the coach and the athlete to recognize when the athlete is ready to perform or train at optimal levels. These sets also allow the coach to evaluate the training program and the progress being made by an athlete over any given period of time. An example of an individual medley test set is as follows:

4 × 250 on 4:00 minutes. Hold 50s at a predetermined submaximal value for speed and efficiency based either on a personal best time plus 10 seconds or individual checking speed values. Where the 100-meter distance is indicated in the following table, the athlete performs this distance and the stroke indicated at goal time for the 400 IM. These values may be halved, along with the distance, for the 200 IM.

Butterfly	Backstroke	Breaststroke	Freestyle
100	50	50	50
50	100	50	50
50	50	100	50
50	50	50	100

Add up the 100 times for a goal-pace 400 individual medley.

I find it beneficial to hold two, perhaps three, events back once a swimmer becomes physically mature so that those events can be used to kick start a training or competition plateau, should either occur at this difficult age.

I recommend that backstroke aerobic work and quality breaststroke pull work be included in every swimmer's aerobic, base-training program at maturation age. By completing a significant portion of their aerobic base training using backstroke, an athlete will develop a free but deep rhythmical breathing technique and a balanced stroke (due to a straight arm recovery). Most important, the athlete will learn the value of applied trunk rotation prior to early application of limb and hand pressure, and force, against the water. This low-intensity, backstroke aerobic work, coupled with limited-stroke, high-quality, resistant breaststroke pull work over short distances, enhances the specific early application of limb and hand force and assists in developing specific power.

The athlete progresses from a training-to-train phase to a training-to-compete phase to a training-to-win phase, and any attempt to short-circuit this process by the coach, swimmer, or parent usually ends in disaster. However, an experienced, artful coach can determine how long each athlete should remain in each phase. The temptation today is to undertrain and overrace swimmers, as opposed to overtraining and underracing them as was done in the not-too-distant past. Together, the coach, athlete, parents, and administrator must use common sense and find the correct balance for each individual.

Scheduling Competitions

Because competition can overstress athletes to the point that they compromise or ignore their distance per stroke and distance per kick, I believe a program must contain a competition black-out period in which they focus on training and preparation only. The black-out period should exist for up to approximately two months per year. During this time, it is ideal to allocate each swimmer 12,000 points (international point score) and have them work to reduce their points to zero. Identify who can do so, how quickly they can do so, and who can do so with the least number of self-nominated, predetermined, stand-up swims or cold starts. This point reduction contest helps swimmers adjust to the pressure of competition by having them practice producing the best result in less than perfect conditions while under a manageable amount of stress.

This competition black-out period should be followed by a competitive period in which athletes move, while maintaining control, from the longer events to shorter, more specific individual race distances as the major meet draws closer. Keep athletes stimulated by offering a variety of competitions: team competitions, single-event, multi-event, front-end/back-end competitions (working only on specific simulated splits), relay competitions, and so forth. But also be selective in competitions. Very few racehorse trainers would take their entire stable to every racing event, yet often swim coaches will take their entire squad to most scheduled competitions. Instead, swim individuals as needed to fit the requirements of the team as well as the individuals on the team.

A model for competitions is that athletes will improve at about 3 percent per year of birth and that they will compete at the same number of competitions as their age within 3 percent of the average of their best time and their goal time. Along with this, athletes should be capable of competing heats within 3 percent of their goal time, semi-finals within 2 percent of their goal time, and finals within 1 percent of their goal time. They should be able to meet these same percentages but of best times at mock trials or in simulated racing at the workout arena.

Profile of the Talent-Maximized Swimmer

The talent-maximized member of a quality program

- has an annual or a two-year plan incorporating academic work, family life, training, and competitions—and distributes copies to all of the relevant and associated people;
- has 100 percent attendance at practice sessions;
- does not arrive late or leave early from competitions or training;
- does not need to be instructed or reminded more than once;
- incorporates both a team and an individual approach to their sport;
- loves to race;
- loves the sport and is committed to it;
- has an open mind and believes that anything and everything is possible;
- has great self-esteem and confidence developed by exposure to and success in defeating challenges and obstacles—and, in fact, enjoys the higher and more difficult challenge;
- always does more than the coach asks;
- has learned and practiced the ability of self-promotion but understands that confidence, not arrogance, is a key factor in performance;

- can handle the press and media in both positive and negative situations with equal ability;
- is very honest in self-assessment of training and competition;
- is competent in turning both ways (right to left and vice versa) in training and competition;
- practices difficult breathing patterns;
- practices circling lanes both right to left and left to right;
- practices pulling first on alternating arms in backstroke and freestyle repeats;
- can repeat exact stroke counts and specific predetermined times with even split, efficient strokes.
- uses two self-prepared (not prepared by parents or coach) drink bottles in each workout;
- carries at all times two suits, two caps, two pair of goggles, and so forth;
- advises the coach of any illness or injury before training or competition;
- is capable of fruitfully using his or her free time to enhance training or competition performance;
- consistently offers the coach feedback on technique, training repeats, best times or sets, heart rates, and so forth;
- practices good self-management in all areas, understanding that focusing on solutions is always better than focusing on problems; and
- practices quality nutritional habits at all times, especially during competition and travel.

While there are many more, these are some of the basic requirements and principles that coaches and clubs must address in developing self-management and coping strategies for athletes. It is not wise to think that the above attributes will be developed without the aid of a team approach within a club or program. The old adage that you must make it happen in the preparation in order to have it happen in the competition, rather than the reverse, applies.

Summary

- The enthusiasm of the coach, the club, and the parents must be directly proportional to that of the swimmer.

- Challenge must be provided at the highest level. Magnificent performance must take precedence over mediocrity, and the basic skills must be taught to perfection and done exceptionally well.
- Coaches must have great empathy for the athletes they lead but must demand great commitment in return.
- Coaches must maintain a clearly defined yearly plan, a training log book, and a current attendance chart in a central coaching office where they can be signed by the athletes on a weekly basis and reviewed by the parents every month.
- The challenges of attaining the maximum performance at the right time for each athlete will reward all involved in the program with an enormous sense of achievement and well-being.
- There is no greater satisfaction or feeling than to play a role in an athlete's success in obtaining the highest possible result, knowing that nothing was left to chance and no compromise was considered.
- Great swimmers always do more than the coach asks, and great coaches always contribute more than the swimmer expects.

PART III

Creating Effective Practice Sessions

CHAPTER EIGHT

Long- and Short-Range Planning

Jill Sterkel

Long-range and seasonal planning and preparation are essential for success in swimming. Without a well-constructed plan and a vision for your program, it is easy to get lost and frustrated. I consider a training plan to be a program's map to success. Properly devising a training plan with attention to detail before the season begins can prevent a coach from losing sight of the goals of the team. I look at the seasonal plan as the foundation for the year ahead.

Long-Range Planning

There are several factors that must be taken into account when developing a long-range plan. The first and most critical question to ask yourself is where do you want your long-range planning to take you? In other words, what is your program's ultimate destination or goal? While each individual in your program will be at different levels of a performance or ability pyramid, the goal of program has to be structured around the peak of that pyramid. Second, start to think about what needs to be accomplished in order to get there. To help answer these questions and to illustrate some of the more frequent issues regarding planning, I will relate some of my experiences as a head coach at the University of Texas at Austin.

There are several factors that influence my basic framework in creating the long-range plan at UT. These include, but certainly are not limited to, the following:

- Where the athletes are now in terms of their fitness, skill level, and experience
- Where the athletes want to go
- How much time there is for athletes to reach their goals

Always the most basic component in analyzing the long-term plan is time. How much time do the athletes have to reach their ultimate destination? Ideally as a high school or collegiate coach you are developing a quadrennial (or four-year) plan and can begin by highlighting key competitions over the four-year period. Decide which competitions swimmers will need to swim in order to reach their goals and map out when these occur within each season. Make a list of these necessary competitions and keep this list handy for your reference as you break down the training. It is necessary to break down the quadrennial plan into smaller pieces, thereby creating yearly or seasonal plans. Even though it is tempting to focus on the smaller seasonal plans, always remember to focus on the long-range objective. Do not compromise the ultimate destination for the sake of smaller seasonal victories. But don't assume your long-range framework is etched in stone, either. I find it useful to evaluate each long-term plan at least yearly and to make updates and modifications where circumstances demand, yet I remain loyal to my basic philosophy and goals. For example, for one of our incoming freshman in 2000, we set the main seasonal goal of getting to the Olympic Trials. As the swimmer progressed faster than we had anticipated back in October, by April we had to shift the goal to making the Olympic team. Our basic plan for the swimmer didn't change, but we did update her goal's focus based on her progression.

I can't emphasize enough the importance of the planning process. It helps you organize your ideas, create a clear direction, and refine your coaching philosophy. Not having a plan is a lot like going to a foreign city and on arrival, trying to find your hotel without a map. No doubt you have been in a situation where you were lost without a map and spent an enormous amount of time and energy trying to get going in the right direction. Sometimes when you are lost you even ask complete strangers for advice on how to get somewhere without knowing if they are even familiar with the area or with your destination. Ultimately, you find you have spent a great deal of time making wrong turns and retracing your steps. Having a solid plan, or map, can help direct you to your final destination without making those unnecessary mistakes along the way.

A long-range plan also creates a record of where you have been and where you are trying to go. At the very least, a written plan provides a record of what you did so that later you can evaluate and make a determination of what worked well and what should be improved on in future seasons.

How much detail should you include in a plan? That is up to you. I view planning as a personal thing. There are some people who have to write down every minute detail and others who don't, yet everyone needs to plan. Choose the style that works for you. But if you are putting any type of plan together for the first time, it's a good idea to write it all down. As you progress and get more comfortable with the planning aspect of swimming, you can incorporate your own particular style and include or omit whatever information suits you.

Once you have picked the major events that will lead to the long-range goal, it's time to look more closely at your seasonal plan.

Seasonal Planning

As with long-term planning there are a few issues you need to consider before you can begin to shape your strategy and begin preparation. Again, you need to begin by looking at time. How many weeks do you have in your season? How much pool time is available to you on a daily and weekly basis? How much time can you devote to weight training and dryland training throughout the season?

— TABLE 8.1 —

Master Calendar

Month	Dates	Mon.	Tues.	Wed.	Thurs.	Fri.	Sat.	Sun.	Week #	Phase
Aug.	21-27					Frosh report	Off	Off	0	Off season
School starts	28-3			Team mtg.	PM	PM	PM	Off	1	Pre-season
Sept.	4-10	PM	PM	PM	PM	PM	PM	Off	2	Preseason
	11-17	PM	PM	PM	PM	PM	PM	Off	3	Aerobic
	18-24	PM	PM	PM	PM	PM	PM	Off	4	Aerobic
	25-1	PM	PM	PM	PM	PM	PM	Off	5	Aerobic
Oct.	2-8	AM PM	PM	AM PM	PM	AM PM	AM	Off	6	Aerobic
	9-15	AM PM	PM	AM PM	PM	AM PM	AM	Off	7	Aerobic
	16-22	AM PM	AM PM	Team mtg.	AM PM	Intra squad	AM	Off	8	Aerobic
	23-29	AM PM	AM PM	Team mtg. PM	AM PM	Relay meet	AM	Off	9	Anaerobic
	30-5					Dual meet	Dual meet	Off	10	Anaerobic
Nov.	6-12	AM PM	AM PM	PM	AM PM	AM	AM	Off	11	Anaerobic
	13-19	AM PM	AM PM	PM	AM PM	PM		Off	12	Race
	20-26	AM PM	AM PM	AM ←——— Thanksgiving ———→ PM				PM	13	Race
	27-3	AM PM	AM PM	PM	PM	Invite	Invite	Invite	14	Competition
Dec.	4-10	Off	AM PM	PM	AM PM	AM PM	AM	Off	15	Aerobic
	11-17	Dead day	Dead day	Finals	Finals	Finals	Finals	Off	16	Aerobic
	18-24	Finals	Finals	AM	←— Athletes	go	home—→		17	Aerobic
	25-31	←— Athletes	home	——→			AM PM	AM PM	18	Anaerobic
Jan.	1-7	PM	AM PM	AM PM	AM	AM PM	AM PM	Off	19	Anaerobic
	8-14	AM PM	AM PM	AM	AM travel	Dual meet	Dual meet	Off	20	Anaerobic
School resumes	15-21	AM PM	AM PM	PM	AM PM	AM PM	AM	Off	21	Anaerobic
	22-28	AM PM	PM	AM PM	AM	AM PM	AM	Off	22	Anaerobic
	29-4	AM PM	PM	AM PM	PM	Dual meet	Dual meet	Off	23	Race
Feb.	5-11	AM PM	PM	AM PM	AM	Dual meet	Dual meet	Off	24	Race
	12-18				Big 12	Big 12	Big 12	Off	25	Competition
	19-25							Off	26	Race
	26-4							Off	27	Race
Mar.	5-11							Off	28	Race
	12-18				NCAA	NCAA	NCAA	Off	29	Competition
	19-25							Off	30	Competition
	26-1		US Ntls.	US Ntls.	US Ntls.	US Ntls.	US Ntls.	US Ntls.	31	Competition

The first thing I do is start with an empty yearly calendar and fill in the blanks. While I take into account the major goals or milestones over the four years that athletes will be in our program, I focus specifically on planning the one season. I write down all the dates that I believe will be important in the planning process. These include the date student-athletes will report to campus, the date training beings, invitational and dual meet dates, travel and vacation periods, final-exam dates, and the date of the designated taper and shave meet for the season. This is all laid out in a weekly format (see table 8.1). In addition to the above information, the layout should indicate how many weeks remain in the season, as well as how many weeks of training have been completed. Table 8.1 illustrates the layout of our upcoming season at UT, beginning with the first week of September and culminating with the NCAA Championships and the US World Championship Trials in the spring. Again, this seasonal plan is created in relation to looking ahead to the swimmers' long-term plans.

The next step is to break the season down into phases. In the past, I have used the guides provided by US Swimming to tailor my season to the various physiological phases (see table 8.2, a and b and table 8.3).

TABLE 8.2A

Seasonal Planning

	Preseason	Aerobic	Anaerobic	Race specific	Competition
Primary (50%)	EN1	EN1/EN2	EN3 (distance) EN3/SP1 (sprint)	EN3/SP1 (distance) SP1/SP2 (sprint)	EN3/SP1 (distance) SP1/SP2 (sprint)
Secondary (35%)	EN2	EN3	EN1/EN2 (distance) SP2/SP3 (sprint)	EN1/EN2 (distance) SP3 (sprint)	SP2 (distance) SP3 (sprint)
Maintenance (15%)	SP3	SP1/SP3	SP1/SP3 (distance) EN1/EN3 (sprint)	SP3 (distance) EN1/EN2 (sprint)	EN1/EN2
# of weeks	1-5	3-8	2-6 (distance) 2-5 (sprint)	1-4	1-4 (distance) 1-5 (sprint)
# of weeks if 8-week season	3	1	2	1	1
# of weeks if 16-week season	5	3	5	2	1
# of weeks if 24- to 30-week season	A season longer than 24 weeks requires cycling through phases more than once to prevent overtraining.				

TABLE 8.2B

Seasonal Planning

Month	Dates	Week	Development phase	Primary focus 50%	Secondary focus 35%	Maintenance 15%	Competition	# of weeks
Aug.	21-27	0	Off season	x	x	x	x	32
	28-3	1	Preseason	EN1	EN2	SP3	x	31
Sept.	4-10	2	Preseason	EN1	EN2	SP3	x	30
	11-17	3	Aerobic	EN1/EN2	EN3	SP3	x	29
	18-24	4	Aerobic	EN1/EN2	EN3	SP3	x	28
	25-1	5	Aerobic	EN1/EN2	EN3	SP3	x	27
Oct.	2-8	6	Aerobic	EN1/EN2	EN3	SP3	x	26
	9-15	7	Aerobic	EN1/EN2	EN3	SP3	x	25
	16-22	8	Anaerobic	EN3/SP1	SP2/SP3	EN1/EN2	Intrasquad	24
	23-29	9	Anaerobic	EN3/SP1	SP2/SP3	EN1/EN2	Relay meet	23
	30-5	10	Anaerobic	EN3/SP1	SP2/SP3	EN1/EN2	Dual meet	22
Nov.	6-12	11	Anaerobic	EN3/SP1	SP2/SP3	EN1/EN2	x	21
	13-19	12	Race specific	EN1/SP1/SP2	SP3	EN2	Dual meet	20
	20-26	13	Race specific	EN1/SP1/SP2	SP3	EN2	x	19
	27-3	14	Competition	EN1/SP1/SP2	SP3	EN2	Invite	18
Dec.	4-10	15	Aerobic	EN1/EN2	EN3	SP3	x	17
	11-17	16	Aerobic	EN1/EN2	EN3	SP3	Finals	16
	18-24	17	Aerobic	EN1/EN2	EN3	SP3	Home	15
	25-31	18	Anaerobic	EN3/SP1	SP2/SP3	EN1/EN2	Home	14
Jan.	1-7	19	Anaerobic	EN3/SP1	SP2/SP3	EN1/EN2	x	13
	8-14	20	Anaerobic	EN3/SP1	SP2/SP3	EN1/EN2	Dual meet	12
	15-21	21	Anaerobic	EN3/SP1	SP2/SP3	EN1/EN2	x	11
	22-28	22	Anaerobic	EN3/SP1	SP2/SP3	EN1/EN2	Dual meet	10
	29-4	23	Race specific	SP1/SP2	SP3	EN1/EN2	Dual meet	9
Feb.	5-11	24	Race specific	SP1/SP2	SP3	EN1/EN2	x	8
	12-18	25	Competition	SP1/SP2	SP3	EN1/EN2	Big 12	7
	19-25	26	Race specific	SP1/SP2	SP3	EN1/EN2	x	6
	26-4	27	Race specific	SP1/SP2	SP3	EN1/EN2	x	5
Mar.	5-11	28	Race specific	SP1/SP2	SP3	EN1/EN2	x	4
	12-18	29	Competition	SP1/SP2	SP3	EN1/EN2	NCAA	3
	19-25	30	Competition	SP1/SP2	SP3	EN1/EN2	x	2
	26-1	31	Competition	SP1/SP2	SP3	EN1/EN2	US Natls.	1

TABLE 8.3

US Swimming's Types of Training

Type of training	Pace	Heart race (bpm)	Distance group (yards)	Middle-distance group (yds)	Sprint group (yards)
EN1	2 to 4 seconds slower per 100 than threshold pace	120 to 150	5,000	4,000	3,000
EN2	Anaerobic threshold or maximum effort over distance	160 to 170	4,000	3,200	2,400
EN3	1 to 2 seconds faster per 100 than threshold pace	180 to 190	2,000	1,600	1,200
SP1	As fast as possible	190 to 200	600	600	600
SP2	As fast as possible	190 to 200	400	400	400
SP3	Maximum speed	160 to 170	100 to 150	100 to 150	100 to 150

TABLE 8.4A

Distance—Weekly Framework

	Morning	Afternoon
Monday	EN1/EN2/SP3 pulling and kicking	Weights EN2-EN3 (2,000 to 3,000) EN1 (3,000) set of 200s to 1,000s
Tuesday	Urge EN1 kicking, pulling, and drills	Weights EN1/EN2 (long, mix in kicking) Weak stroke work
Wednesday	Off	Team meeting EN2-EN3 (300 × 100 at 1:20 [mile pace]); (2 × 150 at 2:15 [mile pace]); (10 × 250 at 4:00 [descend to 500 pace]); (3,000 or 3 × 1,000 [60 second drills])
Thursday	Urge EN1 kicking, pulling, and drills	Weights EN1/EN2 (long, mix in kicking) Distance IM
Friday	EN1/EN2/SP3 pulling and kicking	Weights EN1/SP3 Challenge set day: 3 × 500 at 5:30 (descending); 3 × 400 IM at 5:00 (descending)
Saturday	Urge; empty your tank! EN1-EN3 + SP1-SP3 (could be anything)	Off

In a collegiate season there are generally 30 weeks to work with. While 30 weeks may seem rather lengthy and is the outside limit of US Swimming's guidelines, it serves the school year well and allows for the winter holidays. Table 8.4, a and b highlights the proposed breakdown of a week for UT's distance and sprint swimmers. Generally more distance-oriented swimmers will swim a higher percentage of their training (in volume and frequency) in the endurance (EN1, EN2, and EN3) phases than sprinters will. Likewise, sprinters will spend a higher percentage of their time in the water doing speed work (SP1, SP2, SP3) than distance swimmers will. Our program is generally the same each year as far as the breakdown of the preseason, aerobic, anaerobic, race-specific, and competition phases, but we constantly make adjustments to fine-tune our training plan.

After carefully creating a plan it is time to share it and sell it to your team. I truly believe that a plan will fall flat on its face without the

---

TABLE 8.4B

Sprint—Weekly Framework

	Morning	**Afternoon**
Monday	Weights EN1 SP3 (20 minutes of power sprints)	Medicine ball work; stretching EN3 (1,000-1,500—75s to 125s) EN1/SP3 (starts and turns)
Tuesday	Urge EN1 kicking, pulling, and drills	Weights EN2 threshold swim set (20 × 100 hold specific time)
Wednesday	Off	Team meeting SP2 (200 to 600 per set; 1 to 3 sets (25s, 50s, 75s) EN1
Thursday	Weights EN1 SP3 (20 minutes of power sprints	Medicine ball work; stretching EN2 (2,400-3,200 mix of swim and pull SP2 kick 8 × 35 at 3:00
Friday	Urge EN1 kicking, pulling, and drills	Weights EN1 drill and swim EN2 pulling SP3 starts and turns and short blasts
Saturday	Medicine ball work; stretching Empty your tank! EN1-EN3 + SP1-SP3 (could be anything)	Off

---

support and ownership of the team. Having monthly team meetings in which you give training calendars to the athletes is a good way to keep athletes updated on what to expect in their upcoming training and racing. We meet as a team to discuss team goals and we set up individual swimmer-coach meetings two or three times a year to discuss each swimmer's personal goals and how the swimmer is progressing toward them. Involving your athletes in the process empowers your team. Everyone works harder if they feel that they have had some input during the course of the year as to the team goals and the process by which the team is attempting to achieve them. I also recommend that coaches take the time to sit down with athletes individually and to establish an individual plan that allows them to address their own personal strengths and weaknesses.

The funny thing about a plan is that there will always be minor, and possibly major, bumps in the road that you have no control over. You may have to tweak your plan in order to accomplish what you set out to do. Beware of being so entrenched in your focus that you are afraid to make changes when a particular athlete fails to respond to the training or becomes injured. You have to be flexible. Maintaining focus is important but not worth the expense of losing an athlete. Realize that your plan may not work for everyone. Being able to recognize this and to adjust your plan for each individual will make you a better coach.

Dividing the Season Into Phases

I divide each season into five separate training phases: preseason, aerobic development, anaerobic development, race-specific, and competition. The first two phases (preseason and aerobic development) focus on building general endurance so I have grouped them together for discussion here.

We also break up the season a bit by having a short, race-specific phase in December to prepare our athletes for an invitational meet we hold at that time each year. Our athletes don't taper and shave for this meet, but we do ease up on the training intensity a bit (while keeping volume steady) to help the swimmers feel rested for this meet, rather than dog tired. I find that breaking up the season in this way gives the athletes a little break from aerobic development and a chance to race fast, while keeping them in shape as they head into winter break.

General Endurance

The eight weeks of general endurance are divided into the preseason phase (weeks one through four) and the aerobic development phase (weeks five through eight). The idea behind general endurance is to use endurance (EN) and speed (SP) work to bring the athletes back into good cardiovascular and muscular shape. The preseason phase includes training that is 50 percent recovery or EN1, 35 percent EN2, and 15 percent SP3. The aerobic development phase includes training that is 50 percent EN1/EN2, 35 percent EN3, and 15 percent SP3.

Generally my athletes are returning to school after their summer seasons and have had approximately two weeks off. The goal of the preseason and aerobic development phase is to begin the process of becoming as physically fit as possible. At UT, we start with an emphasis on dryland and weight training. The bulk of our three-hour time slot in the afternoon is devoted to dryland and weightlifting activities. Athletes also begin swimming during this phase. Most of the swim time is spent on drills and general aerobic conditioning in the form of freestyle and individual-medley training. The stress levels start off fairly low and increase in length and intensity as swimmers progress through these sessions, which include double workouts beginning in early October.

Teaching proper technique in all areas of training is essential. Now is the time to practice in order to make perfect. Generally speaking, if bad technique is not addressed in this phase, you can expect it to continue throughout the season. Value and demand proper technique, always.

While this phase primarily calls for the development of the aerobic system, you should not neglect speed work completely; do about 15 percent of training volume speed work. Speed work over very short distances should be used to maintain and to build speed throughout the season.

Anaerobic Development

The anaerobic development phase is very challenging and lasts for three to five weeks. The training in this phase is divided into 50 percent EN3/SP1, 35 percent SP2/SP3, 15 percent EN/EN2. The athlete will be expected to perform at race-pace speeds throughout this phase. Weekly planning for this type of training is crucial. Generally speaking, 24 to 48 hours are needed before lactate tolerance or overload endurance sets are repeated. This provides adequate time for muscle glycogen recovery. Basic endurance training should also be included in this phase and is a good choice for recovery days. Once again you must remember to include short sets of speed work. An excellent way to include speed is to focus on starts, turns, and relay exchanges as well as short sprints (25 yards or less). To ensure the application of all energy systems it is recommended that, especially during this phase, all training sessions be written down.

Race-Specific

This is the two- to four-week fine-tuning phase prior to the final competition phase. Speed work reaches its peak during this cycle, accounting for about 85 percent of work. It is important that the swims in the speed training of this cycle directly correlate to the athlete's overall goal time through race-pace swimming. Swimming at race pace should be precise and on target. All components of the athlete's race must begin to come together; fine-tuning race strategy and race skills are essential tasks during this time. Continue to include an aerobic endurance component (15 percent) during this phase to ensure that the athlete maintains a solid endurance base.

Competition Phase

This phase is generally referred to as taper. Taper means preparing to swim fast. It is crucial that you not allow your athletes to get lazy or sloppy during this final phase, but for the most part, all the hard training is over. You have either done the necessary work to accomplish your desired goals in training or you have missed the opportunity.

From here on out the focus should be rest—rest from decreased training intensity and physical rest away from the pool. Continue fine-tuning and race-pace preparation with this in mind. The length of this phase will vary depending on the individual swimmer and the time you have. Generally, the competition phase lasts about three weeks.

After the collegiate season and a short break in April all of our swimmers are expected to resume training either by swimming for their home club program in the summer or by staying in Austin to train.

Summary

- Planning is your map to success.
- Your long-range plan must have a final destination and must provide guidance as to what needs to be done to get there.
- Your plan must take into account the time period involved.
- Always remember to focus on the long-range objective during seasonal training.
- Allow for adjustments to be made to your plan as needed.

(continued)

- To plan each season, start with an empty calendar and fill in competitions and goals that work toward the major seasonal goal.
- Break each season into physiological training phases.
- Communicate your plan to the team and involve team members in the planning.

CHAPTER NINE

Putting Science Into Practice

Bruce R. Mason

We live in an age in which we can see the effects of science and technology influencing just about every aspect of our lives. In most cases advances in technology have helped to reduce our workload and to improve the quality of our lives. Swim coaching is no different. Coaches who do not take full advantage of the benefits of technology and science will fall behind those in other programs as well as their own swimmers.

Science and technology can make a significant difference in competitive swimming. This chapter provides a brief overview of how sport science and sports medicine contribute to swim performance. Whether your program has the luxury of having a team of sport scientists and sport physicians you can call on, or whether your program relies on you, as coach, to seek out the necessary specialists for your athletes, this chapter illustrates several ways to elevate performance levels in swimming through the use of science and scientific models.

Scientists Who Can Help

Sport science and sports medicine are composed of a number of distinct disciplines. Sport science includes biomechanics, physiology, and psychology; sports medicine includes physiotherapy, massage, and sports nutrition. Each of these disciplines contributes significantly to performance in competitive swimming by *providing a service to* or by *carrying out* applied research.

Providing a service involves testing or treating swimmers in order to specifically enhance their performance as individual swimmers. Servicing provides quick feedback to assist the individual swimmers involved in the testing. Research, on the other hand, is the testing or treatment of a group of swimmers or subjects that is performed to obtain a better understanding of the larger group of swimmers that the research subjects represent. It takes some time for information based on research findings to become available to individual coaches and swimmers. However, the knowledge gained from research investigations should be applicable to many swimmers.

Generally, the way in which a sport scientist can make the most impact in practice is to carry out servicing that affects a large group of swimmers. In this way the swimmers and coaches learn to understand and use the results of the testing. In time the service provided may lead to questions that can be answered through more applied research.

Coaches who travel with national teams may have access to a team of sport scientists. In this situation the coach is responsible for coordinating and prioritizing the services provided by these experts to the swimmers and for implementing their recommendations.

Biomechanists

Biomechanics, the study of locomotion, has a direct application in evaluating the technique swimmers use to propel themselves forward and to perform starts and turns. It involves the study of forces and the actions that occur as a consequence of applying these forces. Biomechanics measures what the swimmer does and identifies technique inefficiencies that can be corrected to enhance the swimmer's performance. Coaches can gain solid, quantifiable information about their swimmers' performances through biomechanics. This information can help them to objectively compare the techniques used by different swimmers and by a particular swimmer at different periods in time.

Physiologists

Physiology studies the effects of physical training on the swimmer by using such things as lactate measurement and heart rate monitoring to identify how well the swimmer is physically coping with training. Physiology also allows coaches to evaluate the aerobic and anaerobic fitness levels of their swimmers. Through physiology you can identify the swim speeds required by a particular swimmer to train the various physiological systems of the body. Moreover, physiologists are able to measure skinfolds to indicate changes in a swimmer's body composition. Physiologists are also well suited to conduct the warm-down swims after competition; they can objectively measure lactic levels to ensure that the swimmers have performed the warm-down swims adequately. This frees the coach to watch other swimmers competing rather than having to supervise swims in the warm-down pool.

Psychologists

Psychology provides a strategy to mentally prepare the swimmer for training and competition. It provides the means by which a swimmer can identify and focus on short- and long-term goals and therefore retain interest in the swim program over an extended period. Psychology provides the swimmer with an understanding of how anxiety levels influence his or her performance, and can offer ways of coping with stress and high anxiety levels as well as ways of raising anxiety levels when necessary.

Sport Physicians

Sports medicine primarily involves the diagnosis and treatment of both illness and injury. In the treatment of ailments, sport physicians must be aware of medications that may affect the ability of the swimmer to train effectively or that may contain banned substances. Most injuries in swimming are overuse injuries, and most illnesses are associated with respiratory infections.

Not only do sport physicians treat injury and illness, they also look for ways of preventing such problems. Prevention may involve educating coaches and athletes or dispensing preventive drugs to avoid illness problems. The sport physician's preventive role is particularly useful to teams that do a lot of traveling to compete and may come into contact with known causes of ailments. The sport physician can also provide protection and treatment related to illnesses that occur with seasonal changes. Injury prevention may involve making suggestions to the coach about lessening the risk of an overuse injury by altering technique.

Sport physicians also have a role to play in educating coaches and swimmers about banned substances that could otherwise be taken deliberately or inadvertently (i.e., in common over-the-counter cold medications, nutritional supplements, and so forth). They can suggest safe, alternative medications so that swimmers avoid ingesting a banned drug.

Physiotherapists and Physical Therapists

Probably the most important function of a team physiotherapist is the prevention, rather than management, of injury. This is best achieved through musculoskeletal screening to identify swimmers who are at risk for injury. A physiotherapist may find, for example, that a swimmer's lack of flexibility is resulting in poor technique as well as potential injury. Physiotherapists are ideally suited to assess the flexibility levels of swimmers, to treat those cases of reduced flexibility, and to prescribe exercises that increase range of motion. Physiotherapists perform an important function in identifying and working with swimmers to rehabilitate certain injuries, particularly soft-tissue, joint, and tendon injuries. The physiotherapist is an ideal person to lead warm-up flexibility exercises for team training sessions while the team is away on tour; they are generally not treating swimmers during the warm-up and thus can fill the need of leading warm-up activities at no extra expense to the team.

Massage Therapists and Nutritionists

Massage therapists are able to provide recuperative massage treatment for athlete recovery from hard training sessions and competition swims. The primary role of a team nutritionist is to supervise the menu preparation for team food. Generally, the nutritionist looks after the supply of extra food and the preparation of the sport drinks for training and competition sessions. The nutritionist has the responsibility of establishing a policy on nutritional supplementation and of providing advice to swimmers in matters concerning supplementation. A significant role of the nutritionist is educating swimmers about eating sensibly. Nutritionists can also teach swimmers the practical skills of how to shop for nutritious food at reasonable prices and how to prepare appetizing, healthful meals.

Adding Science to Your Coaching

In most home-based programs, the coach does not have multidiscipline support at his or her fingertips. In such cases the coach will need to perform some of the more fundamental functions of each of the disciplines and, when necessary, direct swimmers to support outside the confines of the home training environment. In order for this to be effective the coach needs to build bridges between his or her program and local institutions that provide professional support. To perform some of the more fundamental tasks and to fully understand and implement the recommendations that come from outside professional support, the coach will need to pursue in-service training to keep abreast of changes in the science associated with swim coaching. So, you may ask, which of the professional support disciplines is the most important in elevating swimmer performance? All the disciplines are of vital importance; the removal of any one of them cannot be compensated for by increased emphasis on the other disciplines.

Developing a Competition Model

We no longer live in a world where the swimmer wakes in the morning on the day of a contest, feels fantastic, and simply swims with maximum effort to win the gold medal. Major events can now only be won if the swimmer has effectively prepared for the competition. This preparation involves the development of a *competition model*, or race plan, that may be different for each swimmer and for each event in which a particular swimmer is to compete. The coach and swimmer devise the model as a consequence of the swimmer's goals and abilities. The model takes into account the speed of the start, how each swim phase of the race is to be swum (stroke lengths, stroke frequencies, and swim speeds), and the time of each turn phase. To prepare a swimmer to win the event, the model must have as its desired completion time the anticipated winning time for the event.

The idea of the competition model is that the swimmer must maintain the objectives of the model throughout the race. Moreover, the model provides the swimmer and coach with a means of planning training; every aspect of training must have some relevance to the competition model.

So how does one begin to develop a competition model? The competition model can initially be developed from the information derived from a *competition analysis* of the swimmer concerned. Refinement of the competition model would then occur after each competition, with the expectation of improving various aspects of the race.

Using Competition Analyses

Competition analyses are now standard practice in all major swim championships. Such analysis is performed by officials or scientists at major meets and by parents of swimmers or assistant coaches at smaller meets. The analysis breaks all long- and short-course championship events into the following phases:

- 25-meter "free-swim" phases that exclude any part of each 25-meter length that is considered the start, a turn, or the finish
- The start phase, which extends from the starting signal until the head of the swimmer is 15 meters out from the start wall
- The turn phases, which extend from when the head of the swimmer is 7.5 meters out from the turn wall on the way in to 7.5 meters out from the turn wall on the way out
- The finish phase, which extends from 5 meters out from the finish wall until hand touch

In the analysis, time and average velocity are measured for each of the start, turn, and finish phases. For each free-swim phase, the analysis measures average stroke length, average stroke rate, and average velocity, and computes the efficiency index. By definition, stroke length is the distance the head travels from right-hand entry to the next right-hand entry. Stroke frequency is the average number of strokes that would occur in a minute. Average velocity of the swimmer is the velocity of the head as it moves down the pool. The efficiency index for a particular phase is the product of the swimmer's average stroke length and average velocity. When all this information is provided for each swimmer in the race in a spreadsheet format, it is easy to identify why the race was won and where and why other swimmers lost the race to the winner. It is also an easy matter to identify the weaknesses of any particular swimmer in the race.

Before competition analyses were regularly performed, coaches had only lap split times to help them identify weaknesses in technique, endurance, and other aspects that slowed propulsive speed. Such times were of limited value in identifying weaknesses in particular phases of the race. Besides being far more helpful in studying weaknesses, the results of competition analyses are useful in refining individual competition models and in identifying general changes in race strategy that occur as a result of rules changes.

If the competition analysis identifies a weakness in a particular phase of an event, that phase should be examined more closely in a training environment by the coach in conjunction with a biomechanist if possible. For example, if a competition analysis reveals that a sprinter has a weakness in her start, the start phase needs to be broken into subphases and each subphase must be examined for inefficiencies. A start (from the block to 15 meters from the block), for example, may be divided into the following subphases: on block, flight, underwater, and above water. Biomechanical examination of the start phase may identify that the swimmer is weak in a particular subphase. Such a biomechanical evaluation would incorporate distance and timing information as well as above- and below-water videotape of the performance. Weaknesses are most easily identified if a swimmer's timing and distance data are compared with that of other swimmers of equal ability and with that of elite swimmers.

Similarly, the turn can be divided into the following subphases: above water into the wall, rotation, push-off, underwater out from the wall, and above water out from the wall. A biomechanical examination of a free-swim phase would consist of both above- and below-water videotape as well as information concerning stroke length and stroke frequency. Intrastroke velocity and acceleration profiles of the free swimming—measured in a biomechanics lab or training center—would also be of interest in examining the swimmer's technique.

When making any biomechanical assessment, a videotape showing what the swimmer is actually doing, as well as objective performance data for the swim, should be considered. During such testing, it's important that the particular phase under examination be performed at competition pace. If the particular phase under examination is a turn, for example, the testing should incorporate a free-swim section on either side of the turn to simulate competition conditions as closely as possible; in competition a turn is not completed in isolation of free swimming and the swimmer is often not fresh at the time of performing the turn.

All possible causes of an inefficiency or weakness, such as problems with technique, strength, flexibility, or motivation, should be considered when identifying a solution to the problem. Probably the most expedient way of eradicating a weakness is to follow testing with evaluation, followed by coach intervention, followed by swimmer practice, followed by retesting. Repeating this cycle as needed is most effective.

Common Problems Found in Starts

Slow reaction time off the blocks

Poor takeoff angle

Poor body position on entry into the water

Poor streamlining in the underwater subphase

Too steep an ascent angle in the underwater subphase

Ineffective underwater propulsion

Not using enough distance under the water

Poor transition from the underwater subphase into swimming

Common Problems Found in Turns

Inconsistent approach into the wall

Poor adjustment—too far or too close—into the wall

Using head bobs to initiate turn

Slow rotational leg speed

Reversing rather than changing direction

Poor push off

Poor streamlining

Ineffective underwater propulsion

Not using enough distance under the water after the turn

Too steep an ascent angle in the underwater subphase

Poor transition from the underwater subphase into swimming with breath

Maximizing Swim Velocity

Maximum swim speed is determined by two forces:

1. The propulsive forces of the swimmer on the water, which moves the swimmer forward

2. The drag force of the water on the swimmer, which tends to slow the swimmer

When the swimmer is performing with maximum effort and the propulsive and drag forces are in equilibrium, maximum swim speed is limited by the state of equilibrium. To swim faster, the swimmer must either increase the propulsive force or reduce the drag force. Drag force can be reduced by improving streamlining during recovery. This is by far a better method of increasing swim speed, as it requires much less energy than increasing the propulsive force. It is only when methods of reducing drag have been exhausted and stroke technique issues have been addressed that the coach and swimmer should look to ways of increasing propulsive force.

Swim velocity is the product of stroke length and stroke frequency. It is more efficient to have a longer stroke length and a lower stroke frequency than the reverse, for a set swim velocity. However, it is possible to overextend the length of the stroke. Some coaches believe that stroke length should be maximized in order to maximize swim velocity. This is not correct. The stroke length should instead be *optimized* by experimenting with different stroke numbers and stroke frequency counts. During swim competition, a swimmer should aim to maintain the same stroke length through the entire race. The swim velocity toward the end of the race is increased by increasing stroke frequency while maintaining this optimal stroke length.

It is paramount for the modern coach to incorporate sport science and sports medicine into his or her swim program to make that program effective and competitive. In a national elite program, sport scientists and sports medicine professionals are often available to assist the coach. The coach must know what he or she can obtain from these resources and then must be able to effectively integrate that information into his or her swim program. The coach should prioritize which services are needed most and should acquire them in that order.

While the age-group coaches may not have sport scientists to assist them, they can use the principles of sport science in their programs by enlisting parents to help. Parents can videotape athletes to help the coach measure and evaluate swim technique. Coaches can call on sport scientists and sports medicine experts from nearby institutions for advice and consultation. In order to benefit from technological advances, the coach must remain current in sport science and sports medicine. He or she must be enterprising and must show initiative in finding ways to seek out and use scientific information that pertains to swimming.

Summary

- Sport science and sports medicine contribute to the performance of swimmers by providing a service to or by carrying out applied research.
- Biomechanics helps identify technique inefficiencies that can be corrected to enhance swim performance.
- Physiology identifies the swim speeds required by a particular swimmer to train the various physiological systems.
- The competition model is the race plan designed by the swimmer and the coach; it is based on the results of race analysis.
- If competition analysis identifies that a swimmer has a weakness, then that phase must be examined more closely in a training environment.
- Biomechanical evaluations can be made for stroke, starts, turns, and finishes.
- Maximum swim speed is determined by two forces—propulsion and drag.
- Swim velocity is the product of stroke length and stroke frequency.
- Stroke length should be optimized, not maximized.

CHAPTER TEN

Applying the Art of Coaching

Deryk Snelling

As I began to write this chapter, I thought about the essential ingredients for success in swimming, as a coach or a swimmer. I concluded that it comes down to having inner drive, solid role models, and positive experiences. Of course, being blessed with natural talent doesn't hurt either.

To my mind, there are no shortcuts to success and no substitutes for hard, tough swim workouts. You must plan to balance training and racing, and must always be looking to be not only tougher but smarter in your approach. As a coach, this means staying up to date with both the science and the art of swimming and coaching. At the same time, it's important to never lose sight of the basics: health, speed, endurance, power, strength, and technique.

One of the first principles of the art of coaching is to discover whether an athlete has the talent, desire, and ambition to succeed. Next determine if he or she is coachable. Are you going to be able to communicate with each other? Is there a feeling of two-way trust, and do you have the sense that the athlete believes you can take him or her right to the top? Do you truly believe that the swimmer can make it to the top? Are you both willing to put in years of work at an intense but focused pace? The road to the top is not an easy road, and following it calls for far more than a short-term commitment. It can take from six to eight years to develop a great champion. Even if you are fortunate enough to come across talent as great as that of Mark Spitz or Ian Thorpe, it will take at least a full four-year cycle, up to and including an Olympic Games, before an athlete is really accomplished. A little bit of luck on the day of an Olympic event might come in handy too, when the difference between being good and great can be as little as .01 seconds!

My coaching mentor was George Haines, a multidimensional genius, who could work equally well with boys, girls, men, and women in any event, distance, or stroke. He saw only the good in people and was always able to make someone feel special and to tap into each individual's hidden strengths. He could make you believe in the impossible. He certainly did that for me when I was a rookie coach from England who had come to the Santa Clara Swim Club to watch his miracles. I learned from him to set no limits for myself nor for the swimmers who choose me as their coach. Two ideas in particular that I learned from George Haines are central to my coaching:

1. Be optimistically positive in your role as a coach every day. Always try to catch your swimmers doing something good and compliment them on it, filling the air with positive feelings. Let them know how good they are and just how great they are going to be if

they stay on track. I feel that swimmers are sometimes more interested in what you say and do as a coach than in how knowledgeable you are. Still, you should always be sure of the reasons for your actions and be ready to explain them if challenged. As a coach, you must have credibility.

2. We all start out believing we are not only good, but potentially great; it is a coach's job to never to lose sight of that belief. See yourself as a winner, figure out what you have to do to reach your goal, and continue climbing.

So, you may wonder, how can coaches ensure that their athletes are given the opportunities to develop the qualities and experiences necessary to make them successful swimmers? I think the secret lies in building a swimmer's confidence in training and racing, setting no limits on achievement, using team training to each swimmer's advantage, keeping training fun, using the science and resources available, and providing competitive experiences.

Build Swimmer Confidence

Nort Thornton at the University of California at Berkeley, whose success as a swim coach is legendary, has a knack for instilling in his athletes the belief that they can achieve. He does this with some famously challenging workouts. A young swimmer of mine, Graham Smith, in Calgary, Alberta, once told me about his toughest workout ever: a 30,000-yard workout Nort had him do at a training camp. I thought a similar challenge would be a good idea for swimmers at my annual Christmas training camp. I always used the 7- to 10-day camp to encourage swimmers to "go for it," making it long and hard, a kind of survival course. I likened it to "selection," as it is called in the Special Boat Service (SBS), one of Britain's top military units. One hundred and thirty-nine men from the Royal Marine Commandos start selection for the SBS; the rigorous course eliminates them one by one through fatigue until only nine are left. The idea is that once these nine are identified, this select group can be developed and trained with the certainty that they will not quit when the going gets tough, physically and mentally.

To match Nort's tough workout, I decided to have the swimmers try 25,000 meters (equivalent to 30,000 yards). A few dropped out, but most of them completed the grueling workout, and although they were tired, they felt great about having done it—so much so that after we had finished, one of the swimmers who had missed the session altogether and another who had tried it but quit part way through asked if they could do it on their own the following day. Listening to the rest of the team talking about their great achievement, these two felt that they had missed out on something very important.

I was thinking that it would be hard for them to do the workout on their own when someone feeling a bit macho piped in, "Let's all do it again." There and then I said, "OK. But we all do it, and not 25,000 meters, but 30,000 meters in one workout" (even more than Nort's famous 30,000 yards in one day). Everyone said OK, and everyone did it the very next day. That 55,000-meter two-day total is indefensible in sport science, but it gave those swimmers a belief in themselves that no one and no situation could ever take away from them. Accomplishing those workouts helped them to realize how tough they can be when they accept a challenge and adopt a positive mind-set.

I have worked for a long time to build confidence in my swimmers, and have found that this can be done in many different ways. No two swimmers are alike. In planning it is very important to get the right mix of training and racing for each swimmer. I believe that racing is the very best training that anyone can do for all distances, but particularly for the 50-, the 100-, and the 200-meter events. The balance of training and racing will vary more for a middle-distance or distance swimmer. For the 400 up through the 1,500, a coach has to consider things such as the amount and frequency of rest the swimmers need, when they should shave, and how rested they will be for the race. Whether a swimmer will wear a drag suit or one of the new super suits will again depend on the overall long-term racing plan being followed at the time. Coaching swimming is an art-driven process supported by science.

Along these same lines, being in great shape for training isn't the same as being in shape to race. I have been on club swim meet tours where we have traveled for 30 days, racing as many as 50 times, reshaving seven or eight times over that period, and have continued to improve throughout the tour. I have had swimmers who swam in all eight of the World Cup meets, back-to-back, in all different countries, and kept shaving down for each meet. Sometimes a long period of smooth skin helps swimmers (especially those who have a lot of hair) to feel the water better, a sensation that they can lose during the training season. As their tour of fresh-shaven racing continues, their feel for stroke and kick rhythm, water pressures, and streamlining all improve. A speed stroke starts to become natural, flowing, and efficient, quite unlike the unshaved stroke. I believe that you must try many things to find what works for each swimmer. It could even be one rest, one taper, and one shave per year for one type of swimmer and two, three, or even four shaves for others. It's all very individual and can change from year to year for each swimmer.

Set No Limits

Having belief in oneself also means recognizing that no one owns a particular event. When the underwater dolphin kick was first adapted for backstroke, I had a backstroke swimmer who was very good but just did not have the feel or skill to get maximum speed from his underwater kicking. He was ranked number four in the world for almost five years, and in his first Olympics he swam the backstroke leg in the 4 × 100 medley relay to help the Canadian team win silver. Two years later he was second by .03 to the US swimmer in the individual event at the World Championships. Coaches and swimmers have no control over what other competitors do, and in this instance using the underwater dolphin kicking technique wouldn't have helped us, particularly since there was no restriction on the distance of the underwater kicking at this point.

However, once the 15-meter rule was introduced, we once again had a chance. We worked very hard during the pre-Olympic year, concentrating on our strengths rather than our weaknesses. Capitalizing on his advantage of fast turns, this swimmer broke the world short-course record several times and gained valuable self-confidence. The result was that at the Barcelona Olympics, he won the gold medal by .03 against an athlete with a superb underwater kick, despite losing a lot of distance on the start and after the turn. In fact it was a catch-up situation right up until the last six inches of the race, where it all came down to fitness and being the last swimmer to slow down.

Another of my backstrokers developed a bone problem in one leg and had to spend six months with her leg in a full-length cast. We were able to cut off her cast for Commonwealth Games trials, where she swam with a one-legged kick, just trailing the other leg behind. Three weeks later she won a 200 backstroke Commonwealth Games gold medal. Eventually her leg did heal, and two years later she won an Olympic bronze medal from lane eight. I firmly believe that she benefited from the strength and confidence she gained in overcoming her leg injury.

Train as a Team

I believe in team training. The energy is extremely strong when a group works together. Within lanes, swimmers can be grouped with peers of similar strength. Each swimmer in the line keeps the other swimmers focused and thinking about where they are in the lane order, who is in front of them, who is behind, and how well they have to perform the work to survive, to do their part, to not let themselves down. It's just amazing how hard and fast a swimmer can train in a lane with other swimmers without really feeling pain or fatigue. In these close quarters, a swimmer feels alive and hardly has time to let his or her mind drift. This type of exercise trains swimmers to keep their minds focused in race situations.

Another good exercise that takes advantage of the benefits of team training involves having 8 to 10 swimmers in one 50-meter lane do a set of 8 × 400 on either a progressive speed interval with tight turnover or a fast time interval with fast turnover. With each swimmer leaving 5 seconds apart, it takes 40 seconds or so to get the last swimmer off the wall. Therefore the first swimmer is soon chasing the last one off. The current in the lane becomes so strong that the whole line is able to float along, with each swimmer using the drag from the one in front to make his or her own swim easier. I put this kind of workout into the category of assisted swimming; benefits include great speed and very short intervals can be easily attained. In such workouts everyone feels a great sense of achievement. Moreover, doing fast times on short intervals is a great confidence booster.

I personally prefer to coach a large group of 30 or more if they are compatible in their ability to do similar workouts. However, when it comes to taper and coaching swimmers with various personal goals and abilities, unless extra staff members are available to help out, it is better to work with a smaller group of 12 swimmers or less.

Individual medley training is a great way to coach and train a team. Individual medley fits in really well if you work with a team that swims only between 45,000 and 55,000 meters per week during the regular season. All the time that you spend in the water should be productive, and the medley helps ensure that that is the case. If a swimmer is training to specifically race the IM, every kick, pull, drill swim done in IM training works toward the specific event's development, so he or she will do all of the session well instead of possibly drifting through part of the workout. For a swimmer with an individual event other than the IM as the main event, doing a variety of strokes will automatically prevent specific stroke burnout, which tends to occur when all the work is on one stroke only. Thus IM training is a great way to prevent boredom.

Likewise, IM racing can also boost conditioning. Racing individual medley long course and short course over the 200 and 400 (and including the 100 for short course) gives swimmers a great range of distances to develop all physical systems—shorter races for anaerobic fitness and longer races for aerobic fitness. In fact I feel that breaststroke, backstroke, and butterfly swimmers should also race the 50 and 400 distances in their stroke, as well as the 100 and 200. Periodically, breaststroke, backstroke, and butterfly specialists should enter the 50 or 400 freestyle events and race their stroke in these events.

As well as working with individual events, I love to coach relays. They bring out the best in most swimmers. The common goal of a relay fosters unity, and the sense of responsibility to three other team members is often so strong that swimmers achieve some of their best times even when they are tired.

Keep Training Fun

Every workout must be challenging and fun. Boredom will kill the spirit and fatigue a swimmer more quickly than anything else. Challenge your swimmers. Make the challenge as big as you like; the bigger the challenge, the more fun it is and the greater the satisfaction in achieving success. Over the years I have found that cross training is good for swimmers and that the variety prevents boredom.

For morning training I have always offered more than just water workouts. Our weight-training sessions, particularly circuit training, could last anywhere from 20 minutes to over an hour. I might have swimmers do as few as eight exercises and as many 60 circuit stations. Occasional running training also works well. Probably the best motivator and the most fun way to start the day, though, is playing games. Basketball, volleyball, and football have always been popular with my Canadian teams, but the big favorite is floor hockey in a small gym.

For floor hockey games, I like to mix the men and women on the teams. The game can be highly competitive, and it allows the women to be as aggressive as they wish, checking and charging, while the men are not allowed to make aggressive contact with the women or to retaliate in any way. The women can give free reign to their aggression, and the men are encouraged to develop more subtle skills and better self-control, so everyone benefits. These games are so popular that it is not unusual for athletes to turn up more than 20 minutes early for a 6:00 AM workout so that they can enjoy warm-ups, practice shooting skills, and so forth. Some athletes will even ask to come in for a game on their day off. The team goes into the subsequent swim workout charged, excited, and really positive, which is especially important as morning workouts should be just as good as afternoon sessions. In top-class competition, many swimmers don't make finals because they are not conditioned to go fast in the morning heats.

Not only can games provide excellent attendance, happy early morning starts, teamwork development, and a great warm-up, they can also give the coach cues as to how to work with each swimmer in the pool. Games allow the coach to evaluate assertiveness, self-control, attitude, and quickness. Altogether, games are a great way to start the day.

Another way that I have kept swimmers stimulated over the years is by bringing in top foreign swimmers or organizing team visits to go to see world-class coaches and athletes from other sports. Contact with such individuals helps set the standards for the swimmers and myself. Every sport has individual characteristics, strengths, and weaknesses that we can study, adapt, and incorporate into our training methods. For example, Olympic gymnastic coaches know how to develop strength and flexibility, particularly relative to pound for pound of body weight, and track coaches are particularly adept at developing speed, endurance, and explosive power.

I have a good friend who was the leader of a very successful Mount Everest climb; he made a presentation to our team outlining their training regimes and how they learned to deal with stress and fear. He told of his personal trauma when some members of the group were killed on the climb and the team had to decide who would carry on and who would go back down.

On the other end of the emotional spectrum, practitioners in the art of transcendental meditation have come in to teach us yoga skills during our workouts. I believe that you should always be looking out for ideas to improve your basic skills, keeping training simple and focused, tough and consistent, and that you should always try to adapt new perspectives and activities to your training plan if and when appropriate.

Keep Up on the Science

I've been interested in the benefits of altitude training ever since I attended the 1968 Olympics in Mexico City. While I believe it works very well for some swimmers when done correctly, not all swimmers improve with this type of conditioning. Altitude training needs to be integrated into the one-, two- and four-year training plan. The swimmers must be fit but not too tired when they go up to altitude, and they should build up their work slowly over the first four to six days, increasing the volume and intensity. Over the last four days the quality and quantity decrease, which means that they have only 10 days or so as a window of opportunity in which to train long and with intensity. Equally important is the approximately three-week (depending on the individual) recovery and race preparation period. In my opinion, it can take from three to five visits to altitude per year to receive maximum benefit.

Normally our team does our altitude training around 7,200 feet. The best locations I have found so far are Sierra Nevada, Spain, and Flagstaff, Arizona. I have worked at some training centers as low as Thredbo, Australia (1,300 meters), and Font Romeu in France (1,850 meters) and am currently considering the "live-high, train-low" methodology in use at a new training center in Queensland, Australia, which is operated by former Australian Olympic runner Ron Clarke. At this center, swimmers train at sea level, preferably in a 50-meter pool in warm outdoor locations, and live in nearby altitude houses that simulate the atmospheric conditions of a prescribed altitude.

Living high and training low is still quite a new concept that has good potential as an additional training aid. The fact that altitude houses can be built in any location could eliminate the current need to travel to mountain training sites so that in the future they may even become part of normal training environments. Some of the advantages of the live-high-and-train-low approach over the high-altitude training currently in use include the following:

- There appear to be none of the acclimatization problems normally associated with altitude camps.
- There is less risk of overtraining and no interruption of normal training routines.
- These camps can be more easily, and perhaps more frequently, integrated into the normal annual plan.
- The accepted norm of 21-day altitude camp training can be extended to 40 days or longer.

It is ideal to have a physiotherapist, a massage therapist, an exercise physiologist, a nutritionist, and a medical doctor on site for general support during altitude training.

Ideally, our top national British swimmers will train at this type of facility from early November right through late February (during the cold and wet UK winter months when the danger of colds and flu can spoil a healthy training schedule). Currently, this luxury is, of course, only possible if you have the financial resources as well as a flexible school system with the availability of private tuition. However, I believe that this training method will become more common for more swimmers in the future as a greater number of swimmers will have the opportunity to win larger financial awards for themselves and their countries. The standard a winner must meet is becoming increasingly high around the world, and it may be that little extra that swimmers gain from altitude training that will make the difference.

Another important scientific resource coaches should make use of is a sports medicine and sport science staff. I have always brought these specialists into my support staff for swimmers when I could. These professionals provide important help in realizing the racing result that we are aiming for in a given season, year, quadrennial, or lifetime.

There is a very basic method of optimally fitting sport science into a program; the following arrangement works quite well for me. I expect my sport scientists and sports medicine specialists to keep the swimmers healthy and injury free while I apply more quantity and quality to the progressive training and racing loads, and develop and perfect swimmers' techniques for starts, turns, and swimming the race. I work with a sports physiologist at the core of my planning, and I rely on him or her to supply the necessary individual requirements to support that plan through nutrition, flexibility training, strength training, and so forth.

Provide Unique Competitive Experiences

One of the most exciting things you can do to enhance your swimmers' success is to plan a competition trip for your team. Visiting other people and programs is one of the best possible ways for you and your team to expand your horizons and to regain a fresh attitude toward competition.

I planned such a trip with my club team from Britain and took them on a nine-day swim meet tour of Germany. I selected a team of 32 swimmers and a team manager, and we hired a bus. My intention was that we would swim in a dual meet against a top team every day in a different city for six consecutive days of the nine-day trip and that we would be billeted with six different families. Besides cutting down on expense, this arrangement exposed us to a completely different set of challenges and contrasting environments. We had agreed to swim any program chosen by the host team, including relay meets. Our racing schedule was unknown to us until our arrival at each location. One particular night we swam a relay with every swimmer we had, each doing 50 meters. As the host team had their whole club to choose from for their relay, they presented quite a challenge for us. We did in fact win, but only by inches. What excitement! Imagine 16 × 50 relays, with only inches separating the teams.

Another night the final event was a 5 × 100 butterfly relay in a 20-meter pool with the winner of the meet to be determined by the outcome of the relay. All the swimmers gave everything they had; we were halfway into the race when our third swimmer started out so fast that every length thereafter he seemed to be going progressively slower. He managed to touch the wall, but didn't have the strength to climb out of the pool. We were so busy cheering that we didn't notice he was sinking to the bottom. As it turned out, he had swallowed water on the first turn and had been unable to take another proper breath for the next 80 meters. Having managed to finish, he was eventually dragged, unconscious, from the pool. We were all very relieved that he lived to tell the tale of how he almost gave his life to help win the race and the meet for our team.

Our last meet of the tour was against the number-one ranked national team. Once again our teams were so evenly matched that we couldn't afford to lose an event and having won every meet so far (five for five), we wanted desperately to make it a clean sweep. As you can imagine, we were very tired, and I used every means I could think of to motivate the swimmers. At the time I had the national champion backstroker on my team as well as a rookie who was six seconds slower. Both were entered in the 100 backstroke event, where only two swimmers count for points. The last thing I said to them was that I didn't want any DQs, so they should be sure that their turns were safe.

My rookie was really tired, feeling sick, and didn't want to swim. I made allowances and said that if he just went for the first 50 and let the next 50 take care of itself, I would be happy. So, off he went over the first 50 as planned; he made the turn safely, then looked over and saw our national backstroke champion at his feet. Suddenly, he forgot all thoughts of feeling sick, threw back his head, and came in second, beating the other club's two excellent swimmers and doing a personal best by nearly four seconds. What had actually happened was that the number-one backstroker had missed the wall at the first 50, and in light of my warning about being disqualified, had gone back to make the turn again. The rookie had seen him as he made the second turn. It just goes to show that you should never take anything for granted; even the great ones can make mistakes, and if you are ready for the challenge, what seems to be your worst day could turn out to be your best.

Look Ahead

One of the future challenges in swimming that I welcome is the longevity of swimmers in competition. It appears that both men and women will be racing successfully at the Olympic level into their 30s, and as this trend continues, new methods of coaching will have to be developed. Coaching methods will need to be adapted, not only to accommodate the athletes' academic lives, as has already been done to some extent, but also to accommodate the changing professional and social structure. The growing professionalism within the sport is going to challenge many coaches' current ways of thinking and behaving. There will be more than a few shock waves as the parties involved attempt to adjust. I believe that we are looking at a very exciting and turbulent future for the sport. If swimming is to continue to be popular and visible, and is to compete for corporate support, it must become more competitive, particularly in television and the press. Swimming must become a spectator sport, but not at the expense of its present quality and ethics.

The 2000 Olympic year has seen the development of innovative equipment, particularly swimsuits; the next trend to focus on will probably be larger financial rewards. Look to the future, work smart and work hard, have fun, and take one day at a time. You can live your dreams.

Summary

- There are no shortcuts to success. Hard, tough training is required, but you must also train smart.
- The ability to identify talent, desire, and ambition is one of the first requirements of coaching.
- Be optimistically positive. Catch your swimmers doing something right and compliment them on it.
- Keep workouts challenging and fun.
- Vary morning training sessions to create more enthusiasm.
- Always look for ideas to improve your basic skills and coaching knowledge.
- Emphasize team training.
- Individual medley training is productive and develops all physical systems.
- Work to improve the confidence of each swimmer.
- Attain the right mix of competition and training for each swimmer.
- Individualize the training and the taper for each swimmer.
- Use science to support the art of coaching.

PART IV

Teaching Stroke Techniques

CHAPTER ELEVEN

Freestyle Technique

Rick DeMont

I was watching a documentary on the Macupingu Indians in Peru who live at the headwaters of the Amazon River. They are one of the last tribes left untouched by modern civilization. A young boy was swimming with his pet tapir (a 600-pound relative of the rhinoceros that is very much at home in the water). It was obvious that the boy had spent a large part of his life swimming because he was like a fish in the water. At one point he sprinted to get away from his pet and demonstrated a beautiful freestyle stroke. This boy had never had formal swimming lessons; he did this naturally. I thought to myself two things:

1. He chose freestyle in order to swim his fastest.
2. Freestyle must have been around since the beginning of human existence.

The freestyle of today probably contains most of the same elements it has always had. Where did its alternate title "Australian Crawl" come from anyway? From "Aboriginal Crawl," maybe. Whatever you call it, it is still the fastest way to get through the water for anything longer than 15 meters.

I was taught to swim in the 1960s by Ann Curtis, a 1948 Olympic champion. Ann herself had a very traditional freestyle stroke. She taught over-the-barrel high elbow catch, long strokes, and a solid kick. I remember her harping on "technique," often becoming angry about sloppy swimming. It was enough to scare a seven-year-old boy. She was passionate about technique and once even brought in her coach, Charlie Sava (who was an old man at that time), to teach us technique—same story, different voice.

My first experience with seeing amazingly efficient freestyle technique was watching Don Schollander swim in the 1964 Olympics on TV. He was doing exactly what I was being taught to do at that time. He had high elbows and a long, strong stroke driven by a solid kick. It appeared that he was moving an immense amount of water with his arms. His turnover rate was slow compared to the others he was swimming against. I thought to myself, "This is what Ann is trying to teach." A picture is worth a thousand words.

The Two Basic Techniques

During the last 50 years, there have been basically two ways of swimming freestyle. (For all I know, the two methods may go back to the first modern Olympics.) There are obvious similarities, but the major differences between the two lie in the amount of power coming from the hip rotation and from the kick.

One method is characterized by a rapid turnover, arm-oriented stroke, a primarily two-beat kick (sometimes four), and not much hip rotation. This technique has been used mainly, but not exclusively, for distance swimming. Vladimir Burre, Jack Babashoff, Shirley Babashoff, and Shane Gould used this method to sprint effectively. Using this type of stroke, Jonty Skinner, who had a four-beat kick with a rapid turnover rate and little hip rotation, demonstrated what I considered to be the most amazing swim of the 1970s, going 49.4 in the 100-meter freestyle in 1976. A few examples of distance swimmers who have used this stroke effectively are Kieren Perkins, Steve Holland, and Brad Cooper.

Some key elements of this "nontraditional" method of freestyle are the following:

- Very high elbow and low hand in the front third of the stroke. The fingertip to elbow is sometimes almost perpendicular to the surface of the water in the first third of the stroke (see figure 11.1). This is a position not everyone can achieve.
- Very little hip rotation
- Rapid turnover rate
- Very little power created by the kick

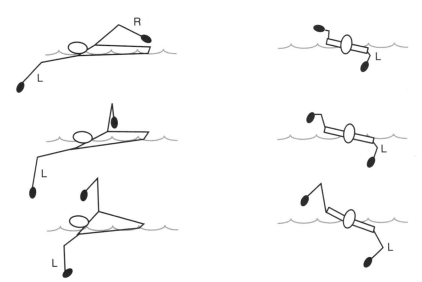

Figure 11.1 Nontraditional freestyle.

Some two-beat kickers do not fit into this category. For example, Janet Evans falls into a slightly different stroke class. She uses a two-beat kick and has a rapid turnover rate, but she generates a lot of power from hip rotation as well.

The second method uses a longer, slower stroke with more power coming from the legs and hip rotation. I call this "traditional" freestyle because this is what I was taught as a child and because it is the form most commonly used by successful freestylers. Most successful freestyle sprinters have used this stroke technique including Steve Clark, Don Schollander, Dave Edgar, Rowdy Gaines, Matt Biondi, Tom Jager, Nicole Haislett, Jill Sterkel, Amy Van Dyken, Jenny Thompson, Dara Torres, and many others. Distance swimmers who have used the traditional method of freestyle include Brian Goodell, Tim Shaw, George DiCarlo,

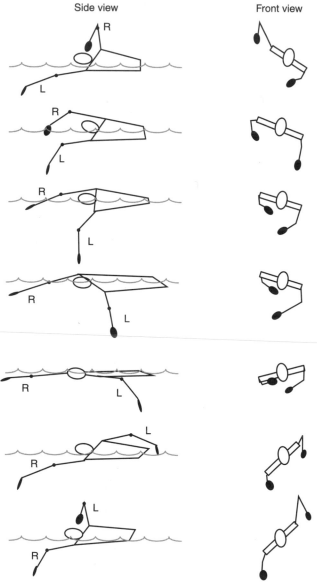

Figure 11.2   Traditional freestyle.

Eric Vendt, and Ryk Neethling. Some important characteristics of this type of stroke are the following:

- A longer glide in the first third of the pull before breaking into the catch part of the stroke (see figure 11.2)
- Greater distance gained per stroke
- A substantial amount of power generated from the kick
- Body roll and hip rotation providing additional power

Finding Your Technique

Of course, there are many variations of freestyle that use a combination of these stroke techniques efficiently. In particular, Ian Thorpe, and Aleksandr Popov to a degree, combine characteristics and elements of both methods. They combine the relatively little hip rotation of the two-beat freestyle pull with a thunder kick, which results in a highly effective freestyle.

For this reason, it's difficult to say that there's one right way to swim freestyle. Different strokes work better for different distances. There is no perfect stroke for everyone. There are certain aspects, common threads, that most great swimmers share such as a relaxed recovery, a high elbow over-the-barrel type of catch, and arm and hand angles that produce power while moving forward. However, each swimmer has a different pull-to-kick power ratio depending on his or her individual strengths.

Personally, I like to build a stroke or a race based on these individual strengths. If an athlete has an incredible kick, I build the stroke around the kick. If he or she has an awesome pull, I build the stroke around that. If he or she has incredible rhythm, I build the stroke around that. You do not want a swimmer to throw away any strengths in order to correct a weakness! The bottom line is that what gets an athlete there the fastest is best.

While strong swimming certainly depends on great strength and power, the best swimmers figure out the minimum amount of effort that they need to produce in order to get the maximum effect. That is the essence of efficiency. The thing I love most is watching someone get through the water in an amazingly efficient way. To me, one of the beauties of sport occurs when the whole seems to be more than the sum of the parts. If the task at hand requires a certain amount of force, it would be foolish to expend more energy than necessary. A swimmer would not want to use 100 pounds of force to do a 50-pound job. Many swimmers use too much force to do the dance. Thus, they die before their time.

A coach must discover and have an open mind about what works for a particular athlete, even if it is something that does not fit the classic "perfect stroke." With that in mind, there are some particular errors a coach should look toward improving.

Common Freestyle Errors

- Not being able to discern how fast one's body is moving through the water (not how fast the hands and feet are moving, but how fast the body glides through the water)
- Not keeping the elbows and shoulders up when the hand enters the water
- Letting the elbows lead the pull at any point in the first two-thirds of the pull
- Stopping the kick to breathe
- Pushing water down in the first third of the stroke
- Pushing water up instead of back in the last third of the stroke

Many swimmers hang on to their old ways as if those habits were their lifeblood. The idea of trying to integrate something new into their stroke scares them. This kind of swimmer would rather remain a national qualifier than risk going through the process of change that could possibly land him or her a place in the finals. A change in technique requires repetition of the new task until it becomes a habit. As a coach, I sometimes have to ask, "Do you want to move to the next level or remain the same?" In my eyes, four hours a day or more is too much time to spend to protect "qualifier" status. Go on, take a risk! The coach must adapt workouts to meet athletes' needs and to help them build a stroke or perfect their technique in order to reach their full potential. To make changes in stroke, both coach and swimmer must reorganize training priorities. One hundred yards of an effective stroke is worth more than 1,500 yards of a lousy stroke.

Because the pull-to-kick ratio is the aspect of freestyle that most affects how swimmers find their most efficient technique, it is important to determine the ratio of power they get from the kick and the power they get from the pull.

Today, sprinting is built from the kick. It used to be said that sprinting was more arms than legs, but I believe that sprinting is more legs than arms. The more power swimmers get from their legs, the more distance they can cover with each stroke and the more water they can travel over with each recovery. Distance per stroke and tempo are variables that always need to be explored. This taps into the philosophy that slower turnover is faster, which may seem strange on the surface. To me, this is the paradox of swimming. The ticket to greater speed is to be able to control large amounts of water at the beginning of the stroke, to accelerate the movement of water through the pull, and to generate power with the kick. A basic prescription for speed is *longest stroke plus strongest kick* while turning over the arms as fast as possible without missing any available water. Swimmers who aim to lengthen their stroke should answer the following questions:

- How far can you extend your arm in front of your body during the stroke without losing the line of your axis?
- How far can you extend your arm behind your body during the stroke without losing the line of your axis?
- How deeply can you pull?
- How much of the time during the pull can you sustain your hand and arm angles as close as possible to perpendicular with the water surface?
- How much power can you generate from your kick?
- How fast can you accelerate your pull and still keep hold of the water?

Careful consideration and review of this information with the coach will pave the way for going to work on the specific aspects of the stroke. The idea is for the swimmer to get the most out of the angles and to stretch out in the stroke.

Perfecting Your Pulling

I like to break the freestyle pull into thirds when teaching it or when drilling a more efficient technique for swimmers.

First Third of the Pull

During the first third of the pull, the hand enters the water between the head and the shoulder. The hand position should be flat (firm, but not tense), the fingers should be together with the thumb either in (touching the fingers) or out. I tell my swimmers to keep the shoulder above the elbow, elbow above the hand, and wrist above the fingertip. As the hand pulls the water down (I call this "down and out"), it should go no farther out laterally than the width of the hand (depending on the individual, maybe more; see first three panels of figure 11.3). If the hand moves laterally too far away from the body, it cancels out the power the swimmer gets from shoulder rotation. The swimmer needs to roll onto the water.

Figure 11.3 Perfect your swimmers' pulling by breaking the stroke into thirds and drilling each third.

Middle Third of the Pull

During the middle third of the pull from the catch to the insweep at the centerline of the body, the hand and forearm should be kept ahead of the elbow as much as possible. The hand should go as deep as the swimmer can handle. If the swimmer is strong enough, he or she can pull the water with the elbow up to as much as a 135-degree angle. An interesting note is that Matt Biondi and Tom Jager both went 21.8 in a 50 free, although Biondi had much more elbow bend than Jager. Jager obtained his power by literally reaching down deep; Biondi got his power with a much shallower pull. This illustrates that coaches and swimmers should go with what works! The stroke should start just outside the width of the shoulder and sweep into the midpoint of the body, just under the belly button (some great swimmers go past the centerline).

Last Third of the Pull

Swimmers should pull from the centerline of the body to well below the hip joint (if a swimmer has long arms, the hand should be closer to the knees than the hip joint.) The angle of the hand should be almost perpendicular to the surface of the water at the end of the stroke. (Swimmers should not push water up into the air, they should push water down to their feet.) Keep in mind the catch-up factor: when one hand is entering the water, the other hand should be between one-third and one-half of the way through the stroke.

Connecting hip rotation with the finish of the stroke is a major power source. With a six-beat kick, it is the first beat and the fourth beat that turn the hips over.

Pulling Drills

All pulling drills can be done with a pull buoy or a kick. However, if the kick is integrated into the drill, make sure it is nonstop. The purpose of these drills is to perfect technique and to improve the power and efficiency of the pull.

Sculling. I like to see the motions of the hands done as fast and as small as possible, so that the hands look just like a propeller. The following can be done with two hands, or with one hand (alternating).

- Two hands in the front third of the stroke, two hands in the middle third of the stroke, two hands in the last third of the stroke, with head and shoulders down so that the propulsion moves them forward, not up
- Traveling scull: two-handed scull that starts at the front of the pull and moves slowly through to the back of the pull throughout the course of 25 yards or meters
- Lying on back, feet first, hands over head
- Lying on back, feet first, hands down by hips
- Fetal position, upright with head out of water and hands out front

Dog paddle. Have swimmers do small dog-paddle movements with their hands in the front third of the stroke, keeping the head and shoulders down. Emphasize forward, not upward, movement. This drill can be used for the middle and last third of the stroke.

Long dog paddle. Underwater version of freestyle done dog-paddle style. Recovery is nowhere near the surface.

Breaststroke pull. You may wonder what a freestyler is doing pulling breaststroke, but the front end of the freestyle pull and a breaststroke pull are similar. Any freestyler should be able to pull breaststroke. Have swimmers do five or six breaststroke pulls without lifting the shoulders or head out of the water (no breath) while maintaining a solid flutter kick. Then they should breathe without stopping to kick, and repeat.

Faster arms. Want to see your swimmers scull or dog paddle fast? Make them do a 25 without a breath and with no kick.

Perfecting Body Position and Breathing

For effective freestyle, swimmers need to establish their best body position in the water. They should start by lying on the surface relaxed, with head position slightly forward. If the head is held too high, then the hips sink too deep. Swimmers should use their energy to go forward, not to pull or push themselves down.

During the pull, swimmers should begin breathing as the opposite hand enters the water. They should not use the front end of the pull to hold the head up and get a breath. Make sure swimmers are just turning the head for the breath. The breath should be on independent suspension, that is, it shouldn't be taken by leaning on the stroking arm. The breath is independent of the actual arm stroke and should be taken on the rotation of the head and neck. Recovery of the pull should be a very relaxed motion.

Many of the recommendations already discussed also apply to distance swimming, the exceptions being the depth of the stroke and the angle of the elbow. Some key points that apply specifically to distance swimming are the following:

- Distance swimmers should not try to move every ounce of water possible, but only the amount of water that they can move at a reasonable tempo. If the tempo becomes too slow, the swimmer should find an easier line through the water, perhaps by using a shallower pull.

- The middle third of the stroke should include an approximately 90-degree elbow bend. Straighter arms, like those used in sprinting, are too difficult to pull for long distances.
- There is likely to be more "catch up" and glide in the front part of the stroke for distance swimmers, especially if they have a lot of power coming from their kick. (Eric Vendt is a great example of this.)
- Recovery should be very relaxed.

Relaxation is one of the keys to peak performance. A good way for athletes to relax is to key on rhythm and breathing. Efficient breathing fuels the engine and relaxes the mind and body. Consciously moving air with the diaphragm is a great, relatively unexplored source of power in swimming. This type of breathing helps one find balance and flow in movements.

Freestyle Drills

Sometimes coaches get into a habit of having a specific workout format that they then have trouble escaping. It is possible to run an entire workout using nothing but drills and obtain the same benefit as the "old square routine."

Catch up. This drill, which involves completing a full stroke with one arm before beginning the stroke with the second arm, is one of my favorite drills of all time, and it is the best drill in the world for beginners. Good freestyle can be built off the catch-up stroke for the following reasons.

- It teaches rookies how to kick through the breath.
- It helps swimmers "square up." It shows them where their best leverage is at the front third of the stroke (shoulder above elbow, elbow above wrist, wrist above fingers).
- It teaches swimmers how to roll onto the power in the front end of the stroke.
- It helps teach swimmers the correct hand positions for taking a breath. An interesting note is that Eric Vendt swims the 1,500 with basically a catch-up stroke. I'm willing to guess that his kick is incredibly strong! Swimmers who do a catch-up stroke without a solid kick should be punished severely (unless they are using a pull buoy, of course)!

Catch-up variations.

- Hands together out front for six beats of kick before starting the next pull.

- Catch up with a pull buoy. (This can really identify pull weaknesses.)
- One-arm freestyle: The left arm stays down against the body, the right arm pulls, breathing is to the left, and the swimmer maintains a solid kick. The swimmer's shoulders should be square to start the stroke. Cranking the hip rotation with the last third of the stroke will allow the swimmer to really feel the connection. At that point, the swimmer should increase the kick tempo and power a little and see how far he or she can glide with each stroke. Reverse for the left arm pull. The swimmer should breathe just before every pull to help get rotation on the opposite side.

Yanko. I got this drill from Eric Hansen, head coach of the Wisconsin Badgers. It starts off the wall with a streamlined kick. Add two breaststroke pulls, without stopping the freestyle kick and without breathing. Follow with a freestyle pull with one arm only. Swimmers should take a breath during this one-arm pull, then take two breaststroke pulls, followed by the same thing with the other arm. Connect the finish of the pull with forceful hip rotation. Don't let the kicking stop!

Recovery. Freestyle kick on the surface of the water with one arm out in front and the other arm moving slowly backward and forward, from point of entry to point of takeout. The moving arm never touches water—it is all done in the air. Again, swimmers must use the kick to maintain body position and get leverage to complete this drill. Repeat with the opposite arm.

Stick-it. A version of the catch-up stroke. Swimmer starts with a solid kick that continues throughout the drill. The recovery arm stops just before the hand enters the water and holds that position for six beats of the kick. The hand then enters water to pull, and the other arm comes out.

Stroke count. Each swimmer swims a series of 25 yards with a specific stroke count to target. (I work with college athletes who use 9 to 14 strokes in this drill. The count varies depending on the individual.) In order to be effective, swimmers need to be under water the same distance off the wall each time. Starting off with medium effort, each swimmer must keep the same stroke count and decrease the time. I really believe this series teaches swimmers how to swim. This is just another version of stroke tempo. I like to tell my swimmers to imagine their hand going into the same hole in the water every time they swim a lap. The faster they can do that, the faster they can go. The stroke count series can also be done swimming against surgical tubing or a power rack.

The cardiovascular system does not know the difference between drills and regular swimming. Drills can be done fast. And drills prevent swimmers from getting into the habit of judging their performance based on the routine.

For example, if you have a standard set of 10 × 100 on 1:05, and at some point you ask one of your swimmers to swim correctly, or to focus on a specific detail of technique during the set, he or she may only be able to accomplish this by swimming 1:15. The slower time might make the athlete feel that he or she is doing the wrong thing; going slower seems to go against swimming logic. But the goal in swimming is to build a race, and it is the coach's job to help build the race by convincing the swimmer that this is the way to go. If the goal is to see a certain technique in a race, practice *only* that technique. Poor technique that is let go in practice is likely to show up at the end of the race. Effective technique can only be taught by massive repetition and must become a habit.

Maximizing Your Kicking

In my opinion, most swimmers (especially beginners) use a little more than half their available power when kicking. These swimmers have a good downbeat but very little upbeat. Swimmers need to learn how to feel and hold more water on the bottoms of their feet during the up kick. The following are some drills I use to increase this skill. I like to picture a strong kick as squeezing water with the feet. If you have a strong kick, you can ride your kick and get over more water during your recovery.

Kicking Drills

Each of these drills can also be done using fins. I especially like the fly up kick and the freestyle kick because they increase neuromuscular awareness of the weak part of the kick.

   Streamlined kick. Swimmers keep the hands out in front for this drill, in a streamlined position on the surface of the water. The head should be down, but looking slightly forward, and the swimmers should breathe straight ahead by lifting the head up without stopping the kick or separating the hands. This is *the* fundamental freestyle drill because it teaches swimmers to breathe and kick at the same time (not doing so is the most common error made by children and experienced swimmers). The streamlined kick can also be done while on the back or the side.

Fly up kick. This drill completely de-emphasizes the down kick and fully emphasizes the up kick. The swimmer slips water on the down kick on purpose, catches as much water as possible on the up kick, then stops and glides as much as he or she can. This drill can also be done with freestyle kick, using one leg for an entire lap (or changing legs in the middle of the lap). The other leg stays still.

Freestyle kick. The goal is to get across the pool in as few kicks as possible. This drill is more effectively done underwater. If the swimmer is getting a good up kick, he or she can squeeze water against the other foot during the down kick. I call it "squeezing water out the back."

Fly kick. This is a variation on the freestyle-kick drill. The swimmer uses the fly (dolphin) kick to get across the pool in as few kicks as possible.

Vertical kick. In this drill the swimmers kick in an upright or vertical position in the deep end while keeping the arms crossed across the chest. The drill can also be done in a streamlined position or done while holding weights or wearing a weight belt.

Barrel rolls. Swimmers do a 25-yard freestyle kick underwater while making a complete rotation: stomach, side, back, side, stomach.

I would like to end this chapter by sharing a few words my grandfather told me. My grandfather was a very successful high school basketball coach in Sacramento, California. Before the race, on the few occasions he watched me swim, he would say to me, "Ricky, swim her pretty!" Looking into his eyes as he spoke, I could see a mischievous twinkle. At the time, I could not make sense out of his statement. I was only 12. I did not quite get it. It took me a few years to realize what he meant. He was pointing out to me that aesthetics are very much a part of athletics. Now, as I think back on those words, I realize that he was familiar with the dance. He wanted to see the beautiful thing occur.

Summary

- Develop a passion for technique.
- There are variations in freestyle swimming; there is no one right way for every individual.
- Traditional freestyle features a long stroke, with the legs and the hip rotation providing much of the power.
- Sprinting is built from the legs, using a kick with both a downbeat and an upbeat.
- Body position must be correct to enable the swimmer to move forward most effectively.
- The coach must match the technique to the swimmer, building on each swimmer's individual strengths.
- Swimmers must be willing to try new technique patterns.
- Effective drills will improve the kicks.
- If a kick is used in pulling drills, it must be nonstop.
- Effective technique can only be taught by massive repetition.
- Relaxation is one of the keys to peak performance.

CHAPTER TWELVE

Backstroke Technique

Dick Hannula

Backstroke isn't the most natural swimming position, and swimmers usually aren't attracted to this stroke in the beginning. Moving in a backward direction and not seeing clearly what is in front of you are disadvantages for beginning backstroke swimmers. This is certainly true in the short run. Still, the stroke has at least one particular advantage for the novice swimmer: swimming on the back allows the swimmer to keep the face out of the water; therefore breathing is easier than in the other competitive strokes. I believe a significant number of swimmers select backstroke because of this advantage over the other strokes.

The Three R's of Backstroke

Success in backstroke technique is best achieved by observing the three R's: rhythm, relaxation, and rotation. Rhythm facilitates power, which is the result of rotation. Rotation refers to the hip-initiated trunk rotation that generates stroking power and reduces drag. Relaxation assists in maintaining steady stroking power. Arm recovery and breathing pattern are the two main components of relaxation.

Rhythm and Rotation

Rhythm requires the body to move past the anchored arm—the arm underwater—evenly and with constant propulsion. The timing of the trunk rotation to arm recovery and entry is critical in establishing effective rhythm. The ideal is to rotate the hips out of the way of the arm and hand that is finishing the stroke. This puts the hips increasingly to the side as the hand finishes the underwater stroke, permitting the arm and hand to recover cleanly. The torque action also unloads the weight of the hips and reduces drag. When the arms are just short of being opposite one another, focusing on trunk rotation will help to ensure effective trunk rotation on the arm and hand entry. Proper rhythm timing and trunk rotation will facilitate a thumb first exit, vertical recovery, and a deep, little-finger catch on entry, all of which are essential components for successful backstroke.

Relaxation

Relaxation essentially requires the arms to recover naturally in a ballistic type of recovery—a continuous movement from the finishing underwater arm stroke into the recovery—as opposed to lifting or carrying the arms into the recovery. The arm and hand also "fall" into the entry, as opposed to being carried and placed into the entry. A regular breathing pattern, inhaling on one arm, exhaling on the second arm, is also important for relaxation.

Blending the Three R's

The key to successful backstroke is to blend the three R's into a backstroke that optimizes distance per stroke. The optimum stroke length is the number of strokes per pool length that is most effective for each individual. Maximizing stroke length by reducing the number of strokes taken for each length of the pool is only a building drill. Maximizing the distance per stroke, in itself, isn't the desired end. Rather, optimizing the stroke length to achieve the most effective reference for sustained speed and to achieve the optimum effective stroking rate is the desired goal in all competitive strokes. The kick, the arm stroke, and the coordinated swimming make up the components that contribute through drills, practice, and training to the three R's of backstroke success.

Kick Training

The kick is a very important component of successful backstroke. Legs are important in every push off from the wall, in starts and turns, when the butterfly dolphin kick is utilized to attain the fastest underwater speed as well as great breakout speed in the surface strokes. The back flutter kick is also very important in maintaining surface speed, maintaining good body position, and keeping drag to a minimum.

The underwater butterfly kick is most effective when the body is in a streamlined, torpedo position (figure 12.1). This kick should be from the hips down with the upper body, from waist to head, reasonably still and extended. This is a narrow, fast kick. The drills that are effective in teaching the underwater butterfly kick would include most of the butterfly kicking drills. The following drills have proved to be effective for this kicking skill:

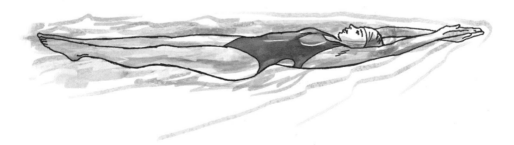

Figure 12.1 The streamlined, torpedo position.

Underwater Dolphin Kick Drills

• **Bursts.** Swimmers kick short, fast bursts underwater in a streamlined position. It's best to do these across the deeper end of the pool or in a diving well in which the water isn't too shallow. Distances of 10 to 15 yards are very effective, and timing or racing other team members can provide increased incentive to improve this kick. Just staying underwater for this short distance usually motivates beginning competitive swimmers, who have to kick fast in order to surface and breathe sooner. You may want to shorten the distance for novice swimmers to less than 10 yards underwater, perhaps having them do only three or four fast butterfly kicks to start.

• **Vertical kicking.** This drill is done in deep water with the body in an upright position, the head out of the water, and the arms extended overhead. This is an effective drill when used in short bursts of 10 or more seconds.

• **Fin drills.** Short swim fins and the smaller monofins such as the "shooter" are good training tools for the underwater butterfly kick. The short cross-pool kick drills won't work here as the distance is too short for the speed generated with fins. Swimmers should do these drills in the main pool over 20 yards or more. Depending on the skill level of the swimmers, the underwater portion of the distance covered can be considerably less than one full length of the pool. The fin drills can also be used in the vertical kicking sets.

• **Flag drills.** Kicking with fins, after pushing from the bottom of the diving well, in an extended torpedo position and attempting to touch the backstroke flags on the kick will also improve the speed and efficiency of the butterfly kick. When your swimmers get good enough to reach the flags with fins, have them try to duplicate the feat without fins.

The backstroke flutter kick is also very important to backstroke success. The back flutter kick actually rolls from side to side due to good trunk rotation. The kick is best when it is continuous, when it operates in a narrow range in which the legs do not separate too much, and when the kick initiates from the hips as much as possible. This will keep the body position more streamlined throughout the swimming stroke. Beginners need to learn to relax the feet and to allow them to rotate in the kick. "Shaking" a shoe or sock off the foot while sitting in the gutter and practicing the back kick is a good beginning step. I've used this technique for decades, but I like what Debbie Potts has done by making a game of this: Who can shake a sock off the foot first? Keeping practice fun for young swimmers always helps to keep them in the sport.

Backstroke Flutter Kick Drills

• **Arms at the sides.** Have the swimmer start with a flat body position to attain the best body position possible for backstroke. Help each swimmer adjust the direction of eye focus to help get the ribcage and hips up in the water. Pressing downward on a pressure point at mid-shoulders (or slightly lower or higher) while on the back can help the swimmer achieve a better body position on the water. Having swimmers count the kicks—1, 2, 3, 4, 5, 6, and repeat—will help swimmers to develop a continuous kick and to position a starting point on the rhythm of the kick to the arms (six kicks to each arm cycle). The torque or trunk-rotated position can also be used with the arms at the sides (see figure 12.2).

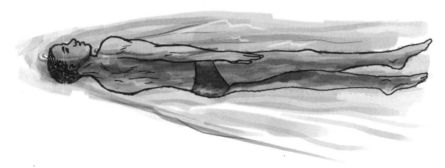

Figure 12.2 The torque or trunk-rotated position with arms at sides.

• **Arms extended overhead.** Swimmers do a streamlined, torpedo kick on the back. This is a flat position that is not a true position for backstroke swimming, but it develops the legs and improves the flexibility of the streamlined position so vital in the starts and turns. The best body position for an individual will vary. The fingertips should be slightly off the water in these drills to get the ribcage higher and to increase the pressure on the legs slightly. This kicking position should also be repeated cross pool over 10 to 15 yards without fins.

• **Cross-pool.** Done underwater in back flutter kick, this drill assists the swimmer in streamlining the kick and in keeping it narrow. This type of kick can also be done effectively with short swim fins but not cross pool. Use the main pool and the normal pool length for fin kicking.

Figure 12.3 The trunk-rotated position with one arm extended overhead.

• **One arm extended overhead.** The swimmer executes this drill in a trunk-rotated position with one arm extended and one arm at the side of the body (see figure 12.3). Swimmers use pressure points to assist with kicking on the side. Swimmers should focus on a pressure point that is one hand-width below the armpit and slightly behind the center point of that side. By pressing down at the pressure point, the swimmer should get the ribcage higher in the water, get the hips and legs up as well, and attain the desired position to the side. The pressure point can be adjusted up or down to meet the needs of each individual swimmer. The "side" indicates more than 45 degrees, and near 90 degrees for some swimmers. Drill on each side using 12 kicks on one side and then 12 on the other, followed by 10/10, 8/8, and 6/6. Stabilize the head, and rotate the hip-initiated trunk from side to side. Another variation would be to add the short swim fins to this kicking drill.

Perfecting Body Position and Arm Stroke

Lenny Krayzelburg, 2000 Olympic gold medalist in the 100 and 200 backstroke, provides a great technique model for backstroke swimmers. He lays well back and his head is flat on the water. Many previous backstroke champions didn't lay back as flat as Lenny does (and consequently as most of the current elite backstroke swimmers do). You can simulate the body position Lenny attains by laying your head back on a very soft pillow; then in the pool, you can adjust the head accordingly to bring the body and legs up higher in the water. Lenny's chest is out of the water, and his hips are up high in the water. The high hips help his effective hip and trunk rotation. Lenny pulls wide, with the elbows somewhat wide. He feels water quite well on his stroking arm. His hip rotation generates more power into his arm strokes, and he attempts to finish his stroke with a relaxed hand.

Lea Mauer described her stroke as being initiated by her thinking hips not shoulders. This is to say the trunk rotation is hip initiated, as the great Australian coach Bill Sweetenham emphasizes. Good shoulder rotation is essential for backstroke success, but it must start from the hips. Lea describes the process in this way: Once the right hand has made its catch, she begins to think about rotating that right hip to the up position. She wants the hip to lead the arm, and she wants to get the hip out of the way at the finish and start of the recovery.

The arm stroke is most effective when the hand is able to maintain the maximum hand surface and "hold" the most water. Reviewing videotape of backstroke swimmers has demonstrated to me that too many swimmers pull with the thumb leading and the little finger trailing too early in the stroke. This technique results in slicing or slipping the hand through the water rather than attaining an anchored position on the water, in which the hand is perpendicular to the water and the elbow is pointed toward the bottom. With the hand and elbow in correct position, the hip-trunk rotation assists the arms in driving the body past the arms. The best arm stroke is one that has the arm entering and exiting at close to the same spot on the water; this is not possible when the hand is slicing through the water. To help your swimmers develop proper arm stroke, place a full-length mirror on the deck at the end of the backstroke lane. I did so for most of my coaching career. It saves a lot of talking; the pictures that your backstroke swimmers see are precise and provide very accurate feedback. Always have the backstroke flags legally in place at every practice session.

The specific pace of the essential progression in the arm stroke and full stroke depends on the ability level of the swimmer. Swimmers must master the basic technique drills before moving on to advanced drills. All swimmers need to review basic drills on occasion.

Basic Technique Drills

1. **One-arm swims.** Swimmers keep the opposite arm stationary at the side of the body. Rotating the hip to the side as the arm finishes the stroke improves the timing and rhythm of the trunk rotation. The swimsuit should be visible and clear of the water at the hip on the rotated upper side. This drill facilitates the feel of moving the body past the anchored and stroking arm. Variations of this drill could include doing a specific number of strokes on one side before changing sides, for example, four left arm strokes and then four right arm strokes. Expand this drill, when the ability of the swimmer permits, by having the swimmer use hand paddles.

2. **Backstroke swims with a plastic coin purse balanced on the forehead.** This drill teaches swimmers to stabilize the head position.

3. **Double-arm backstroke.** Swimmers should recover both arms at the same time and touch at the height of the vertical recovery. This helps to develop a vertical recovery and to get the arms entering the water near the 12 o'clock position.

4. **One-arm backstroke swims.** The nonstroking arm should be carried off the water at the vertical high-point position. This helps swimmers to attain a steady, strong kick and a good deep entry catch position.

5. **Spin-out drills.** These help the swimmer attain an entry near the 12 o'clock position, a vertical rifle-barrel recovery, and a "fall in" arm entry. Swimmers should sit up high in the water, as though they are in an undersized bathtub, and then spin and throw the arms into a rapid backstroke turnover.

6. **Swim the rope.** This exercise involves a rope that is attached at each end of the pool underwater (four to six inches underwater). Have swimmers swim on one side of the rope going down the pool and return with the other arm on that same side of the rope. This drill gives the feeling of anchoring the hand and elbow on the water and rotating the trunk past the stationary arm. It also helps to maximize the distance per stroke.

7. **The "break water" drill with hand paddles.** This teaches the appropriate arm bend on the underwater pull. Swimmers bring the top one-third of each paddle out of the water at about midstroke and then finish the stroke underwater as normal.

Additional Backstroke Drills

- **Touchdown swims** are one-arm swims that alternate the arms after every stroke. The stroking arm must finish at the side of the swimmer before the other arm, which was resting at the side, begins to recover and stroke to that side. This drill emphasizes all the points of the one-arm swims with one arm at the side and adds to the feel and timing of the hip-trunk rotation.

- **The touch-and-go drill** emphasizes hip-trunk rotation and shoulder rotation, the vertical rifle-barrel recovery of the arms, and a deep catch of the hands. This exercise also encourages a continuous and strong kick. The swimmer recovers one arm to the highest vertical position, directly over the shoulder-chin area, and then holds that arm there in a frozen position until the other arm recovers to

Figure 12.4 The touch-and-go drill.

that same position. The other arm then assumes the frozen position as the previously frozen arm takes its stroke (see figure 12.4). The swimmer continues to alternate arms, stroking from the frozen vertical spot. This drill should progress to using hand paddles.

- **Corkscrew drills** aid the swimmer in attaining the feel of the trunk moving past the arm during the stroke. The swimmer swims a set number of strokes in freestyle, then a set number of strokes in backstroke (seven and seven, five and five, or three and three, for example). The transition stroke, from back to free and from free to back, helps the swimmer to be aware of the trunk moving past the anchored hand and elbow. The seven and seven drill would include seven strokes freestyle and seven strokes of backstroke following the rotation of the body into the new stroke. I strongly recommend hand paddles in this drill as they facilitate a greater awareness of the trunk moving past the arms, especially on the transition stroke.

- **Variable sprinting drills** are three-cycle sprints within any training set of kicking or swimming. For example, in a set of 12 × 100 backstroke kicking, the swimmer would swim a three-cycle sprint (left arm, right arm × three) at midpool and at the end of the pool on every length of each 100. This kind of drill contributes to a higher stroke rate and faster turns. Lenny Krayzelburg performs these drills frequently in training.

- **Stroke count sets** optimize the distance per stroke. After maximizing a swimmer's distance per stroke by reducing the number of strokes he or she takes to swim each length, test sets can determine the optimum or most efficient number of strokes taken per length for each swimmer. Using a test set of 10 × 50, the swimmer descends each 50 to a race-pace time while holding to the least number of strokes necessary to attain that race-pace time. This number changes as the swimmer's technique and conditioning level improves. Repeat this test set with new goals as the season progresses.

- **Stroke-rate sets** should be introduced, in addition to the stroke-count sets, to determine the most effective stroke rate for each swimmer. Again using the test set of 10 × 50, record the stroke rate of the swimmer on each length or twice within the length of a long-course pool. Measure stroke rate with a stroke-rate stopwatch that records the number of strokes the swimmer would take in any one-minute period. The race-pace time, the stroke count, and the stroke rate will give your swimmers the foundation for sustaining speed through the complete distance of their particular backstroke event.

Every practice session, have swimmers use a closed fist on any of the swimming drills to help them gain a feel for the water on their hands. Then have them gradually open the hand throughout the set. As you evaluate technique look at all your swimmers from as many viewpoints as possible. This is especially important for backstroke swimmers because they can constantly see you looking at them. The result is better focus on good technique. Watch from a high overhead viewpoint—a diving board, high ladder, or some elevated platform—and from underwater. When on the deck, move from end to end and side to side. The great Canadian coach Howard Firby taught me to look at my swimmers while bent over with my back to them, to peer out at them from under my armpit. Try this method; you will see eddies and water flow like never before.

Lenny Krayzelburg combines the one arm extended and one arm at the side kick drill with a dynamic swimming stroke. He uses a 10/10 kick drill followed by one perfect and dynamic full swim stroke. He swims into all turns on his kicking drills to get speed. He also likes to combine swimming with kicking, for example, he'll swim the first length and kick the second length. He focuses specifically on kicking by doing

50s: one easy, one build, then one at race pace in one breath in underwater butterfly kicking.

Krayzelburg lifts weights after practices; this is an important part of helping to tolerate the necessary stroke rate that he has set as a goal for himself. He watches videotapes often to assess his technique. He always focuses on getting his head back on his underwater butterfly kick and on the breakout.

Great technique is the result of perfect practice. Every drill must be taught correctly and then repeated in perfect form. Move from drills to the full coordinated stroke in your training sessions. Persistence is one of the most vital coaching traits. Be persistent. Never compromise on technique. Find many ways to say the same thing if necessary and always remember that one picture is worth a thousand words.

Summary

- Rhythm, relaxation, and rotation are the key components of successful backstroke.
- The timing of trunk rotation is important to effective rhythm.
- Blend the 3 R's into a backstroke that optimizes distance per stroke.
- Optimizing distance per stroke is more important than maximizing that distance.
- The underwater butterfly dolphin kick should be narrow and fast coming off each wall.
- Kicking and swimming drills, in the right combination, are the best learning methods for the component parts of the stroke.
- Pressure points assist in achieving efficient body position.
- The arm stroke is most effective when the hand holds the most water.
- Progression drills build the arm stroke.
- Hand paddles should be added to many of the arm-stroke drills to further develop skills.
- Great technique is the result of perfect practice.
- Never compromise technique.

CHAPTER THIRTEEN

Butterfly Technique

Pablo Morales

To paraphrase a swim coach I had many years ago, "Butterfly is not for wimps." There is perhaps nothing more instructive or appropriate than this oversimplified assessment of the stroke to introduce a chapter on butterfly training. It serves as a basic acknowledgment of the fact that butterfly is not easy—from the perspective of the athletes (both aspiring and elite butterflyers) or the coach.

For the athlete, there are first the intricacies of learning and perfecting the mechanics of the stroke—the proper timing between simultaneous arm pull, recovery, and dolphin kick. Adding to the difficulty is the significant strength required merely to execute a single butterfly stroke and the resulting susceptibility of the stroke to compromised technique or stroke decay during the course of workout or a race. (The term "easy butterfly" is generally considered an oxymoron). Then there is the subtle blending of contrasting elements—power and explosiveness with grace and fluidity—demanded in advanced butterfly. Finally there are the psychological barriers to butterfly training and racing that most, if not all, swimmers face. The coach, of course, must consider all of the above in devising an effective training program for butterflyers.

Conditioning Aspects of Butterfly Training

At the outset, a coach is confronted with devising a conditioning program for a stroke form that is by nature difficult to maintain for extended distances and repetitions. He or she therefore must first establish a solid foundation on which to build an effective butterfly workout regimen. This foundation should consist of at least three elements—core strengthening, flexibility training, and butterfly technique work—established at the beginning of and maintained throughout the season.

I break down several important aspects of butterfly technique later in this chapter, but maintaining good technique bears brief mention here as an important training prerequisite. A strong foundation in proper technique should be established, as with any of the other three strokes, prior to beginning an extensive program of butterfly conditioning. Furthermore, given the nature of butterfly training, a constant emphasis on technique should continue during each training cycle—to such an extent that it actually controls the scope of the butterfly conditioning program. This is what will be referred to as a technique-based program of butterfly training.

Core Strengthening

The strengthening of the core muscles in the abdomen should be a part of any training regimen, but it has special importance for butterflyers. These stabilizing muscles—especially the lower-abdominal and back muscles—are central to the undulating mechanics of butterfly, creating a powerful kick and greater endurance in the face of the debilitating effects of workout or race fatigue.

Devoting at least a small portion each day to some form of core strengthening is time well spent. This includes but is not limited to dolphin kicking on the back (in a streamlined position) or on the stomach (face down with snorkel, arms extended and holding the back end of a kickboard), monofin training, and the typical assortment of dryland abdominal and lower-back exercises as well as the use of other core strengthening devices such as medicine balls.

Flexibility Training

Most coaches would not dispute the importance of flexibility training in any competitive swimming program. Still, many do not incorporate a flexibility routine beyond some toe touching and a few arm stretches, and often put off stretching until the end of the season or the taper period.

There are several benefits to be derived from a regular, comprehensive, and challenging flexibility program such as an intensive active-static (yoga) routine. These benefits include improved stroke length and streamlined position, proper relaxation during high-effort swims, and a lengthening of muscle fibers for increased resilience against a debilitating accumulation of lactate. A flexibility program also alleviates the tightening and fatiguing effects of intense workloads, allowing for better day-to-day workout performances during crucial times of the season. Clearly these advantages, so important to a butterflyer, should not be put off until the end of the season but should be maximized during the course of the season.

Technique-Based Conditioning

With a solid strength and flexibility foundation in place, a coach ready to get to the heart of the conditioning program faces the question: "How much butterfly is enough?" Given that a butterflyer is particularly susceptible to stroke decay (deviation from the desired stroke form to a significantly less propulsive and efficient mode), any butterfly conditioning program should be sensitive to the development and preservation of proper butterfly technique. Follow this basic guideline: train as much butterfly—with as much intensity—as good form will allow. In practice, this simply means that a swimmer should not swim an amount or intensity of butterfly that is beyond that which he or she can execute with desirable butterfly technique for the entire set. The underlying strategy would be to establish and maintain ideal butterfly form while building capacity over time.

There are several justifications for this seemingly conservative approach.

1. The strength requirements of the stroke make it easy for swimmers to fall into and, consequently, to become accustomed to bad form (what is commonly referred to as "survival stroke"); a butterflyer can ill afford to waste energy on inefficient technique.

2. If a swimmer is constantly training with perfect form (even if, at first, for only a minimal amount of butterfly at a time), he or she is constantly conditioning the proper muscles and ranges of motion associated with good technique.

3. It is a very individualized standard that takes into account the fact that successful butterfly performances may come from individuals with substantially different training capacities. Although the legendary Madame Butterflyer, Mary T. Meagher, had the ability to effectively train endurance butterfly sets that some would consider impossible, other butterflyers have been able to reach world-class status by training with far less butterfly than Meagher.

4. There are psychological benefits to being conservative in this way. Instilled in the swimmer is a greater sense of confidence and less of a feeling of dread toward butterfly training (and racing), since he or she is only doing as much butterfly with as much intensity as he or she can execute with perfect form. Furthermore, the constant emphasis on technique conditions the psychological mechanism that triggers a focus on technique during the physiological stresses of training and racing butterfly. A coach can incorporate butterfly into endurance training (distance and short-rest repetitions), high-quality repetition training, and sprint training.

Endurance Training

Maintaining a conservative approach to overall volume and intensity is perhaps never more appropriate than when dealing with the longer distance, lower rest aspects of endurance training. Endurance training may seem somewhat paradoxical when one considers the difficulty of swimming extended distances of butterfly (beyond 100 meters, for example) in practice without generating significant levels of lactate and slipping into survival-stroke mode. For this reason, a coach should be very conservative about using overdistance butterfly sets (300s or 400s). Endurance training for butterfly should instead consist of

- distance work in combination with aerobic freestyle,
- extensive repetitions of shorter distances with short rest, and
- multiple cycles of repetitions with shorter rest in combination with active-recovery freestyle.

In monitoring the following example sets, a coach should remain vigilant against deteriorating technique by reminding swimmers to stay focused on form and, when necessary, by adjusting the amount of butterfly and rest intervals if correct form cannot be maintained.

Distance (Free/Fly Combo)

Long course: sets of 300s or 400s, 25 fly/25 free, every other 50 fly, or last 50 fly

Short course: 3 × 500, 12.5 fly/12.5 free

Extensive Repetition (Fly Only)

Long course: 24 × 50 fly with 10 to 15 seconds rest

Short course: 40 × 25 fly with 5 to 10 seconds rest

Extensive Repetition (Free/Fly Combo)

20 × 100, last 25 fly; 10 with 15 to 20 seconds rest and 10 with 10 to 15 seconds rest

12 × 200, last 50 fly; 6 with 25 to 30 seconds rest and 6 with 20 to 25 seconds rest

Short Repeat Cycles/Shorter Rest (Free/Fly Combo)

5 × (6 × 25 or 50 fly, with 5 or 10 seconds rest)

5 × (1 × 50 or 100 free, cruise interval)

High-Quality Repetitions

High-quality repetition training or, as some refer to it, lactate-tolerance work, with its longer rest intervals, is well suited for a technique-based system of butterfly training. The extra time allows the butterflyer to physically recover and mentally re-establish focus on good butterfly technique prior to the next intense repeat. But as lactate accumulates, making it increasingly difficult to complete each repeat, a swimmer will need to exert special effort to maintain good form during the onset of stroke decay. Again, it may be necessary in some instances to have a swimmer reduce the amount of butterfly or lower the intensity or effort level. The following are examples of high-intensity repetition training:

8 × (2 × 50 easy free on 1:00)

8 × (1 × 100 all out on 2:00); mostly fly

16 to 20 × 50 fly on 2:00 all out; record times

6 to 8 (× 100, 150, and 200 for time); from starting blocks; one set on 8 to 10 minutes

Sprint Training

Although stroke decay is not typically an issue in the sample sets below, there should be no less focus on technique than in the other two types of training.

25s, 12.5s, six-stroke blasts from wall

Shooters: underwater 25-yard blast dolphin kicks—stomach and back, in streamlined position; adequate rest to complete each underwater

Key Aspects of Butterfly Technique

The key aspects of butterfly technique involve two elements—the essential body undulation and the arm stroke—working in isolation and in coordination with each other. What many consider to be a third key element—the kick—is important, but I address it as an extension of the essential undulation. This viewpoint is in keeping with a recent emphasis toward "front-end" butterfly (see page 171 "The Arm-Stroke Cycle").

The Essential Body Undulation

The central movement, both literally and figuratively, of the butterfly stroke is the head-to-toe undulation of the body. Commonly referred to as a dolphin or bullwhip action, it is perhaps most accurately described as a repetitive, wave-like motion through the body. It is instigated by a slight motion of the head and chest that achieves increasingly greater expression as it travels down the body—to the hips, through the legs, and, finally, to the feet, which add the essential thrust at the end of the undulation.

Head Position and Movement

As the heavy, leading point of the body moving through the water, the head's position and movement deserve double consideration—in the prone, nonbreathing position and in coordination with the arm stroke during the breathing cycle. In the prone position, muscles of the neck should be relaxed and stretched out as the head, essentially face down, establishes a pressure point against the water (usually at a point approximately above the forehead) that facilitates the greatest forward motion (see figure 13.1a, page 174). It is from this position that the head initiates the body undulation with a slight, repeating motion or rocking. The swimmer must take care to avoid excessive motion of the head so as to maintain the essential relaxation of the neck and the established pressure point that assist the body in assuming the most forward-moving position. As during the breathing cycle, the head should undulate as little as possible and stay as close as possible to the forward line of direction.

A Balanced Hip Action and Effective Kick

Probably the most crucial movement in the body undulation is the balanced, or complete, hip action, which involves not only a forcing up but also a thrusting forward of the hips (figure 13.1, a and b, page 174). Note here the necessary contraction of the lower-back muscles on the hip-up action, and the lower-abdominal muscles and buttocks on the thrust forward—thus, you can see the importance of the previously mentioned core-strengthening work. A lack of hip action, especially the forward hip thrust, is usually demonstrated by those who have trouble generating propulsive force from their dolphin kick. There is a good enough reason for this.

An effective and efficient kick requires that the feet assume, on both the upbeat and the downbeat, the proper angle of propulsive thrust against the water in a line directly opposite the desired forward line of movement (see foot action in figure 13.1, a and b). This is accomplished, in part, through adequate flexibility in the foot area, that is, good plantar-flexion in the ankles. But the proper foot angle also comes from a significant and balanced hip action. When the hips make substantial movement upward and downward, the legs essentially follow the hips along the wave path. There is a natural bending of the knees as the legs trail along this path. Next to follow are the feet, which, in aligning on this naturally bending wave, achieve the proper thrust angle. Where there is no forward hip action, the wave motion halts, and in order to position the feet in the proper angle the swimmer must provide a forceful and deliberate bending of the knees in excess of the bending that naturally occurs in the course of the wave action. This is because the feet, being at the end of a shorter line (from knee to foot as opposed to hip to foot), require a more radical bending of the knees to achieve the desired foot angle. This radical movement creates undesirable resistance—not to mention more work for the swimmer—resulting in a downward cycle of energy expenditure. Briefly stated, having the knees stay on the body-wave line not only allows the feet to reach the proper thrust angle but also creates much less resistance against the water than an unnatural, excessive bending of the knees.

The Kick—A Propulsive Finish to the Body Wave

The kick is the propulsive force generated at the end of the body wave. It encompasses the thrusting of the feet (which have achieved the proper angle) and the powerful contraction of the hamstrings and quadriceps. It may be viewed as an additional action or an extra explosive force at the end of the wave—like the snapping of a whip or the exclamation mark at the end of a sentence. Regardless, its effectiveness depends on the correct body undulation.

Despite its propulsive properties, the swimmer should take care not to "overkick" to the point of excessive undulation or bending of the knees. The kicking action should be relatively tight and steady, yet powerful, within the body line. The effects of an excessive kick are addressed later in this chapter in a section dealing with the kick in coordination with the arm stroke (see page 176). From this point forward, the traditional term "kick" or "kicking" will refer to the complete body undulation that includes the propulsive foot thrust at the end of the wave action.

Although it may be viewed as being dependent on and governed by the body undulation, kicking remains an important part of the butterfly training program. The isolation of the kick—whether through intense kicking sets or drills—builds leg strength, increases foot and ankle flexibility, and enforces proper hip undulation.

Kicking sets and drills can be done in a variety of positions—on the back, stomach, or side; with arms up or down—and using an assortment of equipment, including different styles and sizes of kick boards and fins—long fins, short fins, monofins. Coaches have employed monofins with increasing regularity as an effective training device. Monofin training and drills teach the proper wave action of the body (especially the hips), improve plantar-flexion, build core and leg muscle strength, and improve streamlining ability.

The following sets and drills are designed to help condition the legs and to teach or improve the essential body undulation.

Dolphin kick on back
- 8 × 200 streamlined or on stomach with board, descending 1-3, 4-6, 7-8.
- 8 × 100, hands down; all fast, best average.

Sidekick drill. Bottom arm extended, top arm down, alternating sides. Emphasize complete hip action behind and in front of imaginary central line down the body.

Monofin. Repeat blast 25s, moderate to short rest, 8 × 100 with each 25- to 15-meter underwater blast in streamlined position (alternating on back and stomach) plus sidekick drill (alternating right and left sides) into flip turn.

Vertical kicking with weight. Emphasize strictly vertical position and balanced hip action.

Kick and swim. 8 × 100, 50 dolphin kick/50 fly, moderate rest, descending 1-3, 4-6, 7-8 (6 faster than 3, 8 faster than 6).

Shooters. 25 repeats; odd-numbered ones should be underwater blast dolphin kicks; even-numbered ones should be sprint butterfly.

Hands-down dolphin kick on stomach. With center-mounted snorkel, with and without monofin. Emphasize maintaining neck relaxation and forward-moving pressure point despite the slight "rocking" motion of the head.

The Arm-Stroke Cycle

The second element of butterfly technique is the arm-stroke cycle, a double-arm pull down the body underwater followed by a "flying" arm recovery above the water. This motion in coordination with the essential body undulation results in the powerful, yet beautifully rhythmic, butterfly stroke. Over the years, subtle variations of style within this basic butterfly technique have been demonstrated by many successful butterflyers.

Recently, a trend toward "front-end butterfly" has developed. Generally, it reflects a greater emphasis on the front half of the stroke or a shifting forward of balance from the back end of the stroke behind the hips (basically, the legs) to beyond the hips (the upper body). The various characteristics of the front-end butterfly have been successfully developed and demonstrated in the careers of world-record holders Denis Pankratov, Michael Klim, and Jenny Thompson. The butterfly development of Thompson, in particular, illustrates the evolution of this technique.

Initial Scull and Power Phase

The breakdown of the butterfly arm stroke begins at the top end of the cycle—arms extended above the head, hands positioned just inside the imaginary lines extending forward from the shoulders (see figure 13.1b, page 174). From this position, the hands scull, or press, outward and downward. The outward press ceases as the hands reach a point just outside the shoulder line. The hands complete their downward motion at a point just below the relative level of the elbows, as the fingertips rotate downward toward the bottom of the pool. At the same time, the palms rotate inward so that they face directly behind the swimmer. This is the ideal "catch" position (figure 13.1c, page 174).

With a slight flexing of the arms and bending of the elbows, the power phase of the stroke begins. There is an initial pulling back of the hands in a line moving directly opposite the intended forward line of direction (figure 13.1d, page 174). As the hands reach the chest line, the direct pull back ceases temporarily as the palms turn inward, and an insculling of the hands occurs until the hands nearly touch at a point just below the chest line (figure 13.1e, page 174). Here the palms turn back and the direct pull back of the hands, which are now closer together, resumes (figure 13.1f, page 175).

It is preferable that this insculling occur sooner (approximately at the chest line) than later (toward the end of the pull). Setting the hands at the chest allows for a quicker, easier exit of the hands at the end of the pull leading to the arm recovery. The hands remain in ideal pitch for a longer, uninterrupted period of time, allowing the swimmer to build more momentum for the quick and efficient exit. Later insculling results in less time to build momentum for the exit and arm recovery phase and may lead to the hands getting stuck at the bottom or to an inefficient, longer pull.

Pull Through and Exit

This raises the final consideration of the pull phase: at what point should the pull of the hands cease and the arms exit the water? The hands should pull through to a point at which they maintain, in the proper pull-back position, ideal force against the water prior to the natural raising of the fingertips that occurs at the extreme bottom end of the stroke. When the fingertips rise, the hips are pulled down and the hands no longer exert force against the water (figure 13.1g, page 175). The exit is delayed by a longer stroke, which significantly reduces the momentum necessary for a quick and efficient transition to the arm recovery.

In front-end butterfly, the hands pull back only to the final point at which they maintain maximum force against the water rather than wasting time with an additional, ineffective "overpull" at the bottom. Also, because the front-end flyer uses an earlier inscull, he or she creates momentum for a quick, efficient exit leading to the arm-recovery phase.

Arm Recovery

The expedient exit of the hands (in addition to the timing of the second kick, to be discussed later) creates momentum for arms to swing outward above the surface of the water. The arms essentially maintain the extension achieved during the pull-through and exit phases. Here, relaxation of the arms is crucial. A tightening or bending of the arms slows the momentum of the outward swinging motion. It also hinders the forward extension of the arms and shoulders at the top end of the recovery before the landing (figure 13.1, h and i, page 175). The arms should be so relaxed that they feel like dead weight being thrown forward. In this way, the swimmer preserves the greatest amount of momentum in the arm recovery and reaches ideal extension in the front end of the stroke. For the front-end flyer, this relaxed speed of recovery and ideal forward extension, combined with only the most efficient amount of pull through and a quick exit, facilitates a quicker return to the power phase and a more constant, forward-moving action.

Head Motion—Breathing and Nonbreathing Cycles

The swimmer should maintain the essential head position—face down with relaxed neck—as much as possible during breathing and nonbreathing stroke cycles (see figure 13.1b, page 174). In the latter, the initial hand press raises the head slightly to the surface level, and this position is maintained during the arm pull. The head begins to drop downward as the hands exit the water, and it continues to do so during the arm recovery. During a breathing cycle, the head's motion is the same except that there is slightly more pressing to help raise the head high enough for the mouth to take in air. Note that here, as in the nonbreathing cycle, the raised head should remain as much as possible in the essential head position. The result is the leaning forward of the head at this breathing apex. In contrast, the traditional breathing motion involves a lifting up of the head; with a tense contraction of the neck muscles, the chin is pushed forward, resulting in further upward turning of the top of the head. In the leaning position, the head and neck, which remain relaxed, are aligned on an angle closer to the surface and the forward moving line of direction. The leaning motion creates

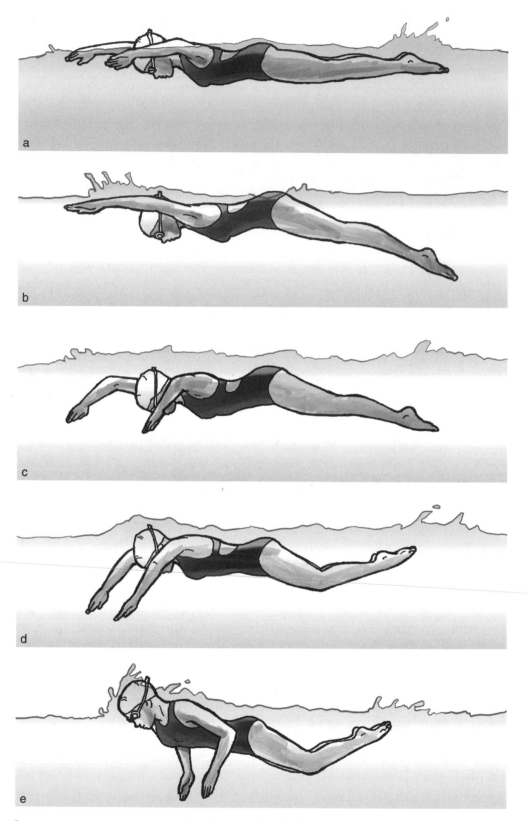

Figure 13.1, a-e Sequence of action for the butterfly.

Figure 13.1, f-i Sequence of action for the butterfly (continued).

significantly less up-and-down activity than the traditional breathing motion.

From a side-viewing perspective, the head-leaning breath is very noticeable in front-end flyers such as Pankratov, Klim, and Thompson. From a front-facing view, less of the face (especially the chin) and more of the top of the head are visible with this method than with traditional breathing. Watching Pankratov, for example, from behind, however, it is difficult to discern a head-leaning breathing stroke—with its more constant head and neck angle and limited up-and-down head movement—from a nonbreathing stroke as he swims away.

There is an additional benefit of the head lean. Because it is a less tense, more relaxed position, the arms and shoulders can achieve more of an unhindered reach at the end of the arm recovery, prior to the landing.

The Landing

Recall that as the arms swing around toward the front of the stroke, the head and neck are dropping toward the water. There should be a simultaneous landing of the arms and head in the water (on the nonbreathing cycle, there is a simultaneous arm-landing and lowering of the head as it returns to its original position). This way—to borrow a theory promoted by stroke analyst Bill Boomer—the head and arms, landing together, combine as an effective throw weight. This throw-weight effect is enhanced by the momentum of the arms swinging forward and the forward alignment of the leaning head position.

To conclude the cycle, the hands enter just inside the shoulder line with the arms extended but relaxed enough to allow for additional extension as the hips rise and the head presses forward against the water. At this point, the hands begin their press outward and downward, and the new arm-stroke cycle begins.

Undulations and the Arm Cycle

There should be two undulations, or kicks, per each arm-stroke cycle—one at the top end of the stroke (see figure 13.1a, page 174), or the landing of the head and arms, and another as the hands complete the pull-through phase (see figure 13.1e, page 174). There are successful butterflyers who have used a "single-beat" kick, but they are typically 200 butterfly specialists and even then it is more the exception than the rule. The motion of the arms in coordination with the steady, uninterrupted tempo of body undulations creates the essential butterfly rhythm.

Again, the kicks should be relatively tight and steady within the line of body undulation. An excessive reliance on the second kick as the hands complete the pull-through phase at the bottom is characteristic of a predominantly back-end butterflyer. This type of kick not only causes extra resistance but also takes longer to complete, and thus interrupts the rhythm of arm-stroke and undulation. This results in the previously mentioned delay or overpull of the hands at the bottom.

In front-end butterfly, the second kick is not excessive but, like the first, effective and efficient. It assists rather than undermines the crucial quick exit of the hands, transferring momentum into the arm-recovery phase and leading more expediently to the next power-generating arm stroke.

Front-End Butterfly— The Shifting Forward of Balance

To review, the following are elements of front-end butterfly: the early inscull at the beginning of the underwater pull phase; pulling back only to the final point that the hands can exert maximum force against the water (the absence of overpull); a swinging, relaxed arm recovery; a face-down head position with a relaxed neck; a leaning-head breathing position; the simultaneous landing of the arms and head; steady, effective, and powerful kicks (no overkicking); and a quicker, steadier stroke tempo overall.

The combined effect of these elements shifts forward the balance on the pivot point (the hips)—from the back half to the front half of the body—and essentially keeps it forward. Think of two children, one heavier than the other, playing on a teeter-totter; the front-end flyer appears to be constantly diving forward, or teetering, to the front side.

Jenny Thompson's development from national-level butterflyer to world champion and world-record holder is a product of the trend to front-end butterfly. As a talented, national-caliber butterflyer, Thompson demonstrated traditional technique, using elements of back-end butterfly such as a strong second-beat kick and an up-and-down breathing motion. Her elevation to one of the world's best coincided with front-end adjustments she made—the head-leaning breathing position; balanced, effective kicks; an efficient amount of pull-back prior to exit; and the simultaneous landing of her arms and head. Her overall hip position now remains high as she constantly teeters forward with a quick and steady tempo of arm strokes. Since her current form emphasizes the most efficient, forward-moving motions and minimizes, or eliminates, inefficient ones, there is little interruption of the forward motion; each one of her strokes builds on the momentum of the previous stroke.

Clearly, the trend toward front-end butterfly is not absolute. As with all stroke improvements, use of the front-end techniques depends upon a swimmer's particular strengths and abilities. Still, with a stroke generally considered grueling, a technique that emphasizes relaxation, balance, and rhythm to yield forward motion and to eliminate inefficient movements has a certain appeal. Also appealing is a technique-sensitive program of conditioning, which is by no means easy but takes into account various levels of butterfly training capacities. Perhaps butterfly, as my coach from years ago stated, will never be for the faint-hearted, but with continued improvements in training and technique, it may become easier to endure.

Summary

- Butterfly combines power and explosiveness with grace and fluidity.
- The butterfly foundation includes technique work, core strengthening, flexibility training, endurance training, high-quality repetitions, and sprints.
- Any butterfly conditioning program must be sensitive to the development and preservation of proper butterfly technique; train as much butterfly as good form allows.
- High-quality repetition training, with its longer rest intervals, is well suited for a technique-based system of butterfly training.
- The central movement in butterfly is the head to toe undulation of the body, or wave-like action.
- A balanced hip action is essential to an effective kick, the propulsive finish to the wave.
- The knees must stay on the body-wave line throughout the kick.
- The recent trend is front-end butterfly with two kicks per arm cycle.
- The recovery is done with relaxed arms; the landing of the arms and head must be simultaneous.
- The face-down head position is the essential head position.

CHAPTER FOURTEEN

Breaststroke Technique

David Salo

We have had our share of excellent breaststroke swimmers coming through the ranks of our club program, Irvine Novaquatics, including 100-meter American record-holder Amanda Beard and 1999 Pan-American Games gold medalist Staciana Stitts. Amanda was the silver medalist in the 100 and 200 breaststroke events at the 1996 Olympics and was the bronze medalist in the 200 breaststroke at the 2000 Games. Staciana also represented the United States at the 2000 Games in the breaststroke, earning a gold medal for her breaststroke leg in the prelims of the 400 medley relay. While I tend to view breaststroke in terms of the basic important characteristics of the ideal stroke, I also leave room for individual variation.

It is important to realize that the nature of the breaststroke is such that the many variations in stroke seen at every level of competition result from variations in human anatomy as much as differences in skill acquisition. Witness any competition and you will see very successful swimmers with tremendously different approaches to the stroke. Anatomical considerations influencing the stroke are ankle, knee, and hip flexibility, as well as shoulder flexibility; flexibility affects the range of motion of the limbs and thus influences heel recovery speed, acceleration of the arm-stroke insweep, and so forth. Of course, there are also differences in muscle-fiber content percentages—that is, some swimmers have a higher percentage of fast-twitch fibers versus slow-twitch fibers; the ratio affects the speed or turnover of their stroke. Some swimmers' strokes are characterized by a strong kick, while others have a kick-dominated stroke (not necessarily the same thing). These different types of stroke may produce equally successful results.

Throughout the 1990s the breaststroke became more popular, largely because of the tremendous success of 200-meter breaststroke world-record holder Mike Barrowman. Barrowman singlehandedly elevated the 200-meter breaststroke to a glamour event through his focus on the one event, his specific training for the stroke, his progressive improvements, and his competitive dominance. His "wave style" approach to the stroke was new, facilitated by rules changes over the past several decades that allowed the head to submerge with each stroke. His technique did much to influence the development of the mechanics of breaststroke as we know it today. While the strokes of a growing majority of today's breaststroke swimmers are characterized by a wave-like action, in which the body seemingly glides over the water surface and lunges into each stroke, our program's approach to breaststroke technique follows some basic tenets that may or may not be considered strictly "wave style."

One criterion that characterizes effective breaststroke is the speed of hand and heel action, because these actions result in forward propulsion. Having mastered the biomechanics of the pull and kick, a swimmer should focus attention on the speed and acceleration of hands and heels in order to develop a successful competitive breaststroke.

The Pull

One of the most important criteria to the overall success in breaststroke is the recovery of the pull into a full streamlined position. The streamlined position, no matter how brief, assures full extension and therefore maximum distance per stroke. One of the major problems for breaststroke swimmers in competition is that they shorten their stroke when they become fatigued—and they lose some turnover rate with full extension. Therefore, I stress to swimmers the need to extend *into* the outsweep of the stroke.

I consider the pull of the stroke to be triphasic, or composed of three phases: outsweep, insweep, and recovery. The outsweep is a "setup" for the more propulsive insweep phase; emphasizing a constant velocity through the outsweep leads to an accelerated insweep phase. If you consider the swimmer as moving through horizontal sheets of parallel planes of water, during the outsweep the arms would remain straight and confined to a plane near the surface of the water (within 6 to 10 inches). At the widest part of the stroke (generally 12 to 18 inches beyond the line of the shoulder, depending on individual strength) the insweep begins to take form (figure 14.1). It is characterized by increased velocity through the pull to the recovery phase.

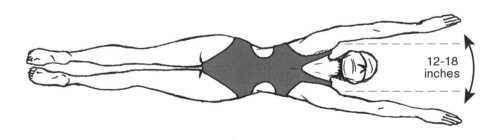

12-18 inches

Figure 14.1 The outsweep sets up the insweep.

Figure 14.2a The blade leads the insweep.

Figure 14.2b The insweep continues.

The insweep continues as the inside (thumbside) edge of the arms (I refer to this as the blade of the arms) begins to take the lead with the insweep. This edge extends from the fingertips to the elbow. Consider this edge as cutting through the series of parallel planes of water with the elbows maintaining their position closely within the original plane (figure 14.2, a and b). The blade therefore cuts through these planes much like a propeller cuts through water, creating resistance and propulsion on the inside of the arm. Through the completion of the insweep the swimmer's hands come toward each other, with the elbows trailing, and end close together. The position of the hands at this point should be above the level of the elbows as the swimmer begins the recovery phase. Throughout the insweep phase the shoulders and back lift while driving the hips forward toward the original position of the chest (figure 14.3). Coaches will want to stress this to prevent their swimmers from creating too much upward motion, thereby sacrificing forward movement. During this phase the elbows remain fairly close to their original planar position.

Figure 14.3 Completing the insweep and beginning the recovery.

As the insweep is completed the hands are close together (within inches) and the elbows are no farther apart than the width of the shoulders. Becoming as streamlined as possible, so as to reduce drag and accelerate into the completed recovery phase, is extremely important at this point. While many swimmers will place significant effort on lifting the hands out of the water at the finish of the insweep, I believe this can be counterproductive. I stress completing the insweep with the hands just at the surface, in front of the chin, and elevated above the level of the elbows. A straight elbow through fingertip position should be maintained, and the swimmer should then drive the blade (elbow to fingertips) straight forward at or near the surface (figure 14.4). As the arms recover, the head maintains a position in line with the back and settles between the arms, ending the stroke cycle in a streamlined position (figure 14.5).

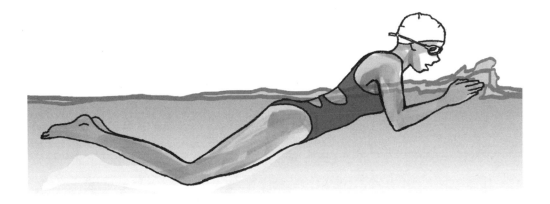

Figure 14.4 Driving the blade forward.

Figure 14.5 The recovery.

The Kick

The breaststroke kick may be divided into two phases: set-up and propulsive. In the set-up phase the heels are driven from the extended, streamlined position to a position at the hip. Then in the propulsive phase the heels accelerate in an elliptical pattern as the pressure of the water against the bottom of the feet is maintained (figure 14.6). The biggest mistake breaststroke swimmers make in kicking is the result of the manner in which they train. Most training places very little emphasis on the set-up phase of the kick, specifically the acceleration of the heels. The heels should be drawn up toward the hips with maximum speed; then the toes are turned outward and downward to initiate the propulsive phase. The heels should continue to be the leaders of the kick; with heels in position outside the knees, propulsion begins.

Figure 14.6 The propulsive phase of the kick.

The heels take an elliptical path as the legs are extended. Pressure is maintained on the bottoms of the feet. At full extension the heels come together, and the completion of the kick occurs as the toes are extended to maximize the streamlined position.

The question of how wide the kick should be, as with the arm pull, depends on the individual swimmer's characteristics of strength and flexibility in relation to the capacity of the pull. This will become obvious to the coach through observation and experimentation. Coaches and swimmers need to ascertain these characteristics in order to fine-tune the appropriate width of the kick and pull. Training considerations should employ various widths of outsweep to develop a greater range and to develop strength and power throughout the range. It is important that the kick not delay the swimmer's arm stroke. If the kick is too wide, the arms have to wait for the kick.

Stroke Timing

In my mind there are certain components of the breaststroke in which timing can be evaluated and corrected. With regard to the pull I look at the velocity of the outsweep and insweep; in particular I look to see that there is a relatively constant velocity through the outsweep with an increase in velocity through the insweep and into the recovery.

In developing proper timing in the arm and leg action of the breast-stroke, it is important to remember that each stroke begins and ends in a streamlined position. From this position, the arm stroke helps to define the timing pattern of all other actions of the hips and heels. While the body remains relatively flat during the initial phase of the outsweep, it is through the phase of the arm-stroke insweep that the swimmer needs to drive the shoulders up and toward the ears while driving the hips forward. The action of the hips will help to drive the heels toward the hips. At the completion of the insweep the focus should be on kicking the hips forward and driving the shoulders and arms forward—back to a streamlined position.

With regard to the kick and the initiation of the heel recovery, I suggest that the swimmer view the recovery part of the kick as beginning with the outsweep of the pull such that as the recovery phase of the pull begins, the propulsive phase of the kick occurs nearly simultaneously. There should be a sense that during the propulsive phase of the arm stroke, the recovery (and hence the drag phase) of the heels is occurring, and that during the recovery of the stroke, the propulsive phase of the kick occurs.

Component Training

I believe that the most effective means of training for the breaststroke is through *component training*. The major problem in training breaststroke occurs when the stroke is not maintained throughout a workout or set; mechanics such as proper timing, body position on the water, appropriate streamlining characteristics, and heel and hand or blade speed must not be allowed to suffer. Continuous long sets of breaststroke can do more damage than good by drilling improper mechanics.

Component training involves breaking down the stroke into its components and training each at high rates of velocity. Components are more specific than kick and pull; they include all elements of stroke mechanics: elbow position, straight arm recovery, heel speed, blade speed, flat back at extension, and so forth. For example, elbow position during the stroke is very important. To emphasize this in training we have developed a drill called the *scrunch scull*. In this drill, swimmers are poised in a vertical position with the head and shoulders out of the water. Knees are bent and held in front of the chest, with the heels positioned below the hips. The swimmer performs a breaststroke pull forward with the elbows held in a high position, without pulling the elbows back. The "blades" sweep across the knees, and forward extension is carried out with high velocity. This drill accomplishes significant aerobic objectives as well as specific training for the breaststroke pull. An example of a set that might also serve as an aerobic training set is 10 × 100 on a 15-second rest interval, 25 streamlined kick, 25 scrunch scull, 25 pull, 25 scrunch scull.

Breaststroke swimmers in our program probably do 70 precent to 80 percent of their training in breaststroke components, with only about 25 percent to 30 percent of that involving the whole stroke. This ensures that they maintain a very high level of velocity throughout their training.

Other suggested drills include various sculling drills in different body positions, breaststroke pull and free or fly kick, and piston kicking—in which the swimmer maintains a horizontal body position on the water creating propulsion by kicking, alternating legs in a piston-like motion.

Training Yardage

Throughout our season, very little changes in terms of overall training yardage requirements. From day one of any given season, most of our work is performed at race velocity with an average practice session consisting of less than 6,000 yards. Except for morning workouts from June to August, training is conducted in a short-course pool. I believe that it is advantageous to the breaststroke swimmer to train in short-course pools throughout the year as opposed to relying on long-course pool training. Short-course training allows swimmers to maintain the kind of stroke mechanics and speed that are lost with excessive long-course training; it is easier to maintain high-speed intensive training when the distance from wall to wall is relatively short. Long-course training, however, promotes timing of the stroke and develops pacing strategies. Prior to the 1996 United States Olympic Trials, Amanda Beard had only two workouts long course (for a total of two hours) while Steve West (Olympic trials third place in the 200 breaststroke; fourth in the 100 breaststroke) had a total of five long-course workouts. Both swimmers performed significant lifetime bests at the trials.

The taper phase, also known as the fine-tuning phase, of our season occurs over the final 10 days prior to the major competition. During this period the yardage drops almost immediately to 2,000 to 3,500 yards with more focus on long, stretched-out swimming interspersed with periods of fast, intense, short swims. I don't time pace 50s or other cruise intervals, as this is a period in which I want swimmers to feel their stroke in the water and to have confidence in their technique rather than focusing on their time. During this period we fine-tune the starts and turns, stroke timing, and so on. A great deal of time is spent during the last month and a half on relaxation and visual imagery training.

Who can predict the changes in breaststroke that will allow swimmers to swim faster in the future? Over the past 40 years there have been more rule changes affecting breaststroke than any other stroke. The current wave style of breaststroke will produce faster swimmers in the years to come, as more young age-group swimmers use the style over many years and gain experience in the stroke.

Summary

- A swimmer's individual anatomical considerations influence his or her breaststroking style.
- The speed of the hand or blade and heel action and the recovery to streamlined position are fundamental for success.
- Pulling includes three phases: the outsweep, the insweep, and the recovery phase.
- The outsweep—made with straight arms and near the surface—sets up the insweep, the more propulsive phase.

- Recovery should occur straight forward, not downward, to reduce drag.
- The kick should focus concentrated effort on heel speed, especially in the recovery phase.
- Velocity must be maintained through the outsweep and increased through the insweep into the recovery.
- The heels lead throughout the kick, maintaining pressure on the bottom of the foot.
- The propulsive phase of the kick occurs nearly simultaneously with the recovery to streamlined position.
- The most effective way to train for the breaststroke is through component training at high rates of speed.
- Swimmers should focus on the feel of breaststroke in the final taper preparation.

CHAPTER FIFTEEN

Starts, Turns, and Finishes

John Trembley and Gary Fielder

How many times have you heard, "He'll never make up the distance he lost at the start," or "She threw the race away in the turn," or "He lost it at the wall"? Too many times? While we all know how critical it is to practice the starts, turns, and finishes of each race, don't we often let the standards slip during training, while concentrating on other things? Whether it's a drill, swim workout, or even a kicking set, every push off, dive, turn, and finish presents another opportunity to perfect the techniques that win races.

Throughout this chapter we'll refer to turns as "changes of direction," as this is what the swimmer is trying to accomplish. This is not just a matter of semantics, but a difference in concept that suggests a different visual image. The implication of the word *turn* is a twisting movement at the wall that considerably slows the change of direction. A rapid change of direction at each wall is the swimmer's objective.

We speak of starts, changes of direction, and finishes as separate entities, just as we segregate each component of a stroke in order to perfect it. Each of these entities can be different depending on the stroke or event. What we must not forget is that each is a part of the whole of the event; there should be a seamless continuity to an entire performance. Let your movements be as fluid as the medium in which your chosen sport is played.

Freestyle Starts

Swimmers spend a lot of time practicing strokes so that technique becomes automatic. Starts are no different and should be practiced accordingly. Every time swimmers step on the block, they should immediately place their feet ready for the start; by making this a habit they can't be rushed into taking their position for a start. When swimmers assume the mark position, their hearing and reflexes should focus on the start signal. For that short space of time, noting else exists but that signal. Adhering to this routine will make every start the same and will minimize the chance of a false start while maximizing the reflex response for a quick start. Simple, but it works.

The good start is a combination of balance and power. By holding under the block and pushing up with the legs, a swimmer increases the tension on the required muscles (the stretch-reflex action). This increase in muscle tension, just prior to the signal, yields an increase in explosive power. As the signal goes and the swimmer pulls down under the block, the center of gravity moves forward, past the point of balance. At this point the swimmer drives with the legs and throws the arms and

─ TABLE 15.1 ───────────

Common Start Errors

Error	Negative result
Thumbs resting on top of block	Too much time is required to move thumbs forward
Elbows bent too much	Center of gravity becomes lower, reducing the potential for height and distance as one leaves the block
Squatting too much	Ineffective hip and leg extension position resulting in a slower start
Leaning back too far	Body mass centered away from the water yields a slower start
Head moves too much	Unless the head motion contributes to the body driving off the block, it should not move
Pike entry	Increased drag

head forward to assist in overcoming inertia. He or she drops the head between the arms and hyperextends the body for a clean entry flowing immediately into a fast, narrow butterfly kick. The best starters are fast off the blocks; they get great distance through the air with a clean entry and a strong kick. These techniques are not hard to develop; some solid practice will result in much-improved starts.

Since you hold at least 200 and as many as 600 practices a season, it is imperative that you begin each practice with a maximum-effort start. The plyometric and strengthening benefit will give your swimmers a better start in races. Also, by beginning with some seriousness, you set a positive tone for the remainder of practice. Here are some techniques to work on during practice.

Block Starting Techniques

- **Dry block with towel.** Have swimmers get into the habit of making sure the block is dry before the start. Going over the block with a towel also ensures that a towel is available in the event of a false start or overheating.
- **Ready throw.** Have swimmers work on making sure that their hands move fast and that their elbows are straight.
- **Ready throw jump.** Swimmers should work on throwing their arms and extending their legs at takeoff. Swimmers who jump well do so

by extending beyond the balls of the feet up through the big toe. This puts tremendous pressure on the soleus muscles in the lower legs. To feel this pull in the soleus for yourself, rock forward and upward from the ball of the foot onto the big toe. Train your swimmers to jump through the ball of the foot and to use the big toe.

- **Track start.** This technique, in which one foot is more forward on the block than the other, requires tremendous explosion of the arms and the back foot (figure 15.1, a and b). Swimmers should hyperextend on entry to the water and begin kicking immediately.
- **Grab start.** In the grab start, swimmers work on leaning their body mass forward and jumping through their big toe (figure 15.1c).

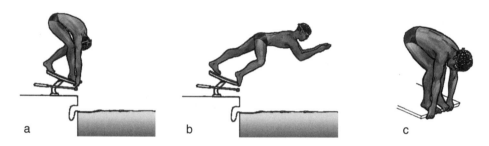

Figure 15.1, a-c The track start (a and b) and the grab start (c).

Freestyle Change of Direction

The objective here is to achieve a smooth, fast change of direction with minimal time spent in contact with the wall. As swimmers approach the wall, they should use the painted T as a visual cue to start preparing for the change of direction. They should not breathe from this point in, as that would require them to take their eyes off the wall. It will take each swimmer some practice to establish the exact point at which to begin the final pull stroke. It should be at the same place each time, as it initiates the change of direction sequence.

The second to last stroke finishes with one hand at the side, palm down, and the other arm at full extension (figure 15.2a). The leading hand pulls through on the final stroke, and as the hand passes under, the body rotates in the vertical plane (figure 15.2b). As the body begins to rotate, the arms remain extended behind the swimmer and rotate medially until the palms face down (figure 15.2c); then they make a short, sharp pull from the elbows to assist body rotation.

Throughout the body rotation, the feet are carried over the surface of the water (the water line should be at a midpoint between ankle and knee) with the legs bent and slightly apart to allow water to pass between them. A tight tuck will keep the heels close to the surface and will produce a faster rotation. The swimmer should begin to open out and punch the feet toward the wall just prior to contact; this activates the hip extensors and quadriceps and results in a shorter contact time, keeping the swimmer from "sitting" on the wall. The feet should contact the wall at approximately a 45-degree angle (figure 15.2d). Having remained behind the swimmer, the arms are fully extended into the streamlined position for the explosive drive off the wall, which is accompanied by an immediate fast, narrow butterfly kick (figure 15.2e).

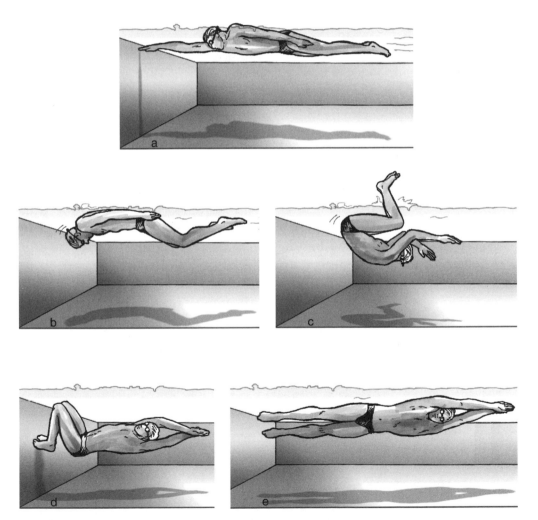

Figure 15.2, a-e Sequence of action for the freestyle change of direction.

Most swimmers whose feet exit too high above the water are keeping the legs too straight. As a baby dolphin kick occurs, the knees must flex immediately to help exit the feet. When the heels clear the surface of the water, the legs must be bent.

Freestyle Change of Direction Drills

These are learning drills to be managed distinct from swimming sets, and therefore should not be incorporated into other swimming sets. Take time, in the early phases of the season and periodically throughout the season, to slow the practice down and do these drills as separate entities.

Arms at sides. This drill works on the approach to the wall by having swimmers practice change of direction movements. Do this drill the first few times five or six feet away from the wall such that no contact is actually made with the wall; swimmers will turn when they reach an imaginary wall. Then, as swimmers progress, they can do the drill close enough to the wall so that they are able to press off the wall on the back.

Swimmers keep the head still and the arms stationary throughout the drill. There must be no twisting from the stomach directly to the back. This drill helps swimmers establish proper chin-tuck timing. Most freestylers mistime when to tuck the chin during the change of direction. Swimmers must tuck the chin to initiate the change of direction at the moment of highest velocity in the pull cycle when they are swimming. That moment during normal swimming is when the lead hand is immediately under the hip. At that point, the chin should be tucked forcefully into the chest. To have this occur at the correct distance from the wall, swimmers should use visual cues from the wall and the end of the center line (the T) and practice commencing the turn from the same place each time. By keeping the arm at the side and under the hip throughout this drill, swimmers can cue themselves to begin the chin tuck.

Often swimmers, parents, or coaches see stroke flaws as problems. They are really opportunities because when the necessary corrections are made the problem turns into a great opportunity to swim faster.

One arm in front, heel slide. This drill is similar to the one before it, but it adds another component in which the swimmers kick toward the imaginary wall from a prone position with one arm in front of the head. Again, as

TABLE 15.2

Common Freestyle Change of Direction Errors

Error	Negative result
Legs split too wide apart	Hips are too close to the wall when feet hit the wall
Legs held together as they recover over the surface of the water	The body sinks as it carries water as legs clear the surface
Change of direction too far from wall	Weak press off the wall
Change of direction too close to wall	Swimming farther than necessary (slower time)
Arching back as feet recover over the surface	It takes the body, from the hips upward, out of hyper-extended position; slows the change of direction
Twisting to the side	Slows the change of direction (one can twist as one leaves the wall)
Passing the wall	Feet are placed deeper underwater than necessary. This brings the hips closer to the wall and forces the swimmer to push off upward and leave the wall too shallow
Hand out of water during change of direction	The out-of-water hand cannot be used to down scull. Down sculling applies leverage and helps the legs get over the surface quicker
Feet clearing the surface too high	Upper body sinks
Breathing into and out of change direction	Slows the body velocity; going into the change of direction, the swimmer takes eyes off the wall

the swimmers progress, they can actually move closer to the wall to kick one arm out, pull the arm to the side, initiate the change of direction, and press off the wall in the streamlined position. This drill works on the recovery of the legs over the surface of the water with the knees bent. Swimmers should work on punching the feet toward the wall such that they are placed shallowly under the surface.

Tennessee drill #1. Swimmers drill proper change of direction mechanics without twisting off the wall. A fast, narrow kick starts immediately as the feet leave the wall.

Tennessee drill #2. Swimmers push off the wall straight on the back with balance as they twist to the side.

Standing flip. Swimmers practice flips starting from a standing position in the shallow end away from a wall. This drill will help swimmers focus on their flip speed and coordination. It's also fun!

Flag in and out. In this drill, swimmers charge hard and fast from the flags into the wall, execute proper turn mechanics, and push off to the flags. This drill emphasizes speed training and can be competitive and fun.

Fin change of direction. Swimmers practice turns with fins on. The fins help emphasize immediately tucking the knees as feet exit the water.

Whole freestyle change of direction. This drill puts all elements of the change of direction drills together into a complete, efficient flip turn.

Freestyle Finish

The swimmer should attempt to finish at full recovery as the arm reaches full extension. The arm is extended from the shoulder as the swimmer completes the final stroke, finishing on the side with the head down, driving for the wall and kicking hard (figure 15.3).

All freestyle finishes at practice should be executed with the swimmer on his or her side, with the fingertips at the same depth as the shoulder. The swimmer should ensure a strong kick into the wall and not lift the head until the touch. When training, it can be more enjoyable and stimulating for swimmers to execute perfect finishes or perfect changes of direction while competing against a rival. If, on each finish or change of direction in training, the swimmer imagines a rival swimming next to

Figure 15.3 The freestyle finish.

TABLE 15.3

Common Freestyle Finishing Errors

Error	Negative result
Crossing center line of body	Increased distance to the wall. The fastest way to the wall is to extend the arm along the axis of the shoulder. The shortest distance between two points is a straight line.
Finish on stomach	Potential reach is shortened and drag force higher on the stomach as opposed to the side.
Weak finishing pull	Loss of power and velocity
Slowing kick before fingers contact the wall	Loss of velocity
Lifting head before fingers contact the wall	Increased drag and loss of velocity

him or her and always beats that rival, the swimmer will be ready to beat that rival in competition.

Butterfly Starts

Essentially, the butterfly start is the same as for freestyle, except that only a butterfly kick is used. It is important not to return to the surface on too steep an angle, as this will slow forward speed (figure 15.4). The swimmer should return at a shallow angle, commencing the arm stroke just below the surface and breaking the surface on the second down-beat of the kick, thus breaking the surface tension at the point of peak power and taking the first stroke without breaking the rhythm of the kick. Swimmers should not attempt to start the stroke too far below the surface or they will find themselves trying to recover the arms while still underwater.

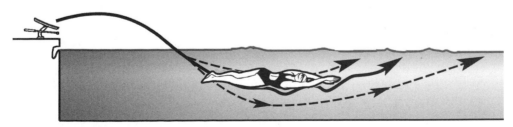

Figure 15.4 The butterfly start.

Butterfly Change of Direction

The goal is to reach the wall with the arms on a full recovery as they reach full extension. As the hands contact the wall, the change of direction is initiated by slightly flexing the elbows and beginning to rotate the body approximately 45 degrees while recovering the legs close to the body to place the feet on the wall at approximately a 45-degree angle (figure 15.5a). During this recovery of the legs, the elbow toward which the body is rotating is drawn backward close to the torso, and the hand drops toward the bottom of the pool with the little finger leading (figure 15.5b). The hand is rotated so that the palm faces upward as the hand continues through an arc to finish pointing back along the lane. The pull of this short arc coincides with the head being thrown back from the wall as the swimmer inhales and assists the change of direction (figure 15.5c). The other arm leaves the wall and is recovered behind the ear to join the lower hand and complete the streamlined position (figure 15.5d). The swimmer leaves the wall on the side with a strong push and immediately begins a fast, narrow kick, rolling back into the flat position and returning to the surface.

I advise swimmers to get in the habit of gauging how many strokes it will take to get to the wall during change of direction practice. Only through practice can they develop the judgment to anticipate whether they will need to lengthen or shorten the last two strokes in order to touch on a full recovery.

Tips for Butterfly Change of Direction

- Swimmers should flex the elbows minimally.
- Swimmers should snap the head back, away from the direction in which they are swimming.
- Before the hands contact the wall, swimmers should begin to flex the knees under the body.
- The first hand to leave the wall should extend toward the bottom and then scull water upward to assist in the body rotation.
- Swimmers should "answer the telephone" with the last hand to leave the wall, bringing the hand as close to the ear as possible. This initiates the hyperextension off the wall.

Swimmers must drill the whole stroke butterfly change of direction. They should start by keeping their heads as far away from the wall as possible by flexing the elbows only minimally. Have them execute a minimum of four or five dolphin kicks off every change of direction in

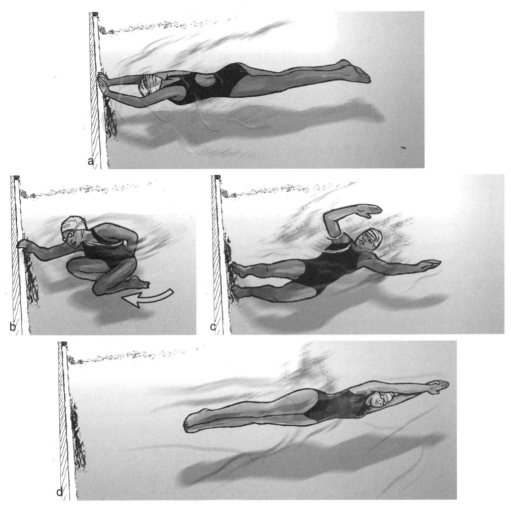

Figure 15.5, a-d Sequence of action for the butterfly change of direction.

TABLE 15.4

Common Butterfly Change of Direction Errors

Error	Negative result
Bringing head too close to the wall by bending the elbows	Too much distance is swum
Pulling the body up/out of the water	Loss of time at the wall
Weak or minimal dolphin kicks off the wall	Loss of velocity
Breathing before the first stroke after surfacing	Loss of velocity

competition and in practices. When butterflyers contact the wall the heels can immediately be seen kicking up, either out of the water or "boiling" the water at the surface (in response to the heels being driven upward). Obviously the feet are going in the wrong direction. They need to travel under the body toward the wall. Swimmers must practice flexing the knees under the body as the hands enter the water prior to contact with the wall. This is especially difficult to master as it is contrary to everything butterflyers have been taught with regard to kick timing during the stroke.

Butterfly Finishes

As with the change of direction, the objective of a butterfly finish is to touch both hands to the wall with the arms at full recovery. The same practice swimmers use in the change of direction for gauging the distance to the wall and deciding whether to shorten or lengthen the last two strokes will be useful here. If a swimmer misjudges the distance and finds that he or she needs to take a half stroke to reach the wall—he or she should not attempt to do so. Trying to take a half stroke usually ends with the swimmer touching the wall with either very bent arms, or in the worst possible case, the face. It is better practice to remain hyperextended and kick, not glide, to the wall.

Backstroke Starts

It is critical with the backstroke start for the swimmers to lift clear of the water. If not, they will give their competitors at least a half-body length advantage, often more.

The hands are placed wide apart of the start handles with the thumbs over the top of the bar to allow a quick release. The feet are placed as high as possible on the wall while remaining below the water line, slightly apart to assist with a straight pushback. To "take your mark," the body is drawn up keeping the elbows out, not down, while the head is placed forward (figure 15.6a).

At the start signal, the arms push back and are recovered out and around to the streamlined position. Recovery should be neither flat, nor directly over the top of the head, but partway between (figure 15.6b). The hips are driven up out of the water, and the head is quickly driven backward until the back is arched and the feet are lifted or flicked clear of the water. The fingertips should enter the water before the hips. The swimmer should maintain the hyperextended position and immediately

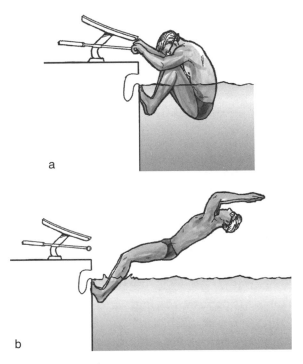

Figure 15.6, a-d   Sequence of action for the backstroke start.

begin strong, fast, dolphin kicks (figure 15.6c), holding a shallow angle to return to the surface. The first stroke is taken so that the swimmer breaks the surface during the final phase of the stroke, achieving peak power to assist in breaking surface tension (figure 15.6d). Remember that starts should be practiced separately before the beginning of backstroke sets so that emphasis can be placed purely on the starting technique.

Backstroke Change of Direction

The change of direction itself is essentially the same as the freestyle change of direction. Naturally enough, the biggest difference lies in rotating from the supine (back) to the prone (front) position at the correct point to initiate the change of direction. The other notable difference is remaining on the back when pushing off from the wall.

The easiest and probably the most standard method of determining when to start the change of direction is to count the number of strokes it takes to reach the wall from the flags and subtract one. Call this the rotator stroke. As the hand exits the water on the rotator stroke, the swimmer completes the stroke by continuing the arm over the opposite shoulder (figure 15.7, a and b), thereby assisting the lateral rotation from back to front and finishing at full extension. It is important that the other arm, extended at the start of the rotator stroke, complete the underwater pull to finish at the side, palm down, in preparation for the vertical rotation at the wall (figure 15.7c). By commencing lateral rotation at the correct point, the swimmer should now be in the right place to initiate a freestyle change of direction (see page /bb/). On pushing off from the wall the swimmer remains on the back, coming immediately into a fast, strong butterfly kick to return to the surface, the same as during the backstroke start.

TABLE 15.5

Common Backstroke Change of Direction Errors

Error	Negative result
Looking over the shoulder for the wall	Unnecessary; slows swimmer down
Change of direction too close to the wall	Swimming farther than necessary; adds time
Flutter kicking off the wall	Slower for 93% of swimmers in the country to flutter kick instead of dolphin kick off the wall
Leave the wall too shallow	Surface tension increases drag. Swimmer must be deep off the wall to dolphin kick effectively.

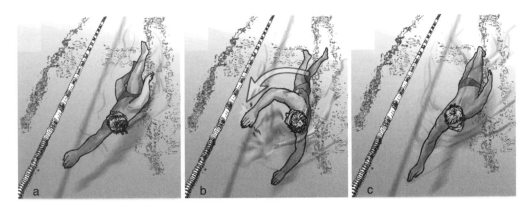

Figure 15.7, a-c Initiating the backstroke change of direction.

Backstroke Change of Direction Drills

Against the imaginary wall. The swimmer focuses on the actual change of direction itself without concentrating on the wall.

With dolphin kicks. During this turn, the swimmer works on hitting the feet high on the wall and drills fast, narrow dolphin kicks off the wall.

Backstroke Finish

The correct technique for the backstroke finish requires the swimmer to count the strokes from the flags to gauge his or her position relative to the wall, just as in the change of direction. This time however, the swimmer will use the full number of strokes. On completion of the last stroke, the swimmer extends the shoulder to achieve maximum reach and drives the head back, finishing partially on the side, kicking hard (figure 15.8). A dolphin kick may be included in this final lunge to the wall.

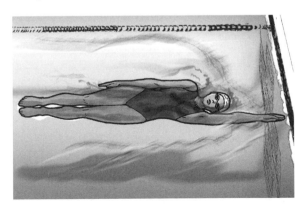

Figure 15.8 The backstroke finish position.

Breaststroke Starts

The start dive will be the same as for freestyle and butterfly. However, unlike the other strokes, there is no kicking on entry to the water. Instead, swimmers maintain the hyperextended streamlined position until they feel the decline in speed (figure 15.9a), at which point they execute a single butterfly pull with the hands finishing by the sides, then hold this position again until they feel the decline in speed (figure 15.9, b and c). As they feel this decline, the hands are recovered underneath the body, close to the torso and continue through the full extension (figure 15.9, d and e). Swimmers must be careful not to come to a complete stop prior to the kick. The kick must carry swimmers toward the surface. Just below the surface, swimmers execute the first arm pull, ensuring that the head breaks the surface before reaching the widest part of the stroke. This entire procedure is referred to as the breaststroke pullout and is used on every start and at every change of direction in breaststroke events.

Breaststroke Change of Direction

From the touch at the wall on a full recovery to the drive off the wall, the change of direction is the same for breaststroke as it is for butterfly, After the drive, however, instead of a butterfly kick the swimmer executes a breaststroke pullout. Refer to butterfly change of direction, including "tips," for more information that is also relevant for breaststroke.

Breaststroke Finish

As with butterfly, the objective is to finish on a full recovery as the arms reach full extension. Remember, if in doubt as to whether to take another stroke or not, swimmers should always kick and streamline for the wall. They should never take an extra or partial stroke on the finish.

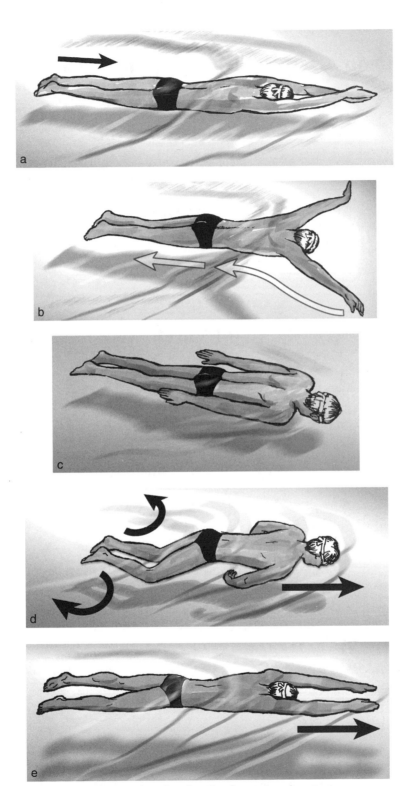

Figure 15.9, a-e Sequence of action for the breaststroke start.

TABLE 15.6

Common Breaststroke Change of Direction Errors

Error	Negative result
Looking over the shoulder for the wall	Unnecessary; slows swimmer down
Head too close to wall	Swimming farther than is necessary
Heels flying up	Heels extending out of the water after the hands have contacted the wall indicate the feet are not going in the proper direction. As with butterfly, the feet need to be going toward the wall when the hands contact the wall
Climbing out of the pool	Spending too much time pulling up out of the pool

Summary

- Practice starts, turns, and finishes during practice to perfect them for races.
- Every practice start should be at maximum effort.
- Swimmers should learn to jump through the balls of the feet and use their big toes.
- Swimmers must change direction in turning with minimal time at the wall.
- The feet are carried over the water and contact the wall at a 45-degree angle on freestyle and backstroke turns.
- Swimmers should streamline off the wall.
- The chin tuck must be a forceful movement into the chest on the freestyle and backstroke turns.
- Swimmers should finish on a full recovery and full extension.
- The change of direction in butterfly and breaststroke is initiated by slightly flexing the elbows.
- Swimmers should lift clear of the water in the backstroke start.
- Subtract one from the number of strokes it takes to reach the wall from the backstroke flags. This final stroke is the rotator stroke into the turn in backstroke.
- The body must not come to a complete stop prior to the kick in the breaststroke start.
- Swimmers should never take an extra or partial stroke on the finish in breaststroke or butterfly.

PART V

Training for Optimal Performance

CHAPTER SIXTEEN

Freestyle Sprint Training

Michael Bottom

If you study any great artist you will understand that he or she did not rise above his or her contemporaries without help. Each had mentors, went to school, or studied the masters. The basic elements of their artistry—how to mix colors, their brush strokes, and even the way they interpreted their artistic vision—were influenced by those greater than themselves.

It has been my goal for over 20 years to learn from the masters of our sport and to give to my athletes that which I did not have: a coach dedicated to sprint swimming. I am dedicated to this end and have studied and applied to the training of sprinters the coaching expertise of many mentors including George Haines, Mike Troy, David Salo, Doc Counsilman, David Marsh, Mark Schubert, Jim Steen, Nort Thornton, and others. I have learned much from their teachings, mistakes, and successes. While I can't possibly pass on to you all that I have learned from these outstanding coaches in one brief chapter, I can give you a basic color scheme for sprint training and my personal guidance on how to apply the colors.

Using the modified United States Swimming training categories (see table 16.1) and a basic understanding of physiology, you can choose the training session or phase that best suits the needs of the athletes in your swim program. Ernest W. Maglischo's *Swimming Even Faster* (2001) is my textbook, and references to the training topics I discuss in this chapter can be found in more detail in the 755 pages of that book.

TABLE 16.1

Training Phase Color Palette

Color	Description	Example set	Pulse rate	Work: rest ratio
Platinum	Speed	25s with band	N/A	> 1:2 to 1:8
Gold	Speed/power	25s against band	N/A	> 1:8
Green	Lactate production	4 × (50 + easy 25) on 2:00	Max	1:2 to 1:8
Purple	Lactate tolerance	4 dive 100s	Max	1:2 to 1:8
Blue	$\dot{V}O_2max$	20 × 200 w/ :20 rest	160 to 180	:20 sec rest; 1:1
Red	Threshold	3 × 400 w/ :20 rest	140 to 170	:10 to :40 rest
Pink	Aerobic	1,000 pull	120 to 150	:10 to :30 rest
White	Minimum aerobic	3 × 400 swim, kick, pull (warm-up)	> 120	:10 to :30 rest

Base Training for Sprinters

The training colors of white (minimal aerobic work), pink (aerobic training), and red ($\dot{V}O_2$max workouts) can be seen throughout a well-balanced training plan. However, the foundation of all swim training must be technique. Nort Thornton, head swim coach at the University of California at Berkeley, is a master of stroke technique. He has taught me that technique is the base or foundation that all fast swimming is built on. The most destructive thing, in my opinion, to fast swimming is the notion that we must build an aerobic base as the foundation to swimming. Miles and miles of indiscriminate swimming develops swimmers with survival stroke technique and shoulders that are often on the verge of requiring surgery. The swimmers that do not quit mileage-based programs are either genetically adapted for this type of training, independent (viewed by coaches as rebellious) enough to protect themselves, or destined to be limited in the long run by poor technique. Thus, aerobic swimming must be accompanied by technique instruction and must be monitored diligently. Ninety-nine percent of the endurance work that my sprinters do in the water has a technique focus. The coach who is truly an artist will apply the aerobic colors of red, pink, and white using drills, games, toys, and dryland exercises.

Aerobic fitness is developed over a longer period of time than other types of fitness, but this area of training is the most accepting. Nonspecific overall aerobic development can have more benefits to a sprint swimmer than miles of freestyle swimming. To build aerobic fitness, we do a circuit every Tuesday afternoon that lasts from 40 to 60 minutes. In one circuit Bart Kizierowski, 1999 NCAA champion in the 100-meter freestyle, does the following:

- Runs a quarter mile in under 1 minute
- Does 10 pull-ups
- Runs six times up and down a basketball court dunking the basketball at each end
- Does 24 plyometric jumps on a three-foot platform
- Runs and dives into a 25-meter underwater sprint kick
- Does 275 meters of backstroke pulling on the lane line
- Grabs a kickboard and does a 31-second 50-meter kick
- Swims 250 meters

Then he is back to the run to begin another round. During the 45 minutes it takes to do four rounds of the circuit, Bart's pulse falls between

150 and 185 beats per minute. Bart does this circuit continuously in his swimsuit. He slips his aqua jogging shoes on and off in seconds for the jumping and running work.

Great sprinters such as Olympic medalist Gary Hall Jr. and world-record holder Anthony Ervin dig their heels in at a straight freestyle swim that is over 400 meters. The first time I saw Gary at practice in 1995, I had been called in to help salvage his season, as he was no longer getting along with his current coach. After hearing how Gary would not do a hard stroke for a whole practice, his coached laughed and said I had to see something. He took me over to the pool where Gary was in the middle of a set of 300s. Of course, Gary was not making the interval and so he was swimming straight through the rest periods. His coach laughed and asked if I had seen Gary do one flip turn in the 20 minutes that we had been standing there watching. I said I hadn't, and he replied, "See!" For the first time, I did see. At the next break I walked over to Gary and complimented him on his brilliance. He didn't believe that I was serious, so I sat down on the pool deck and explained that I understood his logic. I told him I understood that by doing open turns when he was swimming in a crowed lane at slow speeds he was not developing habits and nerve pathways that would be hard to change when he was ready to swim and turn fast. "Brilliant!" I repeated and then went back to observing.

Gary began to trust me as the season progressed. At one point I asked him if he felt we were doing enough aerobic yardage. He laughed and said, "We start with one and a half hours of weights, then do 30 minutes of stretching and core body work, then we get in and swim about 30 to 40 minutes of technique work, and finish up with about 15 minutes of speed work. By the end of warm-down my heart rate has been over 120 for about 3 hours. That is just the morning workout! Yes, I think we are doing enough aerobic yardage." Gary ended that 1995 season with five Pan-Pacific gold medals.

Some of the greatest teachers I have had have been the athletes themselves. In the three seasons that I worked with four-time Olympic gold medalist Jon Olsen, he changed his stroke technique each season. I gave him the tools to work with, and he creatively learned to swim faster. Through our discussions and much experimentation on his part, he found a better way each season. This brings home the point that technique is the base that fast swimming is built on. The endurance colors of white, pink, and red should be applied with technique.

The color blue that represents the training category above a person's $\dot{V}O_2$max threshold is, in my opinion, nonproductive to sprinters. Long-duration, short-rest, high-intensity sets quickly deplete the stored gly-cogen in the muscles. Once ATP (adenosine triphosphate) and CP (cre-atine phosphate)—two high-energy compounds that fuel the muscles—are used up within the first 15 seconds of anaerobic exercise, glycogen stored in the muscles is the only energy source available to sustain fast swimming. When muscle glycogen stores are low, aerobic metabolism must be used to a greater extent. Aerobic metabolism is a much slower process and cannot produce the energy to continue fast swimming. In addition, training in the blue zone also slows the anaerobic reaction that breaks down glycogen into lactic acid. This is counterproductive to a sprinter's need to produce as much energy as quickly as possible.

Anaerobic Training for Sprinters

After graduation from USC, I took an exercise physiology class at UC Berkeley. The professor, Dr. George Brooks, was a world expert on anaero-bic metabolism and the removal of lactic acid from muscles. The class defined and confirmed a truth that had been revealed to me two years earlier, "If you want to swim fast, you have to train fast!" The academic term for this simple truth is "the principle of specificity."

Lactate-Tolerance Sets—Purple

The pain in sprinting comes when the athlete generates energy so fast that the by-product of that energy production, lactic acid, cannot be removed from the muscle cells fast enough. The muscle pH drops from neutral (7.0) to a state of acidosis (6.5 to 6.8), and the muscle fibers go on strike (stop contracting). This "piano-on-the-back" syndrome can be best observed in my favorite race, the 100 butterfly. If you are at all a fan of WWF wrestling, you will enjoy watching butterflyers go from the fluid horizontal position to the vertical "Oh, no" position. The life-and-death struggle begins for some about 10 yards out from the end of the race.

In my opinion, contrary to US Swimming's national "speed though endurance" campaign, the piano-on-the-back syndrome can be best re-duced by a steady diet of purple pain, or lactate-tolerance, sets followed by white and pink levels of aerobic swimming. Purple training increases the muscle cells' ability to buffer lactic acid and at the same time in-creases the muscles' ability to flush lactic acid out of the cells. In addi-tion, acidosis is fiber specific, which means that an athlete can have an innervated muscle fiber bundle going into acidosis while two doors down there is a fiber bundle kicking back watching reruns of the 1996 100 fly

213

at the US trials and cheering on Byron Davis. During purple sets an athlete learns the valuable lesson of adaptation. Slight stroke changes at the proper time can delay total paralysis by recruiting lazy neighboring fiber bundles to help out. Finally, to some extent, the pain of acidosis can be pushed back. During purple sets an athlete will learn that purple pain can be conquered.

Purple, or lactate-tolerance, sets are the most taxing on the athlete. I do not recommend more than three purple sets per week, and I recommend a full day of recovery following each set. My favorite purple set is 4 × (dive 25 meters underwater, 75 meters blast, 300 meters easy backstroke). The goal of the set is that the athlete be unable to move his or her arms as he or she passes under the final backstroke flags and must find a way to get to the wall. *The artistry is getting your athletes to give an all-out effort to experience and deal with acidosis.*

Lactate-Production Sets—Green

Lactate-production, or green, sets are the mainstay for the 50 swimmer. These sets are designed to keep the athlete from going into acidosis. The duration of each swim and the amount of rest between swims must keep the swimmer from experiencing extreme muscle tie-up. There is nothing more fun for a sprinter than to have the experience of swimming fast without the severe pain of acidosis. At the beginning of the season when we are doing our technique base, I use green sets to teach the freshmen how to swim fast without fear.

When I took over the sprint program at Cal Berkeley, the stroke of one of the sophomores on the team caught my eye during the first practice. He was able to enter his hand into the water and instantly hold water. I drooled on myself when I watched him swim. The season progressed, and this swimmer (call him Lance) showed great comeback speed. He was always catching the field in the last 10 yards of the 100. It turned out that this comeback speed, however, never quite overcame the ability of many of his competitors to hang on and finish the race ahead of him. When Lance swam the 50, he was able to get up and go! Yet his first 50 in his 100 lacked aggressiveness. Over and over I talked to him about getting on the first 50 both in practice and at the meets, and over and over in purple sets and at meets he came home strong. There is nothing wrong with coming home strong, but if a sprinter does not go out to make his or her mark in the first 50 of the 100, then coming home strong helps as much as slapping SPF 30 on the blistered skin of a sunburn. Fear of the pain and embarrassment of dying in a race can cripple a sprinter. There is nothing that teaches sprinters to hold back more than breaking them in on purple sets. Let your sprinters learn to enjoy swimming fast with minimal pain. Start them out with green sets before you put them into purple pain.

One of my favorite green sets is 3 × ([3 x (75 + 25)] + 300 easy), descending the 75s so that swimmers work on perfect stroke for the first two and give the last one 100 percent. The 25s are done on the back pulling on the lane line. The 300 after the finish of the third 75 + 25 is directed drilling. The first round is done with no equipment, the second round with fins, and the final round with fins and paddles. Julio Santos, the Ecuadorian national champion in the 50 freestyle, once went under 28 seconds for his final 75 with fins and paddles on. There is no drug available to a true sprinter that will get him or her higher than swimming fast. Julio was a new man after that experience.

Yes, there are physiological benefits to green sets besides the endorphins released. When training this system there is an increase in the amount of key enzymes stored in the muscle cell. These enzymes allow the anaerobic breakdown of glycogen (glycolysis) to occur at an accelerated rate; this, in turn, releases more energy for fast swimming.

Power-Production Sets—Gold

It is one thing to have the strength to be able to lift mass in the weight room. It is another thing to use that strength to swim fast. Gold, or power-production, sets buy you a ticket to transport strength from the weight room to the pool. The idea behind gold sets is to translate the very non-specific action of pushing a weight or other form of resistance up and down to a very specific swimming stroke. This must be done without ruining stroke technique. Any device that increases resistance or overloads the arms and legs can be used in improving power in the water. In my opinion, all gold sets should be done with swimming toys and machines to help increase resistance. Here is a golden list of things to play with in the water:

- Bands (surgical tubing)
- T-shirts, assorted clothing, and drag suits
- An assortment of hand paddles
- An assortment of fins
- The power rack
- The power reel
- Buckets
- Parachutes

- Pull bags
- Lane line segments
- Medicine balls
- Rowboats
- Weights
- Innertubes

Your list can be as long as you are creative. Have fun!

My two favorite pieces of equipment to use in assisting this process are the power rack and the power reel, both developed by a company called Total Performance. The athlete swims against a measured resistance for a measured distance. The progress of the athlete can be measured in time units, and the improvement in power can be charted.

From 1999 to 2000 Gary Hall Jr. dramatically increased his muscle mass. During this time, he almost doubled the weight he was able to lift on the lat pulldown machine. His body weight went from about 180 to 219 pounds during this same year. I was concerned that this increase in body mass would translate into increased resistance in the water and that he might not have a sufficient increase in his ability to generate power to compensate for the additional body resistance. My fears subsided when, while swimming with fins and paddles against the maximum weight of the power rack, he not only beat all the other Olympic sprinters in the water by over a second but almost pulled the machine in as well.

Speed-Production Sets—Platinum

I've added this color to the palette of US Swimming. Platinum (speed-production) work differs from gold sets in that it allows the athletes to feel their bodies, stroke technique, and stroke rate as they move through the water at speeds that match their race velocity. Gold (power-production) work tends to load the athlete and slow both stroke rate and velocity. The secret to platinum training's speed production is keeping the set short and using some type of accelerator to get athletes moving at their end-of-the-year racing speeds. The best device to help do this is the power reel made by Total Performance; unfortunately this device is very costly and is not readily available to most programs. Almost as good are the stretch bands made by several companies and fashioned by innovative coaches out of surgical tubing. However, the key to speed training is not the particular device moving the athlete but the feedback the athlete receives from his or her own kinesthetic awareness and a keen-eyed coach.

Things feel different at high speeds. The exponential increase in the resistance of the water allows athletes to feel their strokes in different ways. This could be positive or negative depending on your eye and the ability of your swimmer to accept and make changes. Anthony Ervin, 2000 NCAA champion in the 50 and the 100 freestyle and world-record holder in the short course 50-meter freestyle, has an incredible kinesthetic feel for his stroke at high speeds. We can discuss a stroke change, and he can go in and alter his stroke with only one or two attempts. Making the initial change, however, is only half the battle. His first comment tends to be, "It doesn't feel right!" He always gets the same response from me: "So? You have been swimming with the same pattern for 10 years; of course it doesn't feel right to change it. The question is, is it faster?" We then discuss if it is indeed faster. I usually avoid these discussions by inserting my standard disclaimer: "I do not claim to have the answer or to know which is faster. The only way we will be able to tell is if you learn them both; then we can time them both to see which is faster." Anthony is all about going faster and is quickly ready for the test. We test our theories on the power reel. When the reel is set at a specific speed, it pulls the swimmer at a constant rate. The stopwatch quickly discerns the truth.

Platinum sets should always be done at race speed and at race-stroke rates. In 1999 Gordan Kozulj, 200 backstroke specialist, finished his NCAA eligibility and was ready to try something different. He asked me to train him as a sprinter. He had done miles of background work and his technique was solid. As we analyzed his race it became clear that there was one glaring difference between Gordan and the top backstrokers in the world. His stroke rate was much slower. His rates were between 29 and 37 cycles per minute. There was not one competitor in the 1996 Olympic final whose rate at any point in the race fell below 37 cycles per minute. Most of the competitors held between 42 and 45 cycles per minute.

When we first started working on increasing his stroke rates, he complained that it was too hard to maintain the higher rates. We used assisted swimming for shorter distances to get him used to holding faster rates, but for half the year he struggled to take his stroke rate to even 37 cycles per minute. Training at the Phoenix Swim Club in Phoenix, Arizona, gave us a unique opportunity to use a tow machine that pulled Gordan up and down the 50-meter course. Using this device helped him learn to hold his rates at 42 to 47 cycles per minute for 300 meters. Gordan won the 2000 European Championships, unrested, in his best time of 1:58.6, and he held his rates from 42 to 47, just as we had practiced.

In 1992 I was working for David Marsh at Auburn University, dreaming of creating a sprint program. "David," I said, "there are two things that would change the face of swimming. The first is drug testing the Chinese women, and the second is moving this bulkhead to 15 meters two times per week." The new pool at Auburn had just been finished, and the bulkheads could easily be moved. David liked my line of thinking, so he accommodated me with the bulkhead and gave me two swimmers to use to try out my theories.

One of the athletes David allowed me to work with was a senior who had had surgery during the summer to remove a growth on one of his lungs. The doctors had removed one-half of the affected lung but had gone out of their way not to cut the latissimus dorsi muscle so that he could still swim. His name was Dean Hutchinson. The other was another senior who had never been on the conference team. His name was Bill Pilczuk.

Dean's best was about 20.1 in the 50, and Bill's was about 20.3. The three of us, in addition to other individuals whom David would cycle through the group, pioneered the speed group. We had many exciting moments; each one exhilarated us and motivated us to keep the experiment going. By the end of the year Dean and Bill went 19.4 and 19.7, respectively, in the finals of the NCAA Championships. Bill was the first person in eight years to beat a guy by the name of Alexander Popov in the 50-meter freestyle. Eight years later both were still swimming and both competed in the 2000 US Olympic trials. I do not claim that the speed training alone did the trick for them. Both Dean and Bill had had three years of solid training under David Marsh; I only had to work on their technique, power, and speed. To this day, as I continue to paint in an unconventional style, I owe much to David for his support and advice.

As a coach-artist, I judge my success by looking at each individual piece of art, and I urge you to do the same. Each athlete is in fact a work of art in progress. If you gear programs to the masses you may develop swimmers who produce—but you will not be a successful coach until you can refine your techniques for each individual. Each canvas can reflect your work, and you can be proud of what you help create. If a season passes and you are not satisfied with your work on a particular canvas, maybe more red, white, or blue is needed; maybe more green, purple, gold, or platinum will help in another instance. The exciting thing is that you are the artist. There is no blame involved in creating; the only consideration is the result. Take responsibility for your artwork and enjoy the process.

Summary

- Technique is the base on which fast swimming is built.
- Aerobic swimming must be accompanied by technique instruction and must be carefully monitored.
- The artist-coach can apply aerobic training in nonspecific aerobic work such as drills, games, and dryland exercises.
- Nonspecific aerobic development can be more beneficial to the sprint swimmer than miles of swimming.
- Training sprinters above their $\dot{V}O_2$max threshold is not productive; limited anaerobic tolerance training is critical.
- If you want to swim fast, you have to train fast.
- Lactate-production sets are the mainstay of the 50 sprinter.
- Power-production sets permit the transfer of dryland strength training to the water.
- Speed work provides valuable feedback and awareness to the athlete. It should be done for short distances at race speed and at race-stroke rates.
- Each athlete is a work in progress, and the coach is continually creating the right blend of training colors to achieve the best results.

CHAPTER SEVENTEEN

Freestyle Middle-Distance Training

Doug Frost

It is not a coach's intention, nor should it be, to specialize in coaching any particular event or distance. Doing so can jeopardize the balance and effectiveness of a swim program. However, it is quite obvious that several very successful coaches tend to produce regularly in certain specialties. Success breeds success as the saying goes, and this applies very much to swim coaching. Having an athlete perform well at the international level in a particular event has a twofold effect on a program: other team members aspire to match that performance, and there is a natural tendency for the coach to emphasize that event when setting up the training structure. Being successful in coaching a specific distance also tends to attract swimmers from other programs. While I believe that all coaches should be in a position to provide opportunities for their swimmers to excel in all events and distances, I realize that this is not always practical or possible. Given the available pool space, time, and funding, programs are often required to be more generalized, much larger, and less workable for coaches than might be considered ideal.

I worked in such a situation from 1979 until 1995 at the Padstow Swim Centre in metropolitan Sydney, Australia, using a five-lane, 25-meter pool (which I still lease and have operated for the last 20 years). The most successful athlete to emerge during those years was Philip Bryant, 1992 Olympian, world championship finalist, and Commonwealth Games medalist in the 400 individual medley. I am very proud of his success, considering the training environment we had to contend with. During all the fuss over Philip, there was another young star in the melting pot, Ian Thorpe. I started to sing Ian's praises in 1995, when he was a young 12-year-old doing fantastic things in the training pool. You might ask, "Who gets excited about 12-year-old age groupers?" I do, particularly if his name is the "Thorpedo."

Since 1995 there have been five years of growth and development for that young man as well as my club program. For about two years, I used both the Padstow Indoor Centre and the Sydney International Aquatic Centre—home of the 2000 Olympics. With the two pools, I was able to combine long-course and short-course training, doing five long-course and five short-course sessions per week. Weary of the increased travel, in October 1997 I took up the position of elite coach at the well-appointed Sutherland Leisure Centre, operated by the Sutherland Shire Council, where I am responsible for the overall program and directly responsible for the National squad. Because of the facilities available at the Sutherland, I am now able to conduct both long-course and short-course training.

Of course everybody wants to coach somebody who is extremely talented, but if you just wait for that talented youngster to appear on your doorstep, it will never happen. Develop an environment that will provide the opportunity for that to occur. One way to develop such an environment is to support and instruct your athletes in *all* areas of development, not just directing what they do at the pool. This includes addressing the way they conduct themselves away from the pool, their education, their diet, and their personal hygiene, as well as providing sport science support in the form of sports medicine, sport psychology, and massage. Advise them of all the advantages associated with swimming: the healthy lifestyle, friends with a common interest, travel, and so on. Remember that the harder you try, the luckier you will get. This is how I went about setting up my practice area and developing my program in middle-distance freestyle so that I could get lucky.

> Succe... afrai... the a... failures and continue on, knowing that failure is a natural consequence of trying. The law of failure is one of the most powerful of all ... you only really fail when you quit trying. –Wynn Davis

What Is Middle-Distance Training?

Middle-distance events have the characteristics of sprint (100 freestyle) and distance (1,500 freestyle) events combined, in that they require the athlete to maintain both speed and endurance. Good middle-distance swimmers do not come about solely because of their physical attributes; the best and most successful middle-distance performances are a function of both physical ability and a proper training program. I believe that the success I have had with middle-distance swimmers is due in part to helping them develop an efficient stroke that incorporates their best technique traits.

There are two main middle-distance events:

- **400-meter freestyle.** I consider the 400-meter freestyle (or the 500-yard freestyle short course) to be the event most aligned with the middle-distance classification; the 400-meter individual medley has very similar characteristics.

- **200-meter freestyle.** Training for the 200-meter freestyle can be incorporated into the middle-distance area. I have found that swimmers moving down in distance tend to have more endurance and thus have a distinct advantage over competitors moving up in distance.

Both middle-distance freestyle events are similar to the 100 and 1,500 events in terms of the areas to address in training. For this reason middle-distance training session preparation is not restricted to any one area. If an area is neglected in your initial program structure, then the preparation and final outcome will suffer.

To be successful in any event on the competition calendar, an athlete must be prepared and have specifically trained for that event and distance. Specialized and personalized preparation for each athlete is most important; training requirements must be addressed *individually*.

It is important to remember when preparing workouts that not all athletes can cope with the same workload. It is your responsibility as coach to assess the athletes' strengths and weaknesses and to incorporate changes in the training structure that will sharpen their particular strengths and help them improve upon their weaknesses.

Once you have assessed swimmers' individual needs, you can group athletes of like ability on a team. Having a middle-distance group as part of the overall program can help the other swimmers do the following:

- Develop good work ethics
- Improve aerobic qualities
- Identify different events that they might swim
- Enjoy variety in practices and within the program

Not all teams provide the opportunity for swimmers to develop as middle-distance specialists; in many cases athletes end up in the distance or middle-distance lanes as a last resort; that is, a coach just doesn't know where else to put them. As a result, many coaches fail in their responsibilities to develop the middle-distance potential of those they are coaching. These coaches miss out on the chance to develop an area of their program that could be very successful if they would only put in the time and effort required to nurture middle-distance athletes.

I believe there are several reasons for the many gains made by our middle-distance program including the testing procedure we use, the suitable workout time and space we allow, and the consideration we give to each group's training needs when preparing the workouts.

The test sets are designed to identify prospective middle-distance athletes. In addition to being capable of enduring an increased workload, such athletes excel in doing the following:

- Repeating even pace sets in a workout
- Maintaining a high floatation position in the water
- Using a balanced stroke—right is as strong as left
- Using an effective stroke for middle distance (optimal speed paired with endurance)
- Using a more powerful than average kick

The tests include the following:

1. 3,000-meter freestyle timed test. This test is the right length to give the coach a basis for setting interval training sets and determining the pace and intensity required for the particular session.
2. 5 × 200 on 5:00 freestyle test set, at the fastest possible speed, holding even pace throughout the set. Record time, heart rate, and stroke count, and measure lactates using a specific lactate monitor.
3. 6 × 100 on 6:00 freestyle maximum effort. Again, record time, heart rate, stroke count, and lactates.
4. 4 × (50 dive timed + 450 active rest)
5. 8 × ([4 × 100 in 1:15] on 6:00)
6. 200/400 freestyle kick. Goal is sub 3:00/6:00.

Each of the first four tests should be conducted every four weeks. For example, in week one test the 3,000 freestyle, week two the 5 × 200 on 5:00, week three the 6 × 100 on 6:00, and week four the 4 × (1 × 50 sprint + 450 active rest). The 8 × ([4 × 100 in 1:15] on 6:00) and 200/400 kick tests are conducted on a more regular basis.

Designing the Middle-Distance Program

To create an exciting and challenging program for each session, I devote several hours prior to the start of each week to preparing for the coming week. It is imperative that workouts be adjusted on a week-to-week basis. Doing so allows coaches the latitude to take into account individual training responses to specific sets and the differences in adjusting to the training demands. The final form of the training program will be governed by each athlete's progress and should be based on the coach's past experiences, involving many years of testing responses and observing athletes of all levels.

Part of my workout preparation time is spent expanding my knowledge by seeking out the expertise and advice of other coaches. I've consulted experts such as Les Lazarus, Terry Gathercole, Bill Sweetenham, John Carew, Laurie Lawrence, the late Joe King, Ken Wood, and Don Talbot. My contact and involvement with these coaches and their athletes at national event camps and on national teams has provided me with a wealth of knowledge. I find it helpful to apply their expertise and insights to my own training program.

I prepare my program and workouts using an overall plan that breaks into four three- to four-week phases. Table 17.1a shows the basic structure of this overall plan including the big-picture layout of the competi-

— TABLE 17.1A —

Overall Plan

Date	Weeks to comp	Competition	Testing	Mid-distance free 21 day	Free 10 day	Free sprint	Breast
17-18 Jan		World Cup	Sydney	Maintenance	Maintenance		
19-21 Jan		NSW Open					
24 Jan	16		No test	Build	Build	Build	Build
31 Jan	15			Aerobic	Aerobic	Aerobic	Aerobic
07 Feb	14	Altitude TBC		Aerobic	Aerobic	Aerobic	Aerobic
14 Feb	13	Altitude TBC	3,000	Aerobic	Aerobic	Endurance	Endurance
21 Feb	12	Altitude TBC	5 × 200 (5)	Aerobic	Aerobic	Endurance	Endurance
28 Feb	11		6 × 100 (6)	Adaptation	Aerobic	Quality	Quality
06 Mar	10		4 × 50 + 450 ar	Endurance	Adaptation	Quality	Quality
13 Mar	9	World S/C	3,000	Endurance	Endurance	Aerobic	Aerobic
20 Mar	8		5 × 200 (5)	Endurance	Endurance	Aerobic	Aerobic
27 Mar	7		6 × 100 (6)	Adaptation	Endurance	Endurance	Endurance
03 Apr	6		4 × 50 + 450 ar	Quality	Adaptation	Endurance	Endurance
10 Apr	5	Aust Age S/C	3,000	Quality	Quality	Quality	Quality
17 Apr	4		5 × 200 (5)	Quality	Quality	Quality	Quality
24 Apr	3		6 × 100 (6)	Precomp	Quality	Precomp	Precomp
01 May	2	NSWIS Camp	4 × 50 + 450 ar	Precomp	Precomp	Precomp	Precomp
08 May	1	NSWIS Camp		Precomp	Precomp	Precomp	Precomp
13-20 May		Olympic trials	Sydney				
15 May				Build	Build	Build	Build
22 May	TBC	Orientation camp	Timed 3000			Build	Build
29 May	16		5 × 200 (5)			Aerobic	Aerobic
05 Jun	15		6 × 100 (6)			Aerobic	Aerobic
12 Jun	14	Altitude TBC	4 × 50 + 450 ar	Aerobic		Aerobic	Aerobic
19 Jun	13	Altitude TBC	Timed 3,000	Aerobic	Aerobic	Endurance	Endurance
26 Jun	12	Altitude TBC	5 × 200 (5)	Aerobic	Aerobic	Endurance	Endurance
03 Jul	11		6 × 100 (6)	Adaptation	Aerobic	Quality	Quality
10 Jul	10		4 × 50 + 450 ar	Endurance	Adaptation	Quality	Quality
17 Jul	9		Timed 3000	Endurance	Endurance	Aerobic	Aerobic
24 Jul	8		5 × 200 (5)	Endurance	Endurance	Aerobic	Aerobic
31 Jul	7	NSW Open S/C	6 × 100 (6)	Adaptation	Endurance	Endurance	Endurance
07 Aug	6		4 × 50 + 450 ar	Quality	Adaptation	Endurance	Endurance
14 Aug	5		Timed 3000	Quality	Quality	Quality	Quality
21 Aug	4		5 × 200 (5)	Quality	Quality	Quality	Quality
28 Aug	3	NSW Age S/C	6 × 100 (6)	Precomp	Quality	Precomp	Precomp
04 Sep	2	Olympic TC	4 × 50 + 450 ar	Precomp	Precomp	Precomp	Precomp
11 Sep	1	Olympic TC		Precomp	Precomp	Precomp	Precomp
16 Sep-1 Oct		Olympic Games	Sydney				

— TABLE 17.1B —

Weekly Training Cycles for
Middle-Distance and Distance Freestyle

Weeks 1 to 3—Aerobic   Week 1—50 to 60   Week 2—60 to 70   Week 3—70 to 80

Day	AM	PM
Monday	Aerobic A2 300 to 500s free Drag suit set Sprint 400 total Kick 2,000 free	Lactate tolerance Descend set 30 × 100 free or IM 2 to 30 × 100 form Kick free, IM, breast
Tuesday	Aerobic A1, Overdistance free 3 to 6 × 1,000/1,500 Include drills 8 × swim ins Kick fly	Anaerobic threshold 100s short rest set 2,000 to 3,000 fly set Kick back Time trial Band fast stroke rate 50s
Wednesday	Off	Aerobic A2 3,000 to 5,000 m as 400s free, 200s form Slow/fast swim Kick 2000 free
Thursday	Aerobic A1 Overdistance pull/drag 6 to 12 × 500 Include drills 8 × swim ins Kick fly	Anaerobic threshold 50s short rest set 2,000 to 3,000 m fly set Kick back Band fast stroke rate 50s
Friday	Aerobic A2 Overdistance free Drag suit set IM-breast set Sprint 400 total Kick 2,000 free	Anaerobic threshold Descend to threshold Slow-fast swim Time trial/club
Saturday	Aerobic A1 500, 800, 1,500s 200, 300, 400s Fly set Kick vertical Band fast stroke rate 50s	Off
Sunday	Off	Off
Sample test sets	3,000 timed 5 × 200 (5) 6 × 100 (6) 4 × 50 + 450 ar	

227

Week 4—Adaptation (same as Week 12)

Weeks 5 to 7—Endurance Week 5—60 to 70 Week 6—70 to 80 Week 7—80 to 90

Day	AM	PM
Monday	Aerobic A2 300s fly set Slow-fast swim Kick free Example 10 × 200 (4)	Heart rate lactate tolerance Example 10 × 200 (4) Kick free, IM, breast
Tuesday	Aerobic A1 Sprint 400 total Overdistance pull/drag 2 to 4 × 1500 Kick 2,000 free/fly	Anaerobic threshold 300s short rest 2,000 to 4,000 m 8 × swim ins Kick back Band fast stroke rate 50s
Wednesday	Off	Aerobic A2 400s free-IM Fly set Slow-fast swim Kick free Time trial
Thursday	Aerobic A1 Sprint 400 total Overdistance pull/drag 4 to 8 × 800 Kick 2,000 free/back	Anaerobic threshold 100 to 150s short rest 2,000 to 4,000 m 8 × swim ins Kick fly Band fast stroke rate 50s
Friday	Anaerobic threshold 200s Slow-fast swim Pull/drag Kick vertical	Aerobic A1 Fly set Drills 400 kick timed Time trial/club
Saturday	Lactate tolerance Free 30 × 50 (60) or IM 28 × 50 (60) (7 each stroke) Kick free, IM, breast Band fast stroke rate 50s	Off
Sunday	Off	Off

Sample test sets	3,000 timed
	   5 × 200 (5)
	   6 × 100 (6)
	   4 × 50 + 450 ar
		Drag suit sets (each session)

Week 8—Adaptation (same Week 12)

Weeks 9 to 11—Quality   Week 9—50 to 60   Week 10—60 to 70   Week 11—80 to 90

Day	AM	PM
Monday	Aerobic A2 Overdistance set Fly set Sprint 400 total Kick 2,000 free	Heart rate lactate tolerance Example 100s or 200s Kick free, IM, breast
Tuesday	Aerobic A1 1,000 to 1,500s Slow-fast swim Drills 8 × swim ins Kick fly	Anaerobic threshold Up to 300s short rest (for max total of 3,000) Time trial or broken swim Kick back 4 to 8 × 50 for pace Band fast stroke rate 25s
Wednesday	Off Inform swimmers of PM set	$\dot{V}O_2$max/lactate threshold Example: 10 to 15 × 400 free 4-(5:00) 30 beats below max 3-(6:00) 20 beats below max 2-(7:00) 10 beats below max 1-broken maximum Kick 200 own stroke
Thursday	Aerobic A1 500 to 800s Slow-fast swim Drills 8 × swim ins Kick fly	Anaerobic threshold Up to 300s short rest (maximum total 3,000) Time trial or broken swim Kick back 4 to 8 × 50 for pace Band fast stroke rate 25s
Friday	Aerobic A2 Overdistance set Fly set Sprint 400 total Kick 2,000 free	Anaerobic threshold Descend to threshold 400s free or 200s form Kick free/IM, breast Time trial/club
Saturday	Lactate tolerance Example 20 × 50 (90) free 20 × 50 (90) IM Band fast stroke rate 25s Kick free/IM, breast	Note AM Lactate tolerance set Increase rest and decrease number each week.
Sunday	Off	Off
Sample test sets	3,000 timed 5 × 200 (5) 6 × 100 (6) 4 × 50 + 450 ar	Drag-suit sets (each session) Fast stroke rate (3 × per week)

Weeks 12 to 15*—Precompetition   Week 12—50/70   Week 13—40/50   Week 14—30/30
*Start 21 or 10 days out from competition

Day	AM	PM
Monday	Aerobic + speed Pull set/drills Kick quality 50s 4 to 8 × 50 for pace Practice push offs	Heart rate lactate tolerance 100s descend to pace Practice turns Jump turns
Tuesday	Off Note projected times for PM practice:	Aerobic A2 Straight swim Race-specific broken swims 100 m best time - 3 sec 200 m best time - 6 sec 400 m best time - 9 sec Practice starts Kick 400s 1 or 2
Wednesday	Aerobic + speed Pull set/drills Kick quality 10 days out—race rehearsal • Warm-up • Heat swim • Swim-down	Aerobic + speed Pull set/drills Kick quality 10 days out—race rehearsal • Warm-up • Final swim • Swim-down
Thursday	Off	Aerobic A2 150s or 75s Race-specific broken swims Practice starts Kick 200s
Friday	Aerobic + speed Pull set/drills Kick quality 50s 4 to 8 × 50 for pace Practice push offs	Aerobic A2 4 to 10 × race distance Descend to 30 bbm Race-specific broken swim Practice turns Jump turns Vertical kick
Saturday	Heart rate lactate tolerance 50s Kick 100s Practice starts	Off
Sunday	Aerobic A2 Race-specific broken swim Prerace warm-up Practice later in morning	Off

tions and the testing sets leading to the goal performance. Table 17.1b provides more details on how we structure the individual workout for a 16-week cycle.

Being innovative is an important part of designing any program. A change is as good as a holiday. It is possible to alter the workouts slightly to keep swimmers challenged and excited without losing the desired effect of a given session.

For example, Bill Sweetenham recommends using a different warm-up at every workout. I incorporate a new warm-up into each session, always preparing swimmers for the change and keeping in mind the warm-up's relationship to the main set. Change the focus regularly on the kick and pull sets with overdistance and short rest repeat sets on a structured basis, depending on the training stimulus required for that session. Don't be afraid to include extra kick in the workout. I include 2,000-meter sets twice per week in addition to the kick sets at every other session.

To provide training variety, I also have several alternative dryland programs in place. For example, swimmers might alternate between running, skipping, circuit training, boxing, or stretch-cord workouts on Mondays, Wednesdays, and Fridays, and vary the types of medicine ball exercises they do on Tuesdays, Thursdays, and Fridays.

Another way to keep the program fresh is to incorporate different training equipment. On our squad, all members must provide the following training equipment for their personal use:

- Mesh bag
- Kickboard
- Paddles, two sizes: finger paddles and large paddles
- Pull buoy
- Drag suit
- Leg tie (band)
- Fins

The program supplies the swim harness and dive gauge. The important thing to remember with accessories is to use them to your advantage, not just for the sake of using them. Our middle-distance swimmers use drag suits for both swim and kick sets, and pull buoys and bands for pull sets. They do kicking sets with and without a board, and they use the fins for swim kick and drill sets as well as speed sets and swim recovery. The swim harness is useful for resistance and speed assistance, and the dive gauge helps swimmers improve their distance off the wall.

Training Camps for Middle-Distance Swimmers

I have been involved with training camps at all levels over the past 20 years and have found that training in this environment has advantages and disadvantages. On the plus side, a well-planned, well-run camp may offer the following benefits:

- The added training stimulus that comes from a change in venue
- Improved climatic conditions
- Different training partners
- Suitable accommodations close to the training venue
- Correct and controlled meals
- Support staff (medical, massage, biomechanical)

On the other hand, training camps may have the following drawbacks:

- Restricted lane space and training times
- Poor timing (in relation to when swimmers need the type of training provided)
- Unprepared athletes
- Accommodations that are unsuitable or too far from the training venue
- Meals that are improperly planned or served at inappropriate times

There are several factors to consider prior to preparing for a camp, be it at the club, state, or national level. The purpose of the camp is paramount. Providing for middle-distance swimmers was our chief impetus in organizing the first National Event Camp for Middle-Distance Freestyle at the Thredbo Alpine Training Center in October 1998. Earlier that year I had spoken with Australian National coach Don Talbot regarding setting up an Australian National event program for 200-meter to 400-meter freestylers; we agreed that at previous camps, these athletes had not received the same degree of specialized training as the other freestyle groups. Introducing a middle-distance freestyle camp enabled us to

- identify athletes specializing in this area,
- give recognition to middle-distance events,
- further develop the skills of these swimmers in a common arena,
- develop the knowledge of the coaches involved, and
- increase the depth of talent and improve the standard in the middle-distance area.

Table 17.2 shows how we set up the first middle-distance specialist camp and includes the daily activities, training, and main sets we used.

— TABLE 17.2 —

Camp Schedule

Date	Morning	Afternoon	Evening
Sunday, 25 Oct.	Travel	11:30-2:30PM Lunch Arrive at Training Centre Room allocation 4:00-6:00PM Pool training Aerobic A1 Overdistance set Skills session Work on pushoffs 50s include turns at start and finish	6:00-8:00PM Dinner 7:30pm Meeting room— team meeting (outline weekly program) Coaches meeting (discuss training programs and workouts)
Monday, 26 Oct.	7:00-9:00AM Pool training Aerobic A2 Overdistance pull set 8 × 500 (6:30/7:00) 2 swim, 4 pull, 2 swim Short rest kick set 3 × (200, 150, 100, 50) (3:40, 2:15, 1:50, 1:00) Sprint 400 total 9:00-10:00AM Breakfast 10:00-12:00 Pool underwater video	12:30-1:30PM lunch Gym TBC 4:00-6:00PM Pool training $\dot{V}O_2$max 3000 timed test Aerobic A1 drill-kick-swim 10 × (150 drill, 100 kick, 50 swim). 3 free, 1 form, 2 free, 1 form, 1 free, 2 form or IM	6:00-7:00PM Dinner 7:30-9:30PM Meeting room— stroke analysis
Tuesday, 27 Oct.	7:00-9:00AM Pool training Aerobic A1 Recovery skills and drills 8 × 800 drills (right arm, alternate arms, freestyle form, left arm, catch up) Aerobic pull set 8 × swim ins 9:00-10:00AM Breakfast 10:00-12:00 Pool underwater video	12:30-1:30PM Lunch 4:00-6:00PM Pool training Anaerobic threshold Spiked 400 quality kick 400 kick timed test Challenge 100s Do as many 100s as you can with a reduced takeoff time	6:00-7:00PM Dinner 7:30-9:30PM Meeting room— stroke analysis
Wednesday, 28 Oct.	7:00-9:00AM Pool training Aerobic A2 Swim mixed or race distance 1 × 800 pull 8 × 50 kick 2 × 400 pull 4 × 100 kick 4 × 200 pull 2 × 200 kick 8 × 100 pull 1 × 400 kick Spiked 400 variable Kick-drill 9:00-10:00am Breakfast	12:30-1:30PM Lunch (pre-packed lunch TBC) Activity planned: "To the summit" chair lift and walk TBC No pool workout	6:00-7:00PM Dinner 7:30-9:30PM Movie *(continued)*

__TABLE 17.2 *continued*__

Date	Morning	Afternoon	Evening
Thursday, 29 Oct.	7:00-9:00AM Pool training Aerobic A1 Pull set race distance 4 × 400, 1 swim, 3 pull 3 × 400, 1 swim, 2 pull 2 × 400, 1 swim, 1 pull 1 × 400, 1 swim Overdistance kick set 8 × swim ins 9:00-10:00AM Breakfast 10:00-12:00 noon Pool starts and turns video session	12:30-1:30PM Lunch 4:00-6:00PM Pool training Anaerobic threshold Threshold 150s 20 × 150s 4-2:00, 3-1:55, 2-1:50, 1-1:45, 4-2:00, 3-1:50, 2-1:40, 1-1:35 Spiked 400 Quality kick set 2 × 200 pull-band timed test	6:00-7:00PM Dinner 7:30-9:30PM Meeting room— Starts and turns analysis
Friday, 30 Oct.	7:00-9:00AM Pool training Aerobic A2 Overdistance pull set 5 × 800 Short rest vertical kick set Sprint 400 total 9:00-10:00AM Breakfast 10:00-12:00 noon Pool starts and turns video	12:30-1:30PM Lunch Gym session TBC 4:00-6:00PM Pool training Aerobic A1 Race distance swim 5 × (300[4:00]100[1:30]) 300-400 pace + 20 100-400 pace + 5 10 × 200 build Kick set drills 20 × 50 kick (3 moderate [:50], 1 firm [:60])	6:00-7:00PM Dinner 7:30-9:30PM Meeting room— Starts and turns analysis
Saturday, 31 Oct.	7:00-9:00AM Pool training 50s quality 5 × 12 50s 1 moderate, 1 hard, 2 moderate, 2 hard, 3 moderate, 3 hard [:60] Aerobic A1 swim-kick 9:00-10:00AM Breakfast Depart	Lunch	Dinner

> * The workouts listed do not include warm-ups, or all kick or pull sets.
> Total sessions = 11; total distance for the week 11 × 7,000 m average

Preparing for National and International Competition

Preparing an athlete for his or her first national competition can be a very difficult undertaking for the coach and the developing athlete. It does help if you have other athletes in your squad who are competing at the national level. These athletes can do much to assist the younger athletes in the transition from age-group to national-level swimming just by training with them.

Introduce national competition to a swimmer by setting up specific, realistic challenges that the swimmer can focus on. For example, swimmers might work on bettering their entry time, improving their ranking, or qualifying for the A or B final (semifinal). Such goals help a swimmer progress, step by step, rather than being overwhelmed.

The greatest satisfaction possible for a coach is having a swimmer selected for a national team. This can lead to several exciting developments. Being selected means the swimmer has passed a major hurdle in reaching his or her potential. The swimmer is now a member of a team that will represent the country, and the sky is the limit. This accomplishment opens the door to winning a medal at the Olympics. In my experience a swimmer who makes the national team (especially the Australian National Team) has a very good chance of being successful in the international arena because of the high level of ability and high standards expected of members of the national team. Furthermore, the prospect of being selected as a coach of the team, depending on your swimmer's rank and the total number of coaches required, is a distinct possibility. I waited a long time to achieve my first ambition as a coach; it was not my last, and I have not been disappointed. Each achievement has been a fantastic, challenging, and rewarding experience.

I include this segment so that all coaches will understand the importance of setting their own goals rather than just having their athletes set goals. Achieving the highest level possible requires that you place no limits on yourself or your athletes. On numerous occasions I have come into contact with coaches who do not project themselves or their athletes as being able to compete at the national level; these coaches and athletes are limited by such lack of vision. Setting limits on what you believe can be achieved will affect the results of your program in the short term and the long term. If you believe an athlete can compete at the highest level and you are not ready or able to take him or her there, then move the athlete to a program that can do what it takes.

Maintaining the Focus of Your Program

An important step for a coach to take is to reflect on each season's results for every athlete in order to establish the best direction to take in the future to produce better results. I assess the attitude as well as the performance of my athletes, taking into consideration the answers to the following questions:

- What was their previous year's performance?
- What makes them committed?
- Did they achieve their goals?

- Is their attendance consistent?
- Are they enjoying the sport?
- Are they managing their swimming and education commitments?

I also assess my own coaching performance over the past season by determining the answers to these questions:

- Have I been well prepared?
- Can I improve my performance?
- What is my overall assessment of the season's results?
- Did I achieve my goals?

Building in time to reflect on the past season highlights the highs and lows, and provides the means to prevent similar lows in the future.

In closing, it is vital that I stress the importance of continuing professional development; no coach is an island. I have learned a great deal over the last 10 years by attending training camps (Hawaii, ASCA scholarship coach); working with elite and senior athletes; working with legendary and respected coaches; attending conferences, team camps, and workshops; making presentations; mixing with international coaches; and using outside resources such as the NSWIS sport scientists.

Without the input and assistance of my peers as well as the cooperation and support of the Australian Swimming Coaches and Teachers Association, Australian Swimming Inc., and the New South Wales Institute of Sport, my level of knowledge would be very shallow. The contributions of these individuals and organizations have gone a long way in advancing me to the level of coaching I enjoy today.

Summary

- Failure is a natural consequence of trying. Successful people aren't afraid to fail.
- Middle-distance freestyle pertains primarily to the 200- and 400-meter events (200- to 500-yard events for short course).
- Having a middle-distance group in a training program helps develop good work ethics, improve aerobic qualities, identify different kinds of talent, and add variety to the program.
- Design a long-range program but evaluate and adjust workouts on a week-to-week basis.
- Continue to expand your knowledge.

- Warm-ups should be specific to the training goals of that session.
- Dryland training adds worthwhile variety to the program.
- Training camps provide special opportunities but must have a specific purpose.
- National team participation and international competition present significant challenges and opportunities.
- Maintaining swimmer and coach focus is a major responsibility of the coach.

CHAPTER EIGHTEEN

Freestyle Distance Training

Dick Jochums

My coaching philosophy has evolved over more than 20 years and is reflected in the Santa Clara Swim Club distance freestyle program that I've developed and that I detail in this chapter. This philosophy was shaped by my parents and by the many fine coaches who have influenced me.

My parents raised me to believe that I could be anything I wanted to be if I worked hard enough. I still believe that this opportunity is what America offers to all its citizens. I learned swimming from the best female coach who has ever coached swimming, Lauralbelle Bookstauver. She was a great advocate of developing proper technique in slow and fast swimming. I swam at the University of Washington, three seasons for Jack Torney and one year for John Tallman. Coach Torney taught me the importance of being a gentleman, and Coach Tallman taught me the real meaning of work (fast swimming) and that the future of swimming was tied to science. Coach Tallman and I didn't have a great swimmer-coach relationship, but after making me beg for a job, he greatly influenced my understanding of proper workout format and its relationship to swim meet results. Ninety percent of what has become my distance freestyle program is directly related to the two years I spent with Coach Tallman as his assistant coach.

I went to Berkeley for graduate work and had a great year helping Pete Cutino, the very best pure coach in terms of quality of workouts and communication with swimmers and staff that I have ever worked for. Anyone who thinks I'm a hard-ass should have seen me before he got hold of me. (While many outsiders may think I am to be feared, those who swim for me know better.) Together, Pete and I started and ran the Concord Swim Club until I took a job in Long Beach, California, under the direction of Don Gambril. At this point in my career I thought I knew it all. I had developed several Division II All-American sprinters. Then Don Gambril came around and actually got me to shut up and learn the most important lesson in coaching: Aim high enough and demand fast swimming so that you don't mess up the kids in your program.

A sport history course I taught brought into focus all that my mentors had preached to me. The course was a survey of recorded western sport history as measured against the principles of those who founded sport, the Greeks. The principles were *agon*, the struggle, and its relationship to *arete*, the victory. Agon meant so much more than just a struggle to the ancient Greeks. It was a process—the good and the bad of the struggle—that led to honor and fame, not merely a win. Arete also meant more than just a win to the ancient Greeks. It could only be awarded by fellow warriors and wasn't fully bestowed until after death. It was the reward for those who truly lived the agonistic system (the process) and in so doing earned honor and imperishable fame.

My heroes in coaching are George Haines, Sherm Chavoor, and Peter Daland. I learned a lot by watching and listening to them, but the coaches I worked with were by far more influential. My program is based on all that I learned from these coaches; each of them, along with my own teaching experiences, have taught me valuable coaching concepts. At Santa Clara we aim at being number one, and the knowledge that we have done everything possible to be the best, within the rules, means that we can accept whatever the end result turns out to be. We don't use drugs because doing so would defeat us before we started. Self-knowledge isn't acquired by using crutches. We don't have easy days because we need to seek the truth about ourselves each and every day. We desire to be tested daily as we search for honor and imperishable fame.

I believe in the ability of the individual to dream a dream and then, through hard work, to make the dream come true. I believe that a properly designed program can help a dream become a reality. I believe that a poorly designed, poorly organized, and poorly administered program can kill a dream. What's worse and most tragic, is that a program that doesn't challenge young athletes to be the best cheats them out of an opportunity to see the beauty of self. My coaching philosophy has developed a few champions as well as a whole lot of people who, according to my definition, are winners.

The Foundation of My Program

My program is based on the fact that as speed is increased resistance also increases, meaning more work (power or distance × speed) must be produced to maintain that speed. In fact, the key ingredient in the definition of work is *speed*. An increase in yards will increase work output only if speed is maintained, while an increase in speed can quite easily produce a tenfold increase in work. This is shown in the power curve (figure 18.1a), the basis for my training methodology. The lactate graph (figure 18.1b) and the power curve, with a little imagination, can be viewed as the same graph. Speed, once again, is directly tied to the production of lactate, and a small increase in speed radically changes this production. Both sides, those coaches who stress quality—or speed work—and those who stress quantity—or a lot of yardage—believe that training must be designed to move both the power curve and the lactate-threshold point to the right of the graph. In fact, this is the crunch point in the argument between the two sides. One side does a majority of what they call work at or close to the lactate threshold, using such work to buffer the power work they actually do. With power tied to the buffering aspect of the program, the threshold point will move to the right because of the full recovery allowed by the nonpower work.

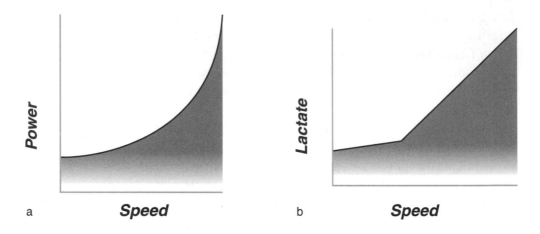

Figure 18.1, a-b The power curve (a) and the lactate graph (b).

The fact is that it's the power element that causes the threshold to move to the right, not the threshold element. It's my opinion that this system works but only if the swimmer does the power elements at the levels at which they're designed to be done. Somewhere in the translation of this system, the word *easy* has come to mean that there is an easier way to get there. The test sets ought to be the power sets—above the threshold—not at threshold.

It's my contention that swimming above threshold as often as possible is the best way to move the lactate-threshold point to the right. This is not more physiologically sound than the buffering system, but it is much more psychologically sound. Doing it this way forces lactate conversion while allowing the coach to work on the swimmer's mental focus during a workout. This way coach and athlete deal on a daily basis with the pain factor that the swimmer must face in a race or over a time period in a meet. The coach can reinforce the daily lessons that the swimmers need to learn and to internalize. I further believe that this approach forces the body to adjust faster, to actually have a more efficient recovery system, and to give the swimmer a better mental outlook that will allow for fast swimming over several competition days, rather than just one day. I think it makes for a tougher and smarter swimmer who isn't as likely to fold if the going gets tough!

What scares me about the buffering system advocates is that they haven't told us the whole story. From what I have read and experienced, they have already taken into account that they aren't getting what is required during the power element. Some of the power required to make this system really work takes much more than a day or two of rest to allow swimmers to sufficiently recover. Have you noticed that the first few days following a meet are not very good workout days? Do you understand that meet performance is work? It's probably the hardest work swimmers do, and because of the real, 100 percent effort required, the swimmers take a day or two to recover from the meet work. I believe that in reality both systems accomplish the same thing physiologically, but the advantages in psychological conditioning in my conversion system far outweigh the buffering system. Since I'm from the old school, the school that still believes that training is 90 percent mental, the choice for me is a simple one.

I looked at the scientific truth of the power curve and decided that it needed to be tied to the principle of specificity, which simply stated says that athletes must train the way they race and race the way they train or the program is wasting time and effort. This means that the swimmer's program should incorporate the actual stroke, distance, speed, and effort used in the race one is training for. Moreover, it is impossible to separate the physical from the mental. I merely took these three concepts—two scientific facts and my belief in the power of the human brain—and developed a program that uniquely stresses a combination of these concepts daily. Every set, every idea, and every technique in my program has been borrowed in some form from some other person. Even the term *lung buster* was borrowed from Peter Cutino, the best coach and best friend I have ever worked for. What makes my program original to is that I've redefined the borrowed concepts through the combinations I use and the way I communicate them to my swimmers.

The Annual Plan

Every swim training program should be based on an annual plan. I believe that one effective way to structure an annual plan is to account for the two seasons—short-course and long-course—that consist of seven total phases:

Short-Course Season

Preseason	September to October
Early season	October to mid-November
Inseason	Mid-November to March
Taper	March to April

Long-Course Season

Early season	April to mid-May
Inseason	Mid-May to August
Taper	August

While these dates aren't set in stone (due to the ever-changing United States Swimming calendar) an annual plan is necessary in order to realize long-term gains in swim performance. It's been my experience that each of these seven phases must be planned for every year to facilitate long-term success. Also, I strongly believe that only one preseason element is necessary each year, but it is a key to the repeating cycles of early season, inseason, and taper. This planning formula is not only the key to season goals but also, and more important, the basis for swimmers' specific career goals.

Each season has its own goals but is also a preparation for the next season. Short- and long-course seasons are geared around a particular big meet, but the short-course and long-course seasons also complement each other. Just as one element or phase of a program is preparation for the next phase, so is each season and each year that a person swims preparation for those that follow. This is as true for the swimmers as it is for the coach. We all make errors and mistakes. Coaches and athletes must learn, review, take some risk, adjust, and improve in light of the experiences they have just completed. Coaches must constantly measure what is happening against what they want to happen. If a program does this, then it has a chance to develop champion swimmers and people.

The program in its entirety is diagrammed in figure 18.2. The solid line is the work output indicator. Notice that after the early season phase, the output increases until the sharp decrease at the start of the taper. The dotted line is used to illustrate energy resources available to produce the work output. Notice that there is a sharp decrease at the start of early season. Further notice that there is a very quick adjustment of resources to meet the work output required during the beginning of the early season and that this resource is maintained at adequate levels throughout the rest of the early season and the inseason. Excess resources are produced during the taper due to the drop in work output.

The preseason involves light work output; the body has enough energy resources to maintain a normal lifestyle. During the early season phases, a jump from almost no work output to a huge work output depletes the body's energy resources. This contributes to a change in lifestyle and is evidenced by the swimmer being constantly tired, having a short temper, and feeling the need for extra rest and food. After about two weeks of this work output, through proper diet and rest, the body builds the ability to produce the required resources, and the swimmer soon gets back to a normal routine and lifestyle. During the inseason, work outputs are increased, but the body has become efficient enough

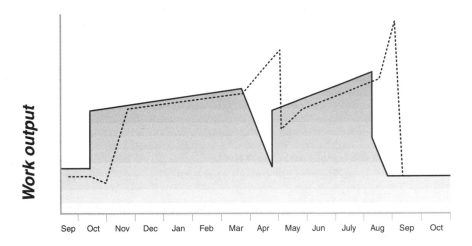

Figure 18.2 Variations in work output (solid line) and energy resources (dotted line) in a typical annual plan.

in resource production to meet usage needs. A normal lifestyle can be maintained without real sacrifice. During the taper phase, a decreased work output causes the swimmers to have excess energy that they may expend in alternate activities (rather than resting as they should). It is important for the coach to encourage athletes to rest during this time rather than expend their excess energy.

Preseason

When I first started to swim, every school in the United States started back up in September, and that was also the time that swim programs headed back into the water. No swim meets were held until late November, if then, so this was the time that coaches introduced or reintroduced swimming skills. September was, and in my program still is, the easiest month of the year, with one-hour workouts stressing stroke technique. The first week we do freestyle; then we add a stroke each week for a total of four weeks of technique drills. All my swimmers participate in these drills; the older and better swimmers become captains of their lanes and help the younger and weaker swimmers. This blending of groups during the first month builds team unity, teaches a common technical vocabulary that will be used at all levels, and gives the more experienced swimmers a chance to shoulder some responsibility and leadership.

The program for the month of September stresses the following principles in order of importance:

1. Swim technique—stroke drills teaching proper fundamentals

2. Proper training procedure
   - Organization: setup of lanes, circle swimming, proper order, streamlining
   - Kicking: single file, no talking, proper grip on board, proper turns
   - Pulling: tubes, hand paddles, pull buoy
3. Starts and turns

In freestyle, stroke drills such as those shown on pages 249 and 250 are designed to stress five fundamentals: press, push, recovery, catch up, and roll.

Press

The press phase is the hand entry or the front end of the freestyle stroke. The natural swimmer has an innate ability to feel water and begin moving the body through it. The rest of us must develop this skill. Quite simply, this ability is nothing more than finding resistance as the hand begins to press back, down, and out as it enters the water. The idea is for the hand to stay still while the body moves through the water, past the hand's point of entry. A perfect pull, which is impossible because water isn't a solid obstacle, would have the hand's entry point and exit point as the same point. The ability to feel water during the press, that is, to find and then maintain resistance, is the fundamental that must be stressed. The press accounts for the first 12 to 18 inches of the hand movement.

The ability to feel water is the difference between natural and average swimmers. The beautiful thing about swimming is that it is a skill that can be learned. It doesn't come easy, but if a swimmer is willing to concentrate and focus enough, a feeling for the water can develop. I have had many swimmers, such as Tim Shaw and George DiCarlo, who have proven that the disadvantage of not being a natural can be overcome by the average person. This is what makes swimming such a special sport!

Push

This is the follow through or back end of the hand movement in the freestyle stroke. The hand accelerates to a full extension of the arm as the hand pushes back through to the surface of the water. Basically this is the same place the hand would naturally hang at the side if standing. This accounts for the last 18 inches of the stroke or hand movement.

The push phase is to swimming what the follow through is to throwing a ball or putting the shot. Having left the hand, the ball or the shot will travel with more speed because of the follow through. Follow through requires a greater range of motion that allows greater velocity through the power phase. Parry O'Brien took the world record in the shot put from 54 feet to over 64 feet by increasing the range of motion he used in performing the event. He simply transferred momentum from one leg to the other with a crossover move after the shot had left the hand; this allowed him to double the speed through the power phase and to increase the world record by over 10 feet in a relatively short time.

The key element in fast swimming is the distance a swimmer travels through the water per stroke. Only with a proper press and push does a swimmer get maximum distance per stroke. This is what is meant by efficiency of stroke or efficiency of motion. When a swimmer feels water and maintains this feel all the way through the push, an S-pull, the desired maneuver during the power phase of the freestyle stroke, will occur. Too many times I have seen coaches attempt to teach an S-pull by explaining what it should look like rather than how it should feel and what makes it happen. Don't waste time trying to teach something that is best accomplished by teaching something else. Teach the fundamentals and good things will result!

> The press and push phases do not produce power. The power phase is the distance the hand travels between the press and push phases. Shorten either of the two fundamentals, and you shorten the power phase. The press sets up the power phase, while the push allows and accounts for the hand speed through the power phase.

Recovery

This is the movement of the hand and arm from the back-end position of the freestyle stroke to the entry position. At the end of the push phase, just as the hand breaks the surface of the water, the arm is lifted from the water, led by the elbow. The elbow is always above the hand and arm through this phase.

A high elbow is a fundamental for two major reasons. First, lifting the arm and hand with the elbow uses a completely different set of muscles than those used to power the hand and arm through the water. This allows the muscles needed in the power phase to relax and recover. Second, the high elbow position helps keep body part movements inside the flow line. Physical law states that any action must be countered by an equal and opposite action. Therefore, any swing of the arm must be countered by an equal swing of the legs in an opposite direction. Keeping the hand directly below the elbow minimizes arm swing and therefore minimizes leg swing.

Catch Up

This is the coordination of both hands at the front end of the freestyle stroke. As one hand passes through the press phase and before it gets halfway into the power phase, the opposite hand must begin its entry and the press phase of the stroke. This must be balanced on each side. That means the catch up (hands getting closer together, not actually catching up) must be the same on both sides.

Freestyle is the most efficient stroke because it allows swimmers to overcome dead or still spots with this catch-up technique. Thus the freestyle stroke generates constant power. If the stroke is swum properly, the result is a constant momentum that the other strokes can't duplicate. All other strokes have breaks in power that result in loss of momentum in the water that then must be overcome in each power phase of that stroke. For this reason, the freestyle stroke is the fastest stroke swum on top of the water at any distance. The speed and efficiency differential increases the farther one swims.

Roll

This is the movement of the entire body through the water from shoulder to shoulder in the freestyle stroke. As a hand enters the water, the swimmer rolls onto that shoulder, then flows through the water, going from one shoulder to the other depending on which hand is entering the water. The swimmer rolls through the water as if he or she were on a barbecue spit, keeping a straight body line or flow line that can't be bent. No "hula dancing" allowed.

The body's naturally streamlined position in the water is on the side. When swimmers roll through the water they are going from streamlined position to streamlined position. They can't stay only in one streamlined position because of the way the arms are attached to the body. When the roll is tied to high elbow recovery, the body flows rather than plows through the water. The recovery and roll, when properly and repeatedly performed, result in all body parts staying within the body's flow line, making for a most efficient stroke.

This fifth fundamental is natural on one side for all swimmers. All swimmers roll onto the shoulder away from the side they breathe on. The key is to see that they roll as well back onto the shoulder they take the breath on.

Preseason Freestyle Drills

KICKING

Action

The swimmer should push off the wall in a prone glide position and use a six-beat flutter kick. As air is required, he or she should take one arm pull and breathe to the side of that arm. The swimmer should take as many one-arm strokes as required, based on the need for air, while maintaining a six-beat kick.

Instruction

- Press the fingertips down, back, and out, feeling for resistance in the water. The hand stays still while the body moves. The kick should be maintained during the arm stroke.
- Push the hand through the back end, accelerating the hand to the surface of the water.
- Recover the hand and arm by lifting at the elbow. Keep the hand below the elbow and as close to the body as possible.
- Enter the water at the front end, fingertips first, by placing fingers on the wrist of the nonmoving arm. As the fingers touch the wrist of the other hand, slide that hand on top of the stationary hand.

Goal

Repeat this drill until perfect. The swimmer must keep the body in a straight line.

SLIDE CRAWL

Action

The action of this drill is the same as that of the kicking drill except that the swimmer first uses one arm, then the other, and repeats the movements over and over again.

Instruction

- Press, push, recovery, and catch up on each side, starting the next stroke as soon as the proceeding arm finishes a stroke.
- Only breathe to one side and maintain a steady kick.

Goal

Teach this drill only after the kicking drill has been perfected. This is intermediary freestyle that keeps swimmers in a straight line position, gives a six-beat kick, teaches proper breathing technique, and stresses four of the five fundamentals—but it breaks the roll fundamental. When they actually catch up, they are flat in the water. For this reason, this drill is introduced and broken the same day by the actual freestyle stroke drill.

FREESTYLE DRILL

Action

The swimmer should do the slide crawl but not actually catch up. He or she should bring the hands about six inches from one another but not let them touch.

Instruction

Allow the body to roll through the water from shoulder to shoulder while keeping the body in a straight line (as if on a barbecue spit). The body stays in line while rolling from side to side.

Goal

This drill doesn't teach a skill; it helps swimmers to understand what they are doing by feeling what is happening. This is best accomplished by having swimmers tell you what they are doing rather than you telling them. Only when they come to know what is taking place can they make the changes that come naturally to the gifted.

Early Season

For senior-level swimmers, the early season phases of the annual plan mark the start of two-a-day workouts. This is the time to give swimmers the required base using the proper technique they drilled in preseason that the inseason and taper depend on. I don't ease into this phase, I jump into it for a couple of reasons. First, most other programs have already been going full bore in the preseason while I was being a stroke coach. Second, I just love the toughening effect that comes with going from doing nothing to doing maximum yardage in a day. It makes swimmers who do it properly psychologically able to handle the real hard work that is to come. This is boot camp, plain and simple. As in boot camp, the "commanding officer" can make points and fit young people into the desired mold during this period.

In reality, this is the second easiest period in the training process because it's quantity work, not quality swimming, especially the first two weeks. In two weeks, your swimmers will adjust to the increase in training and will once again live normal lives and be normal people.

Stroke technique is stressed throughout this phase, as it will be for the entire year. The pace clock is set up and operating, the sets are planned and explained, and the swimmers are ready. The job of the coach on the deck now becomes that of not merely being a timer but a motivator. What better way to motivate than to look like you know what you are doing by talking stroke. Never stop sets to do stroke work. Instead, correct stroke technique in sound bytes during the sets. This will help keep your swimmers focused on the set at hand while ensuring proper stroke mechanics. If you aren't using some of your deck time doing this, then in reality you are nothing but a traffic cop.

What about injuries due to high volume? I don't accept quantity as the culprit! Rather, it's my belief that injuries come from poor technique, not repetition (unless it is repetition of poor technique, of course!). Sore muscles, muscle cramps, and so forth don't really hurt anybody. In fact they give swimmers something to complain about. Complaining, as far as I'm concerned, is just a form of bragging, and coaching wouldn't be any fun if I couldn't cause a little of it. If you don't want to lose swimmers to injury, see that they train the perfect stroke.

My practices are all based on a workout format that consists of a warm-up, minor sets, a major set, and a warm-down. The warm-up is the swim used to get your swimmer's muscles warm and ready to work out. I recommend that the warm-up last 10 minutes, no more, no less. Minor sets are everything that isn't the warm-down, the warm-up, or the major set; they include all kicking and pulling sets. The major set is the main thing to be emphasized that day. It's always a swimming set and could be called it a test set. Once it's done, both the coach and swimmer have an indication of where they are in conditioning and how far they have to go. The warm-down is an easy swim to loosen the shoulders before a swim or the last swim before going to the shower. The following example sets (see tables 18.1 and 18.2) show weekday sets for short course (yards). Examples are for two, two-hour practices.

TABLE 18.1

Weekday Morning Workout

Type	Set	Cumulative yardage	Purpose	Cumulative time (min.)
Swim	800	800	Warm-up	10
Kick	20 × 50 at :50	1,800	Minor set	25
Pull	400 lung buster	2,200	Minor set	31
Pull	8 × 400 at 5:00	5,400	Minor set	68
Pull	400 lung buster	5,800	Minor set	74
Swim	200 to loosen up	6,000	Warm-down	77
Swim	20 × 75 at 1:00	7,500	Minor set	115
Swim	500 to loosen up	8,000	Warm-down	120

TABLE 18.2

Weekday Evening Workout

Type	Set	Cumulative yardage	Purpose	Cumulative time (min.)
Swim	800	800	Warm-up	10
Kick	5 × 200 at 3:15	1,800	Minor set	27
Swim	200 loosen up	2,000	Warm-down	30
Swim	32 × 100 8 at 1:20 form 8 at 1:15 form and fast 8 at 1:10 faster 8 at 1:05 fastest	5,200	Major set	70
Pull	400 lung buster	5,600	Minor set	76
Pull	8 × 200 at 2:30	7,200	Minor set	92
Pull	400 lung buster	7,600	Minor set	98
Swim	100 loosen up	7,700	Warm-down	101
Swim	4 × 200 IM at 3:00	8,500	Minor set	116
Swim	200 loosen up	8,700	Warm-down	120

These examples show 16,700 yards for the day. During early season, regardless of total yardage, the percentages are pretty close to those illustrated here:

Kicking—15 percent

Pulling—45 percent

Swimming—40 percent

The major set or focus of this day's practices is the 32 × 100 set in the afternoon. I want the swimmers to do more than survive the set. I want them to control it, to finish it strong, and by the end, to experience race pain. Each time they take five seconds of rest, they are required to swim faster. This is the goal for the day.

I look at both practices in a day as one workout. Thus, the morning session consists only of the warm-up, minor sets, and the warm-down. The purpose of the morning workout in my program is to get stronger in the water. The emphasis on pulling is my version of weight training.

The morning workout has the same first 1,800 yards or meters each day: an 800 swim or 10 minutes, whichever comes first, followed by 20 × 50 repeats kicking with a board on a set interval. I never change the warm-up. If this bores swimmers, I tell them to count the yardage backward. If they procrastinate a full 10 minutes before they get in the water, that becomes their problem—because everything else will be on a watch, and the group changes to other sets in less than a minute. I see workout starting times like those on a train schedule. Once the train starts to pull away from the station, you either catch up to it or wait for the next train. If the swimmers have had a great week up to that point, I might on Thursday or Friday morning, break the kicking set in two, letting them kick a 500 and then 10 × 50 on the set interval.

Pulling series always start and end with a lung buster—one breath per stroke for the first fourth of total distance (usually a 400), one breath per two strokes for the second fourth, one breath per three strokes for the third fourth, and one breath per four strokes for the last fourth. This is not to drill breath control per se but rather to ease the body in and out of the hard pulling efforts. Breath holding in this drill helps swimmers concentrate on proper technique and actually eases the shoulders into and out of the middle drills. Early season means 4,000 yards or more of pulling each morning workout. The following are examples of pulling sets done by the advanced swimmers in our program:

32 × 100: 8 on 1:20 fast; 8 on 1:15 faster; 8 on 1:10 faster; 8 on 1:05 fastest

4 × 800 on 10:00; 9:30; 9:00

8 × 400 on 4:40

8 × 400: 2 on 5:00; 2 on 4:50; 2 on 4:40, 2 on 4:30

12 × 200 on 2:30; 4 fast, 4 faster, 4 fastest

2 × 1,650 on 19:00; second faster than first

The set is limited only by one's imagination. What works for me is to keep it simple and to do basic sets over and over again. For distance freestyle training, all pulling is freestyle. Every set has instructions that go with it. Only during the warm-up, the loosening-up swims, and the warm-down do we simply go up and down the pool. Every other movement during workout is geared toward accomplishing particular objectives and is so described in the instructions that are given at the start of the set.

If you are like most coaches, two-hour morning workouts during the school year just don't happen. We have 90 minutes to work with in my program, and I hold to the routine just described through the pulling drills. The swimmers are at 5,800 to 6,000 yards in an hour and fifteen minutes. We then have them loosen up with a 100 swim of something hard, let them warm down, and send them to school. Given a short period, I do treadmills, descending 50s, 75s, underwaters, locomotives, and so forth. The following are sets I use with my present team when there are 10 to 15 minutes remaining in practice:

16 × 50: 4 on 45 fast; 4 on 40 faster; 4 on 35 faster; 4 on 30 fastest

10 × 75 on minute: each done form, build, hard

800 every other length IM order—IM hard

Locomotive up to four, repeat four, and back down (1 form, 1 fast; 2 form, 2 fast; etc., up to 4 form, 4 fast [twice], before going back down the ladder to 1 form, 1 fast)

800 treadmill: 200 no pain; 200 little pain; 200 lot of pain; 200 unbearable pain

If there are 30 or more minutes remaining after the pulling sets, I have the swimmers do more with some variety as to stroke. Here are some favorite sets:

2 × 800 IM on 12:00: first straight, second broken at 75s by 10 seconds

Locomotive up to six, repeat six, and back down (1 form, 1 fast, 2 form, 2 fast, etc.)

1,650 leap-frog: swimmer at back of lane moves to front of line each length

800 treadmill; 100 loosen up; 400 treadmill; 100 loosen up; 200 treadmill; 100 loosen up; 100 treadmill

Our swimmers do 1,000 yards or meters of kicking each workout. I believe that if the legs are in shape, the body is in shape. Instead of calling a specific warm-down set, you could use the last few 75s in the morning workout to accomplish the same goal. When I coached college swimming, we always wanted to beat USC, so would call the last four 75s "Trojan 75s," meaning "real slow." This was an effective way to warm swimmers down and let them have a laugh while keeping them focused on beating an opponent.

The evening workout starts with the same basic first 2,000 each day, the warm-up followed by a kicking set of 100s or 200s. I never have swimmers kick the same set two evenings in a row. The 10 × 100s are a straight set, meaning that the first repeat is done at a fast pace but is the slowest of the set, the middle eight will be faster than the first one but will all be the same speed, while the last one is the fastest. The 200s are a descending set, meaning each repeat gets faster, with the last one all out. In fact, the last repeat of any set we do is always the fastest. I do this to reinforce the fact that I expect my swimmers to get the best results from our time in the water and to train using all of their energy sources.

We do a loosen-up 200 after the kicking series to prepare for the major set for the day. It is always done at this point, and during the early season it is a 3,000 to 4,000 series. During the early season we alternate: a day of freestyle and then a day of individual medley repeats. I have found that alternating freestyle with IM training days serves as a great early total-body conditioner. The following are some of my basic sets:

Freestyle Sets

32 × 100: 8 on 1:20 fast; 8 on 1:15 faster; 8 on 1:10 faster; 8 on 1:05 fastest

4 × 1,000; 11:00; 10:30; 10:00

8 × 400 on 4:45

8 × 400: 2 on 5:00; 2 on 4:45; 2 on 4:30; 2 on 4:15

16 × 200 on 2:15

15 × 200: 5 on 2:30; 5 on 2:20; 5 on 2:10

Individual Medley Sets

4 × 800 IM at 12:00: first straight; second broken 10 seconds at 200, third broken 10 seconds at 100; fourth broken 10 seconds at 75)

8 × 400 IM at 5:30

8 × (4 × 100 at 1:20)

- 50 fly/50 back
- 50 back/50 breast
- 50 breast/50 free
- 50 free/50 fly

16 × 200 IM at 2:45: 8 reverse order descending; 8 normal order descending

Each set must have a goal that is explained to the swimmer, and the set must be executed as planned. What a coach calls should make the swimmer better; therefore, each workout must be designed to be a successful experience for the swimmer. Learn what works and what doesn't for each person. Only through careful planning and monitoring will the workouts achieve what they should achieve.

TABLE 18.3

Saturday Workout

Type	Set	Cumulative yardage	Purpose	Cumulative time (min.)
Swim	800	800	Warm-up	10
Kick	500	1,300	Minor set	18
Kick	20 × 50 at :45	2,300	Minor set	33
Swim	200	2,500	Loosen-up	36
Swim	4,800 set	7,300	Major set	102
Pull	400 lung buster	7,700	Minor set	108
Pull	2,400 set	10,100	Minor set	130
Pull	400 lung buster	10,500	Minor set	136
Swim	100	10,600	Loosen-up	140
Swim	10 × 75 at 1:00	11,350	Minor set	150
Swim	300	11,650	Warm-down	160

The intervals mentioned here are for my better swimmers. I use slower sets or cut yardage for my weaker swimmers. Whatever I call must work, and I do everything in my power to make it work. The intervals should really control the quality of effort of early season workouts. The purpose of this phase of training is to build the base fitness that is necessary to do more power-based work in the next phase.

The Saturday workout is the eleventh and last workout offered each week. It's a combination of the two-a-day workout concepts into one workout. The minor sets are tied to the one major set, as seen in the example in table 18.3.

Two of my favorite sets for a Saturday morning during early season are these:

12 × 400 freestyle
- 3 at 5:00 fast; 1:00 rest
- 3 at 5:00 faster; 1:00 rest
- 3 at 5:00 faster; 1:00 rest
- 3 at 5:00 fastest; 1:00 rest

6 × 800 IM set

800 consists of

- 2 × 50 fly at :45; 1 × 100 free at 1:15
- 2 × 50 back at :45; 1 × 100 free at 1:15
- 2 × 50 breast at :50; 1 × 100 free at 1:15
- 2 × 50 free at :40; 1 × 100 free at 1:15

In my opinion, you shortchange everyone in your program if you don't aim high enough. The goal of any program should be to allow all the people in it to reach their full potential. This cannot be accomplished if the program is aimed at the lowest or average performer; therefore, work output should be based on the needs and abilities of the best swimmers. You will be surprised at how fast all the swimmers learn to work at this level.

Inseason

The transition from early season to inseason training is a gradual one that takes into account four significant changes:

1. Emphasis shifts to freestyle in the major set.
2. Quality is determined by effort, not interval.
3. A decrease occurs in the pulling percentage of the total workout.
4. An increase occurs in the swimming percentage.

The basic yardage change from our early season to inseason is a decrease of only 7,200 yards a week, or less than 10 percent (see table 18.4). However, the change in percentage of pulling in favor of swimming affects the workload. No matter how hard swimmers work the pulling and kicking series, they can't duplicate the amount of work involved in the swimming series. Swimming uses the whole body; pulling and kicking do not.

This increase in the swimming percentage alone results in an increased workload. Now add the fact that swimmers are controlling speed in the workout by effort, not merely interval, and it is obvious that the increase in actual work output is dramatic. The key ingredient in determining actual work output is speed. Distance swum in a practice is only a small factor in how much work is actually done, whereas even a small increase in the speed at which those yards are swum results in a measurable increase in actual work output. Thus, the inseason is the period of the training program in which we continuously attempt to increase speed in workouts. This ever faster swimming each week increases work output with no increase, or sometimes even a decrease, in yardage.

TABLE 18.4

Weekly Yardage and Workout Percentages

Day	Early season	Season
Monday	16,000	16,000
Tuesday	16,000	16,000
Wednesday	16,000	16,000
Thursday	16,000	14,400
Friday	16,000	12,400
Saturday	12,000	10,000
Sunday	Off	Off
Warm-up and cool-down	2,400 or 15.0%	2,400 or 15.0%
Kicking	2,000 or 12.5%	2,000 or 12.5%
Pulling	7,200 or 45.0%	5,200 or 32.5%
Swimming	4,400 or 27.5%	6,400 or 40.0%

The principle of specificity requires the distance freestyler to train as close as possible to the actual speed, distance, and time required in the race. To accomplish this, I have standardized the week over this training period. I have three major sets for the first three days of the week. On the fourth day, I choose one of two major sets. I select the same set every fifth day. On the sixth day, I select a set that is specific to a swimmer's race. And on the seventh day I have the swimmer rest unless, of course, we are at a meet.

The key to an effective inseason training phase is doing the preseason and early season phases correctly. If swimmers are going to swim fast in this phase, then they must be using great technique and must have built the necessary conditioning base to be fit enough to do the work. Work output should continue to increase during this phase because each week is designed to increase the ability to swim fast. Everything is adjustable in this program; details can and should be based on what is happening each day in the pool. Time intervals, individual goal standards for each set for each swimmer, the balance between fast and form swimming, and distance totals can be adjusted by the coach as necessary to generate the desired results (see tables 18.5 and 18.6).

Inseason Morning Workouts
Monday through Saturday

Type	Set	Cumulative yardage	Purpose	Cumulative time (min.)
Swim	800	800	Warm-up	10
Kick	20 × 50 at :45	1,800	Minor set	25
Pull	400 lung buster	2,200	Minor set	31
Pull	2,400 set	4,600	Minor set	61
Pull	400 lung buster	5,000	Minor set	67
Swim	100	5,100	Loosen-up	70
Swim	1,000/1,500 sets	6,600	Minor set	88
Swim	100	6,700	Warm-down	90

Inseason Evening Workouts
Monday through Friday*

Type	Set	Cumulative yardage	Purpose	Cumulative time (min.)
Swim	800	800	Warm-up	10
Kick	10 × 100 at 1:40 or 5 × 200 at 3:15	1,800	Minor set	27
Swim	200	2,000	Loosen-up	30
Swim	2,000 to 3,000 set	5,000	Major set	63
Pull	400 lung buster	5,400	Minor set	69
Pull	1,200 set	6,600	Minor set	85
Pull	400 lung buster	7,000	Minor set	91
Swim	100 1,000/2,000 set	7,100 8,100	Loosen-up Minor set	94 116
Swim	200	8,300	Warm-down	120

*Thursday is modified and Friday is over after the major set.

Major Sets—Monday through Wednesday

20 × 100: 5 at 1:15 fast; 5 at 1:10 faster; 5 at 1:05 faster; 5 at 1:00 fastest

3 × 1,000 at 11:00, descending

10 × 200 at 2:15, straight set

Major Sets—Thursday

20 × 100, every other one all out: 4 at 1:15; 4 at 1:30; 4 at 1:15; 4 at 1:30; 4 at 1:15

5 × 200 at 3:00, descending

Pulling set—10 × 100 at 1:30, descending; then go home!

Major Sets—Friday

5 × 400 at 5:00, descending

Inseason Evening Workout—Saturday

Don't ask for it unless it will work! Start with a swim, pull, kick warm-up for 15 to 25 minutes. The swimmer tells the coach when he or she is ready, as in a swim meet warm-up, then swims 1,200 to 4,800 for a major set. Here are some sets I've used:

6 × 200 descending, 2:30; 2:20; 2:10; 2:00; 1:50

3 × 400, intervals of 4:00 and 3:45; last one is fastest

3,300 for time

2,000 for time

2 × 1,650 on 16:30; second one faster than first

Our inseason plan rotates the first three days so that no week cycle can be repeated for at least four weeks. This gives us a four-week period before we begin to look for real improvement. Following a day off on Sunday, Mondays are days when we usually have outstanding workouts. Tuesdays, following a day of hard work, aren't quite as good. On Wednesdays tiredness is showing, and we stress to swimmers that the mind must take over the body. I still expect a great workout, but I do understand that time isn't as important as effort. This understanding, I believe, is the start and the major element of psychological training.

The Thursday workout is more sprint than distance work. Sprint work uses a different physiological system that stresses the swimmer in a different way, thereby allowing recovery of the systems trained earlier in the week. The workout is usually quite fast and provides a very good gauge to measure how tired the swimmer actually is. Since some recovery from the first three days of the week's work has taken place, and since the swimmers know that they get the rest of the day off after the major set, the Friday workout is usually great from the first week, and gets better all through the season. If any of the workouts in a given week are terrible, it indicates just how tired the swimmer is. Adjust the minor sets to allow for recovery as needed.

The Saturday set is determined by all that has happened during the week. It's a chance to make adjustments, to reach agreement with the swimmer on what is going to be done, and then to see that it happens just as planned. This workout sets up the next week, builds trust between swimmer and coach, and establishes goals as something that must be done, not merely dreamt about. If this isn't what psychology is all about, then I'm in deep trouble. The way to reach goals is by setting everything up so that success is the result. This involves both the body and the mind. The mind is the key to swimming, just as it's the key to life. The mind and body can't be separated at any time in anything we are doing. All training is psychological!

The key for the distance swimmer is to get as much short rest work at race pace as possible. The intervals that are shown in the examples are those I use for my best swimmers. For those who need more rest, I adjust the interval or the distance, but only when necessary. Given a little time, some of those average swimmers won't stay average. They just need someone to help them see the beauty of extension of self.

My best swimmers kick 50s on 45-second intervals, holding 39 seconds or better. Most couldn't do that at first, so we started them at 50-second intervals. When they consistently were sub 40 seconds for the set, we changed the interval. Meanwhile they were going 900 yards while others, on the fastest interval, were kicking 1,000 yards.

To help in the development of champions, the coach must call sets that do what they are designed to do. The standard set keeps me and my swimmers informed of where we are and how much farther we have to go. The key is in setting up each day's workout to get maximum effort, understanding what maximum performance is on each day for each person, and building a relationship based on mutual trust.

My favorite set is the 20 descending 100s set, which goes from a 1:15 to a 1:00 interval. This set gives the swimmer and coach a lot of information. Table 18.7 shows the progression I use to get the results I want from the set.

---TABLE 18.7---

Intervals for Descending 100s Set

First set	Goal		Second set	Goal1	Goal2		
5 at 1:30	1:05		5 at 1:25	1:05	1:04		
5 at 1:25	1:04		5 at 1:20	1:04	1:03		
5 at 1:20	1:03		5 at 1:15	1:03	1:02		
5 at 1:15	1:02		5 at 1:10	1:02	1:01		
Third set	**Goal 1**	**Goal 2**	**Goal 3**	**Goal 4**	**Goal 5**	**Goal 6**	
5 at 1:20	1:04	1:03	1:02	1:01	1:00	:59	
5 at 1:15	1:03	1:02	1:01	1:00	:59	:58	
5 at 1:10	1:02	1:01	1:00	:59	:58	:57	
5 at 1:05	1:01	1:00	:59	:58	:57	:56	
Fourth set	**Goal 1**	**Goal 2**	**Goal 3**	**Goal 4**	**Goal 5**	**Goal 6**	**Goal 7**
5 at 1:15	:59	:58	:57	:56	:55	:54	:53
5 at 1:10	:58	:57	:56	:55	:54	:53	:52
5 at 1:05	:57	:56	:55	:54	:53	:52	:51
5 at 1:00	:56	:55	:54	:53	:52	:51	:50

This progression will take some time, maybe years, to complete but the fourth level with the last five on a minute (in yards) is the set the swimmer and coach should be working toward. The third level would be an ideal set to do in a metric pool. First, look for consistency of performance at a level; then either change the level or the time goals in the set. If the swimmer can do either of the last two sets (yards or meters) on a consistent basis, then he or she is about to break the American record for the 500 yards or the world record for 400 meters!

The progression of a swimmer to a world-class athlete can be a planned event. Great swims don't happen by accident but rather through the coordinated effort of a coach and a swimmer. There is a dream you sell to a young person, and a plan of operation for making the dream become something more than a dream. In the majority of cases, with proper guidance, a young person who has guts, determination, and a tough mentality makes his or her reality. Does your program offer each of your swimmers this opportunity?

Every coach has had, seen, or heard of great workout swimmers who don't live up to their workouts on meet day. A coach must set up a program that accounts for the physiological as well as the psychological needs of the swimmer. I believe that the consistency that the descending 100s set demands provides both kinds of training at the same time. If over and over again, a swimmer successfully performs something in practice on a consistent basis that he or she can't explain away, then he or she will eventually end up being a solid meet swimmer.

Taper

Preseason training consisted of technical corrections and stroke adjustments. In reality, very little work output was required but a huge brain output was called for. Early season continued to stress technique but added a huge increase in work output. It was a time of quantity swimming to build a base. The inseason continued to stress technique and added an ever increasing work output as swimmers moved from quantity work to quality work. Ever increasing speed meant an ever increasing output of work. Following these phases, at least twice a year the swimmer and the coach are ready to "let it happen" in a swim meet they've planned for.

The taper, for the distance freestyler, is basically a two-week period of race rehearsal and rest. The ever increasing output from the preseason through the early season and the inseason will now be allowed to be pay off in race results. During a properly planned taper, the swimmer finally gets rid of that tired or heavy feeling; this results in considerable improvement in performance.

I have swimmers treat each workout in this phase as a swim meet. They do a meet warm-up (kick, pull, and swim). The coaches watch just as at a meet. I time the swimmers in something (rehearsal); they tell me how much and what they have done; then I tell them what I want them to do before they get out of the water. I continue two-a-days during the taper. After all, meets have two sessions, and swimmers should plan on swimming twice a day at the meet. We start by cutting the yardage at least in half, then proceed to bring it down to almost nothing. An important part of loading is "feel"! Do sets that will work toward a swimmer getting a feel for the water and for racing.

As in the early season and the inseason, I treat the two-a-day workouts as one workout with one major set. The major set for the first eight days is 3 × 100 descending with 10 seconds rest one day and 8 × 100 at their own distance race pace with 10 seconds rest on the alternate day. The morning workout times are either 3 × 75 on 1:00 or 50s on 45 seconds, depending on whether the meet is meters or yards. After these first eight days, we begin to prepare more specifically for the first race. At this stage we cut the work down to include only an actual meet warm-up.

Much more than merely timing the swimmer is accomplished at the taper stage. The times are important but so are the swimmer's mental state, stroke rates, and stroke techniques. It is also important to ensure that what is happening is a rehearsal and not work. The purpose of the taper is to allow the body to experience total recovery so that all the training that has been done will result in a great performance. Don't "just one more" the taper to death. If you have done what you planned to do and things still aren't quite looking exactly the way you want them to, step back and stop. Let rest take over. "Just one more" rarely stops at one, and additional practice undermines the whole concept of the taper.

Rehearsing means swimming repeats at race speeds and race efforts. Reaching this ultimate speed takes time, rest, and technique work. I use stroke rate and stroke count as tools during this phase. During the inseason, with heavy work outputs, the turnover or stroke rate (number of strokes taken per second) tends to be slower than it is when the swimmer is rested. If the swimmer uses proper, efficient stroke technique the entire year, he or she will usually have a set stroke count (number of strokes taken per length) for racing. The way to increase racing speed is to maintain distance per stroke while speeding up stroke rate.

Say, for example, that a swimmer takes 16 strokes per length at a stroke rate of 7.5 seconds for five strokes. During the taper he or she maintains 16 strokes per length but over two weeks brings the rate to 6.5 seconds per five strokes. The swimmer's time for the length must have dropped by 1.6 seconds.

In my program the taper is the time to rehearse race speed, to set stroke rates that will result in this speed, and to make sure the swimmer understands the concept. At the end of one of the 100 repeats, my swimmer may be given the following information: 53.1, 27.2, 6.5, 6.5, 6.5, 6.5. What this means is that the time for the 100 was 53.1 seconds, the middle 50 was 27.2 (which translates to a 54.4 100, feet to feet), and the stroke rates were 6.5 seconds for a five-stroke cycle for each length. That's a lot of information. The athlete now knows what pace he or she is holding, and the stroke rate reflects just how hard it is.

Stroke rates must be based on distance per stroke. Each swimmer has his or her own most efficient rate. It takes time to get the stroke rates tied to a particular distance per stroke. I've never seen it done in less than 10 days, because the key to it is the total muscle recovery that comes from rest. When stroke rates are brought down to the desired goal too quickly, a simple full-length stroke count will reveal that the swimmer has added a stroke or two.

Two hundred plus yards in the morning along with either 300 or 800 yards in the evening over the first 8 to 20 days of the taper can't be considered work. For swimmers who have been going 2,000 to 3,000 yards a day at race speed during the inseason, this reduced level at race pace is indeed rehearsal (see table 18.8).

TABLE 18.8

Taper Sets

AM Level	3 × 75 at 1:00 (form, build, hard) Form	Build	Hard	Time
1	:15	:14	:13	:42
2	:14	:13	:12	:39
3	:13	:12	:11	:36

Once swimmer is consistent at one level, move him or her to the next.

PM Level	3 × 100 with :10 rest, descending Rep 1	Rep 2	Rep 3
1	:59	:58	:57
2	:58	:57	:56
3	:55	:54	:53
4	:54	:53	:52
5	:53	:52	:51
6	:52	:51	:50
7	:51	:50	:49

Set goal to start at; once completed, note which set is most appropriate for the swimmer.

PM Level	8 × 100 with :10 rest, pace work Reps 1-7	Rep 8
1	:59	:58
2	:58	:57
3	:57	:56
4	:56	:55
5	:55	:54
6	:54	:53
7	:53	:52
8	:52	:51
9	:51	:50

Set goal to start at and then go up a level each day. The last repeat is always the fastest repeat, but still pace work.

The actual swim meet's timed pace work for the distance races is as follows:

400/500	strong 100
800/1000	3 × 100 with 10 seconds rest—race pace
1500/1650	5 × 100 with 10 seconds rest—race pace

While the psychological aspects that control a person's training should be tied to the program design in every phase of your overall plan, consideration of psychological factors is of the utmost importance during the taper. If a taper depended only on the work on which it should be based, then it would always be effective for those who had done the work and would always result in failure for those who hadn't done the work. A person's brain can do amazing things, producing both positive and negative results that shouldn't be possible in a given race according to workout performance.

Nothing in the world is 100 percent reliable, works perfectly all the time, or behaves exactly as drawn up on paper. Murphy's law, *If it can go wrong, it will go wrong,* seems to have been stated by someone who understood what coaches face during the taper. The pace work times planned never happen in the taper exactly the way they were laid out on paper. The first week is usually tough, with both good and bad performances seen in each workout. This is when coaches earn their money. If the swimmers have done the work as you designed it, or even if they didn't and they stayed in the program, it is the coach's responsibility to carry them to a positive experience on race day.

This is the time when the coach shows no doubt and no negative emotion; he or she is strong each and every day. Every time swimmers look up for support, they hear the truth as you see it. If you don't believe it's going to happen, then you are doing something wrong. Even if some swimmers only did parts of the program, they can swim fast. It's better if they have done the work, a point you should emphasize during the other phases of the program or after the big meet but *not* during the taper. During the taper, every swimmer should hear comments like: "You're fine, right where I expected you to be at this stage!" "Great set!" "Stroke looks great; how's it feel?" "Times will come! I expected this!" "We're about four days out; we're right were we want to be!" You must also believe in your program, give rest the chance to work, and stick to the plan. No matter how bad things look early, the taper will work if the coach stays cool, strong, and positive. The swimmers, at this point in time, not only want it to work, they will make it work.

During the taper, all coaches have days when things just don't look right and the swimmers start to show fear. Your job is to never, and I mean never, let them see your doubt or fear. Go around the corner and cry if you must but show confidence in front of the swimmers, the parents, and the team. All too many times I wanted to scream at a swimmer, "What the hell is going on?" But I was smart enough to keep a bright face and to let my frustration out only after the garage door came down behind my car at home. Because I have always shown confidence in myself, the program, and my swimmers during the taper, my swimmers have picked up this confidence—and the result has been many great performances. By this time the swimmers want to believe. Give them someone to believe in—you!

The Big Picture

Look at the program as a whole. See the blending of the phases one into another. Look at the sets as indicators. Sets can be used to promote the physiological truths that the program is based on and as opportunities to build swimmers psychologically. A repetition set system helps swimmers to understand themselves by letting them know where they are rather than having to guess. See the program for what it is. It has accomplished and will accomplish its goal: to produce champions, not merely gold-medal performers.

I don't need or want swimmers who expect to be entertained. I need people who want to be the best—not only the best in the world but the very best that they can be. I need people who take responsibility for their actions, who understand that it's up to them to get the job done, and who can accept defeat with pride if they know that they have done everything possible and morally acceptable to win. I need people who come out of a defeat or a win with the same attitude and the same question: "What do I need to do to get better?" I need people who do more than talk and dream. I need people who do the work and walk the talk that makes them winners no matter how they place.

My program puts the responsibility on the participants. It is designed to let the swimmers measure themselves against themselves, first and always. It demands the truth from them about their own desires, dreams, goals, and accomplishments. Since they also measure themselves against the best in the world, my swimmers know where they stand and how far they have to go. We're not scared of the best; in fact we want to race against the best. If we can't beat the best the first time, then we want to at least make them think about us, perhaps scare them a little or, better yet, make them hurt so they'll know they were in a race. We want the best to know that there will be a next time and that between now and then we will be working to become the best ourselves.

Is my program boring? No way! It's challenging. It puts responsibility where it belongs. It's simple, truthful, and easy to understand. It's designed for the people in it. Those who have come through it are proud of the program and of themselves. To this day, they can tell you how good they were with pride, no matter what their place in American or world swimming. They know who they are and just how much they have accomplished and learned through their full participation in the program. They tested and measured themselves on a daily basis, and they have come to understand the importance of the process and how it has defined them. They are individuals who take responsibility for their own lives, for both the successes and failures, and who always strive to be the best they can be. Such individuals can be beaten but never defeated.

My program teaches the beauty of work and effort. It teaches that the only discipline that counts comes from within the self. It teaches that pain is a necessary ingredient in life, one that can be seen as an opportunity for accomplishment and fulfillment. What makes me proudest of what I'm sharing with you is that this is a program that has produced a whole lot of great people and a few great swimmers. I would have it no other way.

Summary

- A program is a plan of action to realize specific goals.
- The power element is more important than the threshold element in training.
- Every swim training program should be based on an annual plan.
- The progression of a swimmer to a world-class performer can be a planned event.
- Preseason training stresses stroke technique.
- Early season provides the quantity base necessary for later success.
- The transition from early season to inseason training is gradual.
- Inseason training is characterized by emphasis on freestyle in the major set (specificity), by quality being determined in terms of effort, and by an increase in the swimming percentage over pulling.
- The key for the distance swimmer is to get as much short-rest work at race pace as possible.
- The taper is basically a two-week period of rehearsal—repeats of speed that will be used in the race—and rest.
- The taper will work if the coach stays cool, strong, and positive.

CHAPTER NINETEEN

Backstroke and Butterfly Sprint Training

Eddie Reese

Not everyone can be a sprinter. Not everyone wants to be a sprinter (at least that's what I tell my team). There are some basic keys to sprinting that must be drilled consistently and often in practice: a solid aerobic basis of conditioning, proper stroke technique (including starts and turns), and increasing strength. In addition, butterfly and backstroke sprinters also need to perfect their underwater dolphin kick and have a sound seasonal and career training plan.

Build an Endurance Foundation

There is no easy way determine early who is a sprinter and who isn't. With that in mind, all swimmers should learn and hone their technique in all strokes and should train their overall fitness properly through aerobic and anaerobic conditioning. This means that a coach may have to give up fast, short swimming on the part of younger swimmers now in order to protect their long-term potential.

For these reasons, I recommend that all younger swimmers—13 and under—train their endurance as if they were training for a future in distance swimming. That doesn't mean they have to swim only distance freestyle. Rather, that means that if there is one, one-hour workout per day, then three out of five workouts should focus on longer, easier swimming, kicking, or pulling in all strokes, while the other two workouts can be faster and can include IM sets, relay training, or kicking.

Tom Jager, who held the world record for the 50-meter freestyle and who is still the American record holder for the 50-yard free, made his first junior national qualifying cut in the mile swim. At one time in his career he was also the American record holder in the 100 backstroke, and he was a very fast butterflyer. He swam a 21.4 split in one of the few 100 fly races in which he competed. As a collegiate swimmer, he swam a consistent 1:36 for the 200 free split of the 800 relay at each NCAA Championship meet in which he participated.

Nate Dusing is another example of an eventual sprinter whose first achievements were in distance events. As a 12-year-old, he trained 5,000 meters per practice and few doubles (two practices a day). It was distance-oriented training. The first qualifying standard he met was in the senior national mile event. After his sophomore year in high school, he swam 8:17 in the 800-meter freestyle, 3:59 in the 400-meter freestyle, 1:52 in the 200, and a :52 in the 100 (still very good times). By his senior year in high school he had progressed to swim 47.1 for a high school record in the 100-yard fly, 53.1 for a national age-group record in the

100-meter fly, and 48.0 in the 100-yard back. In the 2000 Olympic trials Nate made the team in the 200 meter free with a time of 1:48.99

All the speed that Tom and Nate gained throughout their careers didn't (and doesn't) just happen. These gains would not have been possible without a solid distance and endurance background. In addition to paving the way for such gains, an endurance-building program for younger swimmers also provides ample opportunity for the coach to drill proper stroke technique while building a solid aerobic base. A swimmer must acquire the most efficient technique possible at an early age and then continue to work on it. In this way stroke work is like yard work—if it isn't monitored and kept up on a regular basis, it will continuously get worse and will take more work to fix later.

It is critical that a swimmer train for distance ability and race the endurance events at a young age. The best time to build up an aerobic conditioning base is before puberty. After puberty, the swimmer will become more specialized in events. If a young swimmer trains aerobically but does not become a sprinter, he or she will still be conditioned to swim what he or she is genetically gifted to excel in—distance events. If a swimmer who did not train aerobically decides to specialize in sprints, his or her conditioning will not be complete; this swimmer won't come close to reaching his or her true swimming potential.

Collegiate swimmers who are sprinters must continue to do aerobic training in order to maintain the base they have built. This is absolutely necessary to enable them to continue to improve in the NCAA season and to be successful during the summer.

Sharpen Proper Technique

The key to optimum speed in fly or back is to make the strokes as mechanically solid as possible. For example, there are many nationally ranked 11- and 12-year-olds in the backstroke who put their hand in the water on its back instead of perpendicular to the water. In the finals of the US Nationals or NCAAs, there may be one swimmer every four or five years whose hand entry is incorrect. At the highest levels of competition, fewer stroke technique errors are observed because the fastest swimmers are those with the most efficient technique.

Backstroke

The body position for backstroke starts with the head placement on the water. The body always follows the head. In the backstroke, the head should be in a position that allows a cup of water to be balanced on the swimmer's forehead. This is true whether the swimmer is streamlining off the wall, breaking out of the water, or swimming. The best way to get swimmers used to this head position is to place a paper cup half full of water on the forehead of each of your backstrokers. The swimmers should then swim 25s balancing the cup on their heads. Do this drill consistently—a minimum set of 8 × 25, four or five times per week—to ensure that this head position becomes natural for your backstrokers.

There are some good drills to help your backstroker learn to place the hand in the water perpendicularly. This placement allows for the easiest entry with the least amount of resistance. I recommend the one-arm drills in which one arm remains at the side while the swimmer focuses on the stroke of the other arm.

The best drill for hand speed is the spin drill. To begin, the swimmer sits up with the head and shoulders out of the water and the legs and hips horizontal. The swimmer then holds the head still and moves the hands very fast. All drills must be monitored so that any mistakes can be corrected.

Butterfly

In the fly, younger swimmers often have a problem with the recovery phase of the stroke. The overwater recovery is influenced by the underwater pull pattern. This in turn is influenced by the strength of the swimmer relative to arm length. The best butterflyers draw an hourglass pattern with the hands underwater. The insweep that occurs near the stomach and finishes at about the hips should almost cause the hands to touch. The faster the swimmer goes, the more narrow an hour glass he or she creates. There isn't enough time for wide sweeps in the pull when moving fast. On the recovery, the swimmer should bring the little fingers out of the water first. The hands should recover about six to eight inches above the water, entering shoulder-width apart. The entry out front should be shoulder-width apart with the hands almost flat relative to the surface of the water. The swimmer must never let the wrist bend on the entry and should keep the arms as long as possible.

In most butterfly races, the swimmer should use a breathing pattern of every other stroke or one up, one down. Many swimmers tend to breathe every stroke in races; however, most swimmers are faster with the head down. So there needs to be a balance between breathing and speed. Putting the head down for every other stroke or using a one up, one down pattern helps get the hips up and therefore makes the swim easier. Of course, in the 50 and 25 fly, the swimmer should greatly reduce the number of breaths he or she takes. The swimmer should lift the head forward to breathe as the last underwater outsweep takes place. The head enters the water slightly before the hands do. The swimmer looks at the bottom of the pool, the hips come up, and the feet are kicked downward.

Increase Strength

The best way to increase strength in swimmers under age 10 is to simply have them come to practice and swim. The next step to increase strength is to add body-weight exercises—push-ups, pull-ups, walking a horizontal ladder, sit-ups, and running will increase strength safely in children this age. These exercises should not be timed for this age group. It is best to give them a numerical limit of repetitions to do. This helps the athletes concentrate on good technique instead of speed.

Dips done on a set of parallel bars should not be used for most children under the age of 10. The shoulder girdle of children under 10 is typically not developed enough to support their weight in that manner.

The 11- to 13-year-old age group can safely gain strength by doing the body-weight exercises recommended for younger children as well as dips on the parallel bars. You can start timing this group on the exercises, but give them a number to do for dips. Add lunges and hops. Limit the amount that the knees bend when hopping by having them keep the angle at the knee greater than 90 degrees. (Sometimes jumping, landing, and then sitting in a chair or on a bench helps prevent the closing of this angle.)

The 14-and-over age group can be all over the map when in comes to strength gain. Athletes who are new to the sport will be best served by doing resistance training in which they must lift their body weight. Swimmers who have come through the program may be ready to exercise with weights. The amount of weight for each exercise should be light enough for the athlete to do 12 to 20 repetitions.

Safety is always the main concern. Therefore, those beginning a strength program using weights are safest when using machine weights rather than doing free-weight exercises. These machines force good technique and provide for safety.

Most collegiate swimmers have been in a strength program for a period of at least three or four years. They are ready to progress into a free-weight program that is set up for strengthening. For optimal strengthening, the weights should be heavy enough to cause fatigue in four to six repetitions. The athletes should always have a spotter or two when lifting free weights.

Perfect the Underwater Fly Kick

A big part of Nate Dusing's success was his ability to quickly learn and perfect his underwater fly kick. He was the best fly kicker in the nation during his senior year of high school. If the kick is important, and we know it works to help butterfly and backstroke sprinters to win races, then it's worth spending time on it. While most swimmers may not be able to kick like Nate, all 100 fly and back swimmers should have the goal of continuing to improve their underwater fly kick. This improvement can be accomplished by ensuring that the fly kick is consistently trained as part of the overall program.

There are two ways to start the training necessary for a better fly kick.

1. Try the vertical fly kick for improving the speed or frequency of the kick. Swimmers perform this with the arms crossed in front of the chest and the hands resting on the opposite shoulder. The kick starts from the shoulders and moves to the feet with a snap forward and backward. Have swimmers count these kicks for 5 to 10 seconds, aiming for 2.5 to 3 kicks per second. (Count every forward kick as one.) One good way to incorporate this into practice is to add it to the warm-up. Give swimmers an interval that is 5 to 10 seconds slower and have them follow this order: Finish the rep of the warm-up, take 5 seconds, do 5 seconds of vertical fly kick, rest, and then continue on the next interval. Another method is to have swimmers do the fly kick three to five times off each wall for every stroke but breaststroke. The best way for swimmers to focus on the kick is to do the four to six sets of five to eight seconds just as fast as possible.

2. Doing fly kick on the back with the hands at the side is one of the best ways to gain the strength necessary to get better at the kick. On every push off from the wall, the swimmer should be streamlined, take five to eight kicks off the wall, pull the hands to the sides, and continue the fly kick on the back. He or she should take one backstroke stroke into every turn. My team times 8 × 100 of this set on two minutes every two weeks. This drill works the abdominal and quadriceps muscles. The improvement is very fast and continues throughout the year.

Once swimmers have become accustomed to kick training, they may need or want more of a challenge. One of the hardest drills for improving the fly kick is to kick against the resistance of surgical tubing and to kick with it coming back. I have swimmers kick out "as far as they can go" against the tubing, then kick a few more times. At that point they pull themselves along the lane line to the other end of the pool, then sprint back with the cord pulling them. This drill is more intense than the other two drills and should not be jumped into immediately with young swimmers. Do not skip any steps; there are no shortcuts.

A great way to work on maximizing the distance a swimmer gets off the wall is to tie surgical tubing from lane line to lane line across the middle of the pool (25 yards at 12 + yard mark); you can select the lanes to tie across. The swimmer kicks out underwater with the butterfly kick and breaks out to the surface stroke after passing the surgical tubing. This drill also works for older breaststrokers and their pullouts. Repeat 25s work best for the younger and less advanced kickers; 50s and 75s work for the better kickers. It is more difficult to do the kickouts from a turn than from a push off. Flyers should not breathe on the breakout stroke.

Construct a Solid Training Plan

We plan our collegiate season around three main phases: preseason, midseason (also known as dual-meet season), and championship season. This three-phase season begins six to seven months before the swimmer's "goal" or championship meet.

Preseason Training

The daily workouts during the preseason training of the collegiate athletes I coach include primarily aerobic swimming. Of course, the younger the swimmer, the bigger part that all four strokes play in this aerobic training. Swimmers race as a function of how they practice, therefore when they train aerobically they need to train all the strokes often in order to keep their technique in these strokes polished.

During the preseason, the collegiate swimmer should also make time for anaerobic training, which builds strength and speed. Anaerobic training offers a coach the best opportunity to see the swimmer's stroke when it is most "normal," or most like the swimmer's race stroke.

The workouts in table 19.1 are examples of a typical week of training our swimmers do in the preseason. I have used these warm-ups and sets a few times. They accomplish what I want from training at this time of year, and they are aimed at the end results that will come six to seven months down the line.

The morning practice can be used to work on weaker strokes or any component that needs to be fixed. If there is extra time, planned or not, left at the end of practice, use it to work on turns or starts. The turns my swimmers do when they circle swim in the lanes during most sets are not the same turns they should use in a meet. Therefore, it is important to allow swimmers to regularly practice turns straight in and straight out from the wall.

┌─ TABLE 19.1 ─────────────────────────────────────┐

Preseason Training

Monday
400 free, 3 fly kicks off every wall, breathe every 3 strokes; rest :15
100 fly or back drill, 5 fly kicks off every wall, breathe every 3 strokes; rest :15
300 free, 3 fly kicks off every wall, breathe every 3 strokes; rest :15
100 fly or back drill, 5 fly kicks off every wall, breathe every 3 strokes; rest :15
200 free, 3 fly kicks off every wall, breathe every 3 strokes; rest :15
100 fly or back drill, 5 fly kicks off every wall, breathe every 3 strokes; rest :15
100 free, 3 fly kicks off every wall, breathe every 3 strokes; rest :15
100 fly or back drill, 5 fly kicks off every wall, breathe every 3 strokes; rest :15
3 × 200 freestyle kick on 3:30
6 × 100 streamlined fly kick (no kickboard) on 1:45 (8 kicks off every wall underwater on the back, pull arms to sides and continue fly kick)
6 × 50 kick drills (follow the appropriate pattern for specialty stroke)
Fly: 5 kicks, 2 strokes
Back: 8 kicks off the wall, pull hands to sides, flutter kick with hands sculling
Breast: 4 kicks, 2 strokes
Free: 10 kicks, 1 single-arm stroke
3 × 100 free on 1:25, 100 IM on 1:30
2 × 100 free on 1:20, 100 IM on 1:35
1 × 100 free on 1:15, 100 IM on 1:40
2 × 100 free on 1:20, 100 IM on 1:35
3 × 100 free on 1:25, 100 IM on 1:30
12 × 25 swim choice, on :35; 90% effort
Easy 200

Tuesday
800 (100 free/100 back) Kick 3 to 5 times off every backstroke turn; rest :20
600 IM (odd 25s proper order swim; even 25s freestyle; rest :20
400 kick; rest :20
200 freestyle
2 × 8 × 25 on :35; 95% effort
2 × 8 × 6 line or 15 meters on :25; 98% effort (dolphin kick on back)
2 × 4 × 25 drill on :45
4 × 400 swim of best stroke, intervals based on individual. Fly can be done fly/free by 25s or 50s or by alternating 50 fly, 50 left arm, 50 fly, 50 right arm
8 × 100 (25 fly, 50 free, 25 fly) at 1:45. Designate number of kicks per stroke, how often to breathe. Allow free to be moderate.
Easy 200
6 × 50 swim on 1:30. Have swimmers swim fast for best average.

Wednesday
300 free on 5:00
200 back or fly drill/free by 50s on 3:30
400 free on 6:00
300 back or fly drill/free by 50s on 4:30
500 free on 7:30
12 × 100 free at 1:35 (:06 vertical dolphin kick at the end of each 100—15+ kicks)
Easy 100 on 2:00
3 × 3 × 100 free kick on 1:45
3 × 4 × 50 kick (choice) on :55
3 × easy 50 swim on 1:00
8 × 300 free on 4:30 (descend 1 to 4 and 5 to 8)
Easy 200

Thursday
8 × 25 on :45 from a one-step dive off deck, fly kick first half/choice last half
8 × 50 free on 1:00. Breathe every 3, 3 fly kicks off each wall
8 × 75 IM (fly, back, breast) on 1:20, 5 kicks off fly and back walls
8 × 100 free on 1:35, 25 fast, 50 drill, 25 fast
Easy 200 drill at 4:00
Do the following three sets three times through, subtracting :05 off interval and two repeats each time:
8 × 25 on :40, fly breathing pattern first half/back spin drill second half, 8 kicks off wall.
8 × 15 underwater kick on :40
4 × 25 drill on :45
1,500 fly/free (25 fly/25 free or 25 fly/50 free or another combination that fits the strength of that swimmer) OR 1,500 back. Time and record for average splits.
Easy 200
Friday
100 free on 1:40; 100 IM on 1:40
2 × 100 free on 1:35; 100 IM on 1:40
3 × 100 free on 1:30; 100 IM on 1:40
4 × 100 free on 1:25; 100 IM on 1:40
5 × 100 free on 1:20; 100 IM on 1:40
8 × 50 drill on 1:00. Stroke or kick drill
8 × 200 back on 3:30, best average with five kicks off each wall OR 8 × 200 fly on 3:30, 50 fly/50 free with five kicks off each wall
Easy 100 on 2:00
800 kick choice on 15:00
8 × 50 kick (fastest interval) on :50 (or whatever is appropriate) best kick
8 × 50 drill on 1:00
6 × 50 swim best stroke on 1:30 (fastest)
Easy 200

Midseason

During the midseason or dual-meet season, practices are very similar to the preseason workouts. In the midseason, intervals get faster and distance swims become less frequent and shorter. The focused or timed fast sets increase to three times per week—usually Tuesday, Thursday, and Saturday. Sometimes Saturday is a dual meet and therefore definitely counts as a fast day.

During the midseason I continue to have swimmers do sets of 25s and 15-meter swims and kicks. In the preseason phase those sets precede the distance swimming sets, but during the midseason they are done either early or late in practice. I try not to allow the identity of our dual-meet opponent to dictate the workouts we do leading up to the contest. Sometimes when there is a tough meet coming up, swimmers will institute the SIT method (self-imposed taper). Usually the best direction to take before a big meet is to decrease intensity and keep the yardage up.

Once again, make time during this phase to work on starts and turns. Usually the best swimmers have the best starts and turns. Get them to help you teach the others. Starting to work on turns just three weeks before the big meet is better than not training them at all, but not much better.

Championship Season

This is what coaches and swimmers work for all year. Some swimmers end their year three or four weeks earlier than those who go to the national meet, but the following questions must be addressed for all swimmers:

- When is their big meet?
- How have they trained?
- How many practices have been missed?
- How much swimming and dryland improvement has occurred?
- Where are they in their mental preparation?

It's helpful to participate in a meet three or four weeks out from the goal meet—in our case, the conference meet usually fits into this time slot nicely—to evaluate the swimmers' status. Some swimmers need more of a taper than others. I use the times and the way swimmers look in the water to determine what to do with their training from this meet until the final meet. The workouts in table 19.2 represent a typical week of training for swimmers in the championship phase.

TABLE 19.2

Championship Phase Training

Monday after setup meet (3 or 4 weeks from championship)
Easy 2,000 yards or meters
Tuesday
1,500 warm up (5 × [200 free/100 drill] :30 rest)
800 kick
8 × 50 swim on 1:00 (88% effort; below anaerobic threshold)
Easy 200
Wednesday
1200 warm up
500 kick
6 × 25 swim at 90% on :35
6 × 15 kick at 93% :35
Easy 200
4 × 50 at 90 to 96% (depending on swimmer) on :45 to :50
Swim down
Thursday
Same as Monday; concentrate on streamlining
Friday
Similar to Tuesday
Saturday
More warm-up for pace work

During one of our conference meets, one of my swimmers went 46.8 for the 100-yard fly and 25 minutes later swam 46.6 for the 100-yard backstroke in a 25-yard pool. He was unshaved but wore one of the full bodysuits. He was as fast as he would have been from resting, but we thought he'd drop some more time by the NCAAs with shaving. Regrettably, the NCAA pool was 25 meters in length, and thus it is difficult to determine the gains he made from the conference meet to the national meet. Still this swimmer's training schedule for the next two or more weeks would be different than someone who didn't look "high in the water" or fast at the conference meet.

Summary

- Successful sprint training is built on a foundation of endurance conditioning.
- Young swimmers need to develop an endurance base.
- Anaerobic training is most effective when added to training after puberty.
- The key to optimum speed is the most efficient technique.
- Increasing strength is essential for fast sprinting.
- Backstroke and butterfly swimmers must perfect the underwater butterfly kick.
- Preseason training should be primarily aerobic.
- Intervals get faster in midseason training.
- The taper for the championship meet is highly individualized.

CHAPTER TWENTY

Backstroke and Butterfly 200-Meter Training

Bill Rose

The 200 butterflyer and 200 backstroker are special athletes who require specific training that meets the demands of their events. The 200 fly and backstroke races include all the elements that make the sport of swimming so worthwhile and exciting; fine-tuned aerobic conditioning, technique, strategy, speed, and control all come into play. In my opinion, in no other race is victory determined by as many factors.

Just as the two races include many of the same demands, training for these events is similar as well. To excel in both the 200 butterfly and backstroke, I believe athletes must first understand and agree to training within a distance-based program. It is rare that a 100 butterfly or backstroke champion is able to double up to the 200 and vice versa. The 100 events are power events, whereas the 200 event relies more on muscle endurance and stamina; the raw speed required in the sprint back and butterfly isn't enough for success in the 200 events. Currently a larger number of 100 fly champions repeat at the 50 and 100 free than at the 200 fly.

The 100 backstroke champion is not often the main contender in the 200 backstroke, in part because of the kicking speed and endurance necessary in the 200 backstroke. With the introduction of the underwater dolphin kick, it is now more common for sprint backstroke swimmers to have increased difficulty "holding on" in the back half of the 200.

Before the dominance of the underwater dolphin kick, Kaye Hall set American and world records in the 100 backstroke. At the national championship meet where she won her first 100 backstroke title, she finished last in the 200 backstroke. Her coach then trained her to control her stroke rate and stroke count. The emphasis on holding the optimum stroke rate and count enabled her to better her 200 race by holding the second 100 with a minimum drop off. The following year, Kaye won both the 100 and 200 backstroke races at the short-course national championship meet. She became successful in the 200 as well as the 100, even though it wasn't her favorite distance. Eventually, she won the gold medal in the 100 and a solid bronze medal in the 200 at the Olympic Games. She also continued to lower her 100 backstroke time throughout the period of improvement in the 200.

Lenny Krayzelburg is one exception to the rule that current 100 and 200 backstrokers tend to excel in one event or the other, but not both. He was a better 200 backstroke swimmer who trained to bring his 100 backstroke to success as well. (He won gold in both backstroke events at the 2000 Olympic Games.)

The only swimmer in history to win Olympic gold medals in both butterfly events is Mark Spitz. Mike Bruner, the swimmer who broke Spitz's world record in the 1976 Olympics in Montreal, did not even have the 100 butterfly time standard necessary to enter the US Nationals. In fact, Bruner hit his lifetime 100 fly best of 57.9 on the 100 split of his world-record 200 fly performance of 1:59.23.

The pacing strategy used by the 200 butterflyers and backstrokers often determines the outcome of the race. Swimmers can choose from several different ways of splitting the race to affect the outcome of the final result: even splitting, negative splitting, positive splitting, or the "fly and die" method.

The largest percentage of 200 butterfly races are swum (and won) with a positive split—the split for each 50 is progressively slower. The reason for this is that in butterfly, sustaining the fine balance of control and technique with speed is more difficult than in any other stroke. At the top of the competitive pyramid, however, statistics show that world-class performances are achieved with even splits (after the first 50 from the dive, the splits for each 50 are the same.) It is not efficient to negative split a 200 butterfly due to the difficulty of maintaining the proper body position in the water at slower speeds. In reality, many butterflyers need to think that they are negative splitting in order to evenly split the race. Needless to say, the fly and die method of swimming the 200 fly is not recommended for optimal results.

In 200 backstroke races, even splitting and negative splitting are more commonly used than positive splitting. In particular, the move from the underwater fly kick in backstroke to a surface backstroke and flutter kick has resulted in more even splitting in backstroke.

During the last 20 or so years of competitive swimming, sport science has made huge strides in identifying, testing, and evaluating everything that makes up a champion. These worldwide efforts have been wonderful for the sport of competitive swimming. However, it's important for coaches to remember that training is not necessarily rocket science. It still comes down to a few simple facts.

1. The human body ultimately adapts to stress (training) that is repeatedly given.
2. Every human being is unique. Genetically no two humans are the same. The gene pool creates endomorphs and mesomorphs, buoyant and nonbuoyant frames, fast-twitch muscle fibers and slow-twitch muscle fibers, and so on.

3. The mental capacity to train and compete is also unique to every individual.

With these three things in mind, coaches must simply apply what Doc Counsilman called "the *x* factor" to the training of each athlete. The daily distance swum will vary depending on the time of season (early season, midseason, and taper) and the energy system being emphasized (aerobic, anaerobic threshold, etc.).

Early Season Training

Early season training, the first six to eight weeks of training, starts with 5 to 6 workouts a week and gradually builds to the normal midseason regimen of 10 to 11 workouts per week. Our swimmers normally train twice a day on Monday, Tuesday, Thursday, and Friday, and once a day on Wednesday and Saturday. Sunday is usually a complete off day unless there is a swim meet. The emphasis during the early season is on developing proper stroke technique and building up aerobic capacity.

Throughout this phase of the season, main sets are centered around gauging stroke count, stroke rate, and distance per stroke in order to achieve the optimal stroke technique and a controlled pace. Almost all the training sets are descending and negatively split to emphasize the importance of learning to understand and control pace. By stressing these concepts in training, you pave the way for successful races. The body and mind cannot be expected to be able to produce during the stressful period of a race what has not been repeated in practice to the point of becoming mental and physical habit. The percentage of the workout done swimming butterfly or backstroke will vary with each swimmer, depending on his or her experience, fitness level, age, and the degree to which he or she specializes in the 200 butterfly or 200 backstroke. Generally my most advanced 200 butterfly specialists do no more than 50 percent of their total workout butterfly, whereas my less advanced butterfly specialists do no less than 20 percent of their workout butterfly. The same percentage ranges apply for backstroke specialists.

The buoyancy and balance level of each swimmer will be different. Those who are very light on the water will usually be able to control their body position and rhythm for a longer repeat or for more repeats than swimmers who are less buoyant and are more powerfully built. This is true for all strokes but especially for the fly; however, both types can be world-record holders in the 200 fly. Two cases in particular come to mind: Pablo Morales and Mike Bruner.

Pablo Morales had one of the most powerful strokes I have ever seen. Pablo is probably best known for his famous comeback to win the gold medal in the 100 butterfly in the 1992 Olympics after the devastating disappointment of not qualifying for the 1988 Olympics. The 100 was totally suited to his style and strong physique. The 200, in my mind, was about 104 meters too far for him, but to his credit Pablo was one of the fastest 200 butterflyers in the world in the early years of his international competitive career.

Mike Bruner, on the other hand, was able to train megadistances of butterfly in practice without suffering any stroke or body-position problems. He certainly could not be considered a powerful swimmer either in stroke or body type. During his younger years, his body simply did not develop at the same rate as those of his peers. In fact, Mike was the brunt of a lot of "dough boy" jokes. To compensate for his lack of power and speed at that point, Mike developed himself into one of the most highly conditioned swimmers of his time.

Proving his worth was very important to him, and the only way he knew to do so was to take anything his competitors could do and do it longer. He repeated to himself daily, "Your speed will come some day, but until it does, you have to prove to everyone that no one in the world can swim butterfly as far and fast as you can." For years, Mike was famous for doing wacky things in workouts. When swimmers were doing a set of 10 × 400 meters free on 5:00, Mike would commonly say, "I want to do it fly." It got to the point that his teammates and competitors considered him unbeatable if they ever got into a race with him when he was right there with them after the first half of the race. I believe that Mike's reputation, and the effect it had on him and his competitors, was the key factor in his winning the most important race of his life—the 200-meter butterfly contest in which he took the gold medal in 1976.

Midseason Training

Midseason training includes the 16 to 18 weeks following early season training. During midseason training all the physical and tactical elements of the race are repeated and repeated and then repeated some more. To develop the endurance necessary, 200 butterfly and backstroke conditioning combines middle-distance to distance freestyle training with that of a 400 IM swimmer. During this phase of training, a national-level swimmer training for the 200 backstroke or butterfly will average approximately 80,000 to 100,000 yards or 73,000 to 92,00 meters a week (50 percent of which will be done in his or her specialty stroke).

During the midseason training phase, our 200 butterflyers and backstrokers repeat a weekly cycle over the entire 16 to 18 weeks (see table 20.1). Each workout has a different set of objectives. Three of the morning workouts are dedicated to fast kicking. The main set is from 800 to 1,200 meters of quality kicking. Threshold training is scheduled for Monday evening, Saturday morning, and various other mornings.

On Tuesday evening, and sometimes on Saturday morning, swimmers do what is affectionately termed a "butt-buster workout." The object

— TABLE 20.1 —

National Team Weekly Midseason Cycle (April–July)

Day	AM	PM
Monday	8,000 meters Aerobic swim Fast kicking Pulling Descending set	8,000 to 9,000 meters Threshold freestyle set Specialty mix Descending set Negative split
Tuesday	8,000 meters IM work or pace work Pulling and kicking sets Short-spurt sprints	10,000+ meters Short rest, aerobic work All swimming or pulling sets Mixed strokes
Wednesday	Off	~5,000 meters Pace and technique work Starts and drills
Thursday	8,000 meters Aerobic swim Fast kicking Pulling Descending set	6,000 to 8,000 meters Test set Pace work and drills Pulling Short alactate set
Friday	8,000 meters Aerobic and pace work Descending set IM and stork work	7,000 to 10,000 meters Max $\dot{V}O_2$max set Pulling and negative split sets Starts and finishes
Saturday	8,000 to 10,000 meters Potpourri workout (coach's choice)	Makeup workout for those who missed a workout

— TABLE 20.1, *continued* —

National Team Weekly Midseason Cycle

Monday AM	Monday PM
Warm-up (1,600) Swim 4 × 200 on 3:05, build an IM choice after 1st repeat. Pull 800 on 11:30, alternate back and breast every 3rd 50.	**Warm-up** (1,700) Swim 400, kick 300, pull 3 × 200 with 1-2 rm. Rest. Swim 400 (odd 50s choice, even 50s drill-swim IM order) You have 26:00 to complete.
Pull (3,100) 3 × (4 × 50 on :45 descending + 300 at 4:00 negative split and descending)	**Scull-swim** (2,700) 4 × 250 (50 back scull, 50 back swim, 50 front scull, 50 free swim, 50 specialty swim) on coach's interval. Keep efficiency and technique in mind.
Fast kicking (main set) (4,100) 4 × 50 on 1:00 descending; 800 fast on 12:30 or whatever comes first	**Threshold freestyle swim** (3,900) 2 × (10 × 50). First repeat of each set at 1:00, drop interval by :05 per repeat to :35 before adding :05 to each repeat interval again. Object is to set a time (i.e., 200 race pace) and hold through all 10 repeats. Swim 100 easy.
Aerobic swim (4,200) 100 easy on 3:30	**Pull** (5,100) 1,200 on 16:00. Work off all the walls and the first 15 m of each 50.
Descending swim (7,800) 6 × (300, 200, 100). First set on 1:30 per 100 pace, drop each set :05 to 1:10 before adding :05 per set	**Swim (descend** (6,000 to 8,700) **and negative split)** * Distance, mid-distance, 400 IM and 200 fly 3 × (3 × 400) on 5:15, 5:00, and 4:45 by the set. Descend and negative split each set 1 to 3. Take :45 rest between each set. * Stroke and sprint 3 × (3 × 100) on 2:00, 1:45, and 1:30 by the set. Descend and negative split each set 1 to 3. Take :45 rest between each set.
Warm-down (8,100) Swim 3 × 100 (pace, moderate, easy).	**Warm-down** (6,300 to 9,000) Swim 2 × 150 (moderate and easy) on 2:25.

of the workout is to stay at the top on the aerobic scale (heart rates ranging from 130 to 150 or higher throughout the workout) for 10,000 or more meters using a mixture of strokes and distances and never taking more than 30 seconds rest between the already short-rest sets. The swimmer is encouraged to "hit the wall" in this practice, and then to attempt to push farther to find out if it is the mind or the body that is rebelling.

— TABLE 20.1, *continued* —

National Team Weekly Midseason Cycle

Tuesday AM	Tuesday PM
Warm-up (1,600) Swim 4 × (300 on 4:30 [descend by set] + 100 reverse IM on 1:35 [breast on 1:45]).	**Warm-up** (2,000) Swim 400 choice on 6:00, 2 × 300 (last 100 IM on 4:35) 3 × 200 (last 100: 50 back, 50 breast) on 3:10, 4 × 100 choice descending on 1:30
Pull (3,600) 1 × 400, 2 × 300, 3 × 200, 4 × 100 on 1:20 base. Hold same pace (your choice) throughout.	**Swim** (6,800) 800 on 10:00, 20 × 50 on :45, :30 rest 600 on 7:30, 16 × 50 on :44, :30 rest 400 on 5:00, 12 × 50 on :43, :30 rest 200 on 2:30, 8 × 50 on :42 Ladder (800 to 200) is at 140 to 150 bpm and evenly split. 50s are done at the ladder pace minus :01 (i.e., 800 time of 9:00 = 33.7 average per 50 - :01 = 32.7). 50s may be done specialty with coach approval.
Swim—sprints (4,200) 9 × 50 variable sprints on :55, then 150 easy on 3:30	**Swim (may use zoomers)** (8,400) 2 × (4 × 200) on 2:40. First set is freestyle with last 50 back. Insert an additional 50 back each repeat. Second round is backstroke inserting butterfly.
Swim—IM work (6,200) Swim a ladder by the 50. Start with 300 and add a 50 per repeat up to 500. First repeat is 150 IM order, 150 free. Each 50 is added in IM order to the end of the first repeat. First repeat is on 4:30; add :45 to the interval each repeat.	**Pull or swim** (10,400) 2 × 400 on 4:45, :30 rest 2 × 300 on 3:45, :30 rest 2 × 200 on 2:40, :30 rest 2 × 100 on 1;25, :30 rest First repeat of each set is holding pace. Second repeat is faster than first by going the last 100 fast.
Kick-swim (7,700) 6 × 250 (200 swim, 50 back) on 3:45. Descend total time 1 to 3 and 4 to 6.	**Warm-down** (10,700) Swim 3 × 100 (pace, moderate, easy)
Warm-down (8,000) Swim 3 × 100 (pace, moderate, easy)	

Wednesday is a recovery day. There is no morning workout and the afternoon session emphasizes technique, drills, starts, and turns. The total amount of meters covered is usually between 5,000 and 6,000.

Thursday evening is set up as a "quality day." Swimmers do a five-week revolving test set cycle which includes 8 × 100 on 3:00, 6 × 200

National Team Weekly Midseason Cycle

Wednesday PM

Warm-up **(1,500)**
Swim 500, 400, 300, 200, 100 on a 1:30 base with every 5th, 4th, 3rd, 2nd, each 50 backstroke by the repeat.

Swim-kick **(3,200-3,400)**
4 × (swim 200 IM, swim 100 specialty, kick 100) on 6:00. IMers go IM order on specialty rep. Breastrokers and IMers go 50 instead of 100 on the breaststroke repeat. Keep heart rate 135 to 145 bpm. Swim 300 easy on 3:30.

Swim-pull **(6,000-6,200)**
400, 300, 200, 100 choice on a 1:30 base with 2 × 300 pull between each rep on 4:15. Each swim rep is at threshold speed (150-160 bpm) and negative split. Each pull set is aerobic.

Warm-down **(6,300-6,500)**
Swim 200 on 3:00 pace, 100 easy on 1:45

Thursday AM		Thursday PM	
Warm-up	**(1,600)**	**Warm-up**	**(1,600)**
Swim 4 × 300 on 4:30 choice, drop interval :10 per repeat. Kick 200, pull 200 on 6:40.		Swim 400 on 6:00, then 4 × 100 choice on 1:35, 50 descend by the round on :50. Kick 300, pull 300 on 10:00.	
Pull	**(3,200)**	**Swim**	**(2,600)**
4 × 400 on 5:30, descend 1 to 4.		400, 300, 200, 100 on 1:30 base. All aerobic except last 50 of each repeat which is specialty, build to finish.	
Kick (main set)	**(4,000)**	**Swim**	**(3,200)**
400 on 8:00 at approximately 80% effort. Then 4 × 100 descend to best effort on 2:00 starting at the average 100 for the 400.		9 × 50 on :55 variable sprints, 150 easy on 4:00	
Swim	**(6,600)**	**Test set**	**(4,400)**
100 easy on 3:30 5 × (5 × 100) on 1:20 (1:30). In each set 1 to 4 are aerobic, best technique; 5 is threshold specialty. Rest :10 after each set.		Swim 6 × 200 on 5:00. Try for best possible average, specialty, record all swims.	
Swim (choice of equipment)	**(7,700-8,000)**	**Swim (choice of equipment)**	**(6,000)**
800 (700) on 10:00, 400 (250) on 5:00, 200 (150) on 2:30. Everything is to be done "speedplay."		800 speed play on 11:00 4 × (100 [drill 50, swim 50] on 1:45 + 100 aerobic on 1:35), descend each set	
Warm-down	**(8,000-8,300)**	**Warm-down**	**(6,300)**
Swim 3 × 100 (pace, moderate, easy).		Swim 6 × 50 on :55, 1-3 pace, 4-6 ascending	

National Team Weekly Midseason Cycle

Friday AM		Friday PM	
Warm-up	**(1,600)**	**Warm-up**	**(1,600)**
Swim 4 × 300 on 4:35. Drill swim last 50 of each IM order. Kick 200, pull 200 on 6:40.		Swim 400, kick 400, pull 400, drill-swim 2 × 200 IM on 25:00 or whichever comes first.	
Pull	**(3,100)**	**Swim**	**(6,600)**
5 × 300 on 4:30. 3rd and 6th 50s are breaststroke.		60 minute sustained swim. Coach will randomly stop swimmers up to 5 times during the swim to perform whatever time and distance asked on demand. Swimmer then continues until stopped again. Choice of equipment, but may stop only long enough to change equipment; random times must be with no equipment.	
Swim	**(4,700)**		
4 × 400 on 5:30. Odd 50s IM order, even 50s choice. Keep heart rate between 130 and 140 bpm.			
Swim (with zoomers)	**(6,200)**	**Swim**	**(7,400)**
6 × 250 on 3:30 1st, 3rd, and 5th 50 backstroke. Keep heart rate between 130 and 140 bpm.		8 × 100 from a dive on 2:00. Work the dive and 1st 10 meters in and out of the turn. Everything else is form.	
Swim (choice of equipment)	**(7,800)**	**Swim and warm-down**	**(7,900)**
8 × (150 [hold pace on 2:00] + 50 specialty [on :40 at 80% effort]).		10 × 50 on :50. 1 to 5 build to finish choice, 6 to 8 ascending.	
Warm-down	**(8,100)**		
Swim 3 × 100 (pace, moderate, easy).			

Saturday AM	
Warm-up	**(1,700)**
Swim 4 × 200 on 300. Rotate reverse IM through each repeat. Kick-swim 900 (50 kick, 100 swim continuous) on 14:30.	
Swim	**(2,700)**
20 × 50 on :45. First person in line will sprint, and then go to the back of the line, the rest of the swimmers will swim moderate until they rotate to the front of the line.	
Pull	**(3,900-4,200)**
1,500 (1,200) on 18:00. Come down at the 500 (400). Do at 150+ heart rate.	
Swim	**(7,900-8,200)**

2 sets of   • 4 × 100 on 1:25 (descend and evenly split each set)
          • 3 × 200 on 2:40 (swim each rep faster)
          • 2 × 300 on 3:45 (second set is faster than first)
          • 1 × 400 on 4:40	

Swim (may use equipment)	**(9,300-9,600)**
2 × (1, 2, 3, 4 × 50 on :40 fast with 1 × 50 form on 1:00 after each section.	
Warm-down	**(9,600-9,900)**
Swim 3 × 100 (pace, moderate, easy) on 1:45.	

on 5:00, 5 × 400 on 7:00, 4 × 800 on 12:00, and a fifth-week test set of the coach's choosing. Results are recorded for comparison purposes.

Friday evening usually features a $\dot{V}O_2$max set along with more pulling and negative split work. Short 15- to 25-meter sprints are incorporated into the workouts at least five times a week in the midseason training phase. Including shorter sprints during this phase reminds the athlete what it feels like, mentally and physically, to swim fast.

On Saturday morning, the workout is a potpourri of aerobic, pace, and descending work, as well as IM and stroke work. The distance covered is anywhere from 8,000 to 10,000 meters. Simply speaking, it is whatever the coach feels is necessary to tie the week together based on the accomplishments of the previous five days. For example, if it wasn't possible to fit in a descending set earlier in the week, it could be included here. Or if swimmers hadn't done any specific start and turn work, they could do so at this time.

During the midseason phase, our swimmers face competitions approximately once a month. We do not allow "resting" for a meet to interrupt the training cycle leading up to these monthly competitions. The swimmers are expected to perform in whatever situation they face. I have found that swimming tired is a great way to develop mental toughness. It is a win-win situation. If a swimmer does well in an event like the 200 butterfly or backstroke while enduring heavy training, that's great. If he or she does not do well, so what? The swimmer has the built-in excuse of being tired. I tell swimmers that in this situation they can't lose by failing, so there's no reason not give it their best.

Taper Training

The taper phase of the season should be quite individualized; for this reason it is the most difficult phase for the coach to incorporate into the training. The length of the taper can vary from four to six weeks to four to six days! A rule of thumb that I use is the larger and older the athlete, the more rest he or she needs. For example most of my 200 fly specialists who are under age 18 have a three-week taper (of which one week is full rest). Swimmers over age 18 have the experience to know how much of a break is appropriate for them. Keep in mind that the taper is as much a mental break that mentally prepares swimmers to compete as it is a physical rest period. Sprinters tend to want a longer taper than distance swimmers. The 200 fly or back events, considered to be more middle distance, dictate that the athletes who swim them may need more cardiovascular endurance than those who swim certain other events. Therefore, endurance needs must be considered when deciding what type and what length of taper to use.

Once the optimal length of the taper for an individual athlete is determined, approximately the first half of that time should be spent doing a gradually decreasing version of the midseason training phase (see table 20.2). The daily emphasis remains essentially the same, but the total distance of the workout is gradually lessened, and the rest between sets and interval repeats is lengthened. The last half of the taper is based on two aspects: rest and mental preparation. This is the time when all the visualizations are stressed. It is the time when the swimmers are told that everything that happens both in and out of the water is geared toward the body welling up with strength and power, and toward the mind becoming clear of purpose. The coach goes through as much difficulty as the swimmer during this time. Everything the coach says must be positive. When the athlete says, "I feel awful," the coach must answer, "That's great! The taper is working and the mind is telling the body that it refuses to waste the rest that is needed." If the athlete says, "I feel great," the coach again must respond, "That's great; the taper is working just as planned." In other words, nothing must be construed as being bad during a taper. Of course, many coaches go home at night during a taper and find themselves unable to sleep worrying about whether or not the desired end result will actually come about.

The bottom line of the taper is rest. If the work has been done during the season, rest is the best course of action. If the work and effort have not been put forth, it's too late to fit it all in now. I have always thought of the taper as being a love-hate proposition for swimmers and coaches. The swimmers love it and the coaches hate it.

One common mistake that is made in a taper is oversprinting—doing too many high-intensity sprints, without enough rest. The phrase, "speed comes with rest," needs to be remembered.

Training for the 200 butterfly is a beautiful thing. It is the best of middle-distance, distance, and 400 IM training all rolled up into one great package. The swimmers willing to train for the 200 butterfly, are, in my opinion, the kind coaches dream of training—swimmers like Mike Bruner, Craig Beardsley, Mary T. Meagher, Pablo Morales, Melvin Stewart, and most recently Tom Malchow. I truly believe that most coaches would agree that the swimmers who have given them the most joy as well as challenge over time have been their 200 butterfly specialists.

A case in point is an up-and-coming 16-year-old butterflyer, Juan Veloz. Juan asked me one day if he could try something that my former swimmer, Mike Bruner, had neither done nor attempted to do. I thought for a

TABLE 20.2

National Team Weekly Taper Workouts

Days away from meet	Yards	Workout
15	5,000 to 5,200	**Warm-up:** Swim 300 on 4:00, kick 300 on 6:00, pull 300 on 4:15, swim 300 on 3:30 **Swim:** 4 × 100 on 1:10 (1:20 back or fly, 1:30 breast) 4 × 100 on 1:05 (1:15 back or fly, 1:25 breast) 4 × 100 on 1:00 (1:10 back or fly, 1:20 breast) 600 descending on each 200 (distance swims 800) **Kick:** 500 on 10:00, then 6 × 25 fast on :25 **Pull:** 500 on 7:00, then 6 × 25 breath control on :35 **Swim:** 16 × 25 on :30, descend to fast in groups of 4 **Turns:** Practice 20 **Swim:** Timed 50 specialty **Warm-down:** 2 × 100 together 3 × 3 and out
10	3,500	**Warm-up:** Swim 300, 200, 100 on 1:30 base (all negative split); kick 3 × 100 on 2:00 descending; pull 2 × 200 on 3:00 descending; swim or drill 4 × 100 IM order on 1:40 **Swim:** 5 × ([(3 × 25 free) + (1 × 25 specialty fast)] on :30); all repeats 80% effort or higher 3 × 300 (250 for breast) on 4:30; descend to 85% 100 easy 3 × 50 on coach's interval at 200 pace **Warm-down:** Swim 2 × 75 moderate, easy
5	3,400	**Warm-up:** Swim 300 choice on 4:30; kick 300 (back, free, choice by the 100) on 6:00; pull 2 × 150 on 2:20 descending; drill-swim 6 × 50 on 1:00 (IM order + 2 choice) **Swim:** 8 × 50 on 1:00, hold steady pace for 1-4 and descend 5-8 **Kick:** 200, then 4 × 25 fast on :30 **Pull:** 200, then 4 × 25 on :40 with solid breath control **Swim:** 200 negative split holding heart rate < 161 4 × 200 on 2:00 specialty, should feel easy but fast **Starts:** Practice 5 **Warm-down:** Swim 200

minute and then came up with the challenge of going 100 × 100 meters butterfly on 1:30. Juan didn't even blink; he just asked when. I replied,

"Tomorrow, but the stipulation is that you must hold your stroke, and if your times for each 100 are not within four seconds of each other you must stop." He said "Let's do it." The next day, after a good warm-up, we sent him on his way and recorded every 100 time. The results were heartwarming for Juan, myself, and the whole team, who stayed and watched in awe. His average 100 was 1:10.2, the worst being 1:12.3 and his best a 1:05.1, his last repeat!

This chapter has covered one method of training for the 200 butterfly and backstroke. Is it the only way to success? Absolutely not! That's the beauty of our sport; there are many "different strokes for different folks."

Summary

- Training for the 200 backstroke and the 200 butterfly is very similar.
- Endurance and the splitting strategy are important aspects of these two events.
- Sprint champions in the butterfly and backstroke don't often repeat in the 200s of these events.
- Early season training involves a gradual buildup in the number of sessions per week and in the intensity of the sessions. Technique and aerobic buildup are emphasized.
- The percentage of the training in butterfly or backstroke depends on the individual swimmer.
- Midseason training emphasizes the adaptation to higher and higher stress levels.
- The mental capacity to train and compete is unique to every individual.
- Fast kicking is an important set of the morning training sessions.
- Recovery days and quality days are both important in the training.
- Swimming tired is a great method of improving mental toughness.
- Taper training is highly individualized.

CHAPTER TWENTY-ONE

Breaststroke Training

Jon Urbanchek

Breaststroke is the oldest of the competitive swimming strokes. It has gone through numerous transformations during the 20th century due to rule changes, some relating to underwater swimming and some relating to mixing breaststroke with the butterfly. Finally, during the 1950s, breaststroke became the stroke we know today, in which the head breaks the surface with each cycle except at the start and turn when one full stroke may be taken underwater.

As far as the technique is concerned, the biggest change has been the advent of what is called "reverse breath taking." Instead of taking a breath at the outward sweep of the hands (glide and breathe), in reverse breath taking the swimmer takes a breath during the inward sculling. This style started in Asia in the late 1950s and 1960s, and in Europe in the 1970s. David Wilkie, 1976 Montreal gold medalist in the 200 breaststroke, had a similar technique. Reverse breath taking was introduced to the United States in the mid 1980s by the Hungarian coach Jozsef Nagy, who converted Mike Barrowman's traditional (flat) breaststroke into the "wave" breaststroke. Mike Barrowman brought the new wave breaststroke to the University of Michigan in 1987. The wave-like technique then became the standard technique for breaststroke swimming throughout the world, and it remains the standard technique today.

The main difference between the flat breaststroke and the wave breaststroke is that the flat stroke is driven by the feet and legs (rear-wheel drive), while the wave breaststroke is driven by the lower arms (front-wheel drive). The wave breaststroke is more energy efficient than the flat breaststroke because it reduces the deceleration between the arm pull and the leg drive. The results of this reduced deceleration are evident in the upper-body lunge that occurs between the completion of pull and the beginning of kick phases. The arms give the initial speed, the upper body lunges forward, and the kick follows shortly thereafter. The shoulders rise and fall in perfect symmetry. These three continuous interlocking movements—pull, lunge, kick—result in a smooth wave-like appearance.

Even with this continuous, efficient technique, breaststroke still has the highest energy requirement of any stroke. It uses more total muscle mass than other strokes mainly because of the necessary contribution of the leg muscles to propulsion in breaststroke. This higher energy requirement means higher energy consumption and lactate buildup for breaststroke swimmers. Thus, in addition to training the body to tolerate lactate, training effectively for the wave breaststroke technique requires specific stroke-related training that focuses on the three major components of the stroke: the pull, the lunge, and the kick. Training for the 100 and 200 breaststroke events is similar because breaststroke is such a technique-driven stroke.

The Pull

The breaststroke pull itself incorporates three distinct components:

1. **The outsweep**—Arms are fully extended, palms face outward (wall-eyed position) to approximately the 9 o'clock and 3 o'clock positions (9:30 to 2:30 to be most accurate).

2. **The downsweep**—Elbows remain close to the surface. The forearms, led by the hands, bend the elbows to about 90 degrees. At the same time the shoulders are hunched until they touch the earlobes.

3. **The insweep**—Hollowing of the back begins here. The quickest movement of the hands takes place; movement is in an inward and forward direction. Head is kept facing down until the insweep is completed.

The Lunge

The lunge involves changing the shape of the back from hollow to round, resembling a dolphin's back. This is the most distinct movement of the wave breaststroke. Then hands and forearms are thrust forward on the surface of the water. The palms face down for added support and to keep the shoulders from falling down too fast (continue the wave). The head will be the last part to jump into the lunge.

The Kick

The heels begin to rise at the end of the insweep of the hands. Swimmers use the hamstring muscles to accelerate the feet until they touch the buttocks. The key point in timing the kick is that the heels and shoulders are at their highest points at the same time. The feet should thrust out and backward with gradual acceleration; ankles and feet are extended and pointed to hold a streamlined position for minimal resistance during the body's highest velocity.

For additional breaststroke technique and drills, see chapter 14.

Training Technique

When setting up a breaststroke training program, a coach has to take into account the importance of the timing and rhythm of the three components—the pull, the lunge, and the kick—of the wave breaststroke.

It's important to train each of these parts separately and to use the full stroke for only about 20 percent of total training time. The total amount of breaststroke and breaststroke-related drills could total 50 percent or more of total training for natural breaststrokers. The coach must take individual differences into consideration, especially for "man-made" breaststrokers who might train breaststroke for individual medley swimming purposes only.

Breaststroke Drills

  Sculling. With chin up, keeping the head steady, the swimmer sculls with the hands, being careful to avoid any up-and-down movement of the shoulders. The dolphin kick should be kept to a minimum. Have the swimmer try going forward with the sculling movement of the hands. This exercise helps swimmers develop a feel for the water and correct hand pitch.

  Pulling. This drill should take up a majority of breaststroke training. It can be done with or without small paddles (big paddles slow down the insweep and lunging) and with or without fins. I do not recommend using a pull buoy because it gives a false buoyancy to the swimmer's body. Instead, I recommend that the swimmer use a very slight dolphin kick not for propulsion but just to keep the lower body afloat. Pulling drills should be done with a very fast lunging movement. This drill can be used also as a training set of repeat 25s, 50s, and 100s.

  Pulling mixed with underwater pulling. Underwater pulling helps develop continuous arm movement (there is no dead time in the stroke because the swimmer does not come up to breathe). A coach can mix the drill by alternating two pulls on top and two pulls underwater, three and three, four and four, and so on. This drill can also be used as a training set. Swimmers should keep the dolphin kick light and use only one dolphin kick per pull cycle.

  Kicking. Swimmers kick without kickboards but can use paddles. Have the swimmer perform two or three rapid kicks underwater while in a streamlined position with the arms fully extended and shoulders locked on the earlobes. The swimmer should then come up for a full stroke, and after taking a breath, dive back underwater. This drill can also be used as a training set. It is best used in 50s and 100s in intervals. This drill builds great rhythm, and the controlled breathing helps to develop anaerobic capacity.

Swimming. These drills mix breaststroke swimming on the surface with breaststroke swimming underwater, such as two strokes on top and two strokes under; combinations of three and three and four and four also work well. This drill can be used as a good training set from 50s to 400s in length. The timed 400 can be used as a test (four up and four down) throughout the season to monitor anaerobic capacity improvement.

Breaststroke Training Sets

Most main sets for breaststrokers are essentially made up of the above training drills in some combination. I do not recommend using straight sets of long duration. Use straight sets only for testing purposes and for short duration (up to 800 total) in interval swimming (e.g., 8 × 100 meters at 1:45 or 4 × 200 meters at 3:30).

Resting intervals for breaststroke need to be longer than for freestyle or backstroke training. Usually 30 to 40 seconds of rest is required (regardless of the distance of interval) to be able to maintain proper technique. Use this same rest interval when any of the drills are done in underwater-overwater combinations.

Training the Anaerobic System for Breaststroke

Because of the high energy requirement in breaststroke, it is important to do training that develops the body's ability to use anaerobic energy. This can be incorporated into the daily workouts by having swimmers perform most of the breaststroke training drills for kicking and pulling underwater. Because of the nature of breaststroke training (mostly component work: pulling, lunging, and kicking), it can be very difficult to establish an accurate threshold for training speed. Instead, I recommend using heart rates to guide anaerobic training. Using the manual counting method for 10 seconds is a reasonably accurate way to determine which energy system is used:

Moderate intensity aerobic (EN1)—120 to 150 beats per minute

Anaerobic threshold (EN2)—150 to 170 beats per minute

Maximal oxygen uptake ($\dot{V}O_2$max, EN3)—170 to 190 beats per minute

Higher lactate production (SP1-2)—190 or more beats per minute (maximal heart rate)

Because breaststroke swimming is the least economical of the strokes coupled with underwater (hypoxic) swimming, it elicits higher heart rates during training than other strokes. When training at altitude, the stress in breaststroke training (increased lactate buildup) is greater than for other strokes and must be taken into account in designing training sets.

Periodization of an Annual Training Plan

The University of Michigan training cycle includes two mesocycles or semiannual plans: a 30-week short-course collegiate season from September through March, and a 20- to 22-week long-course summer season from April through August. Figure 21.1 depicts a model of the 30-week collegiate training season. It indicates the total amount of meters or yards per week along with the percentage of training that occurs within the specific training zones that train specific energy systems.

This short-course mesocycle includes four macrocycles. The first macrocycle is 12 weeks long, from September through November, with a major competition at the end. During this macrocycle, the first 6 weeks are devoted to aerobic training and skill development with the heart

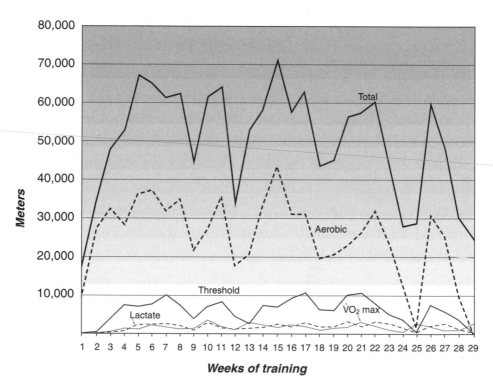

Figure 21.1 The collegiate training season.

rate pulse not exceeding 150 beats per minute (bpm) in any workout. The second 6 weeks include aerobic and anaerobic threshold training with heart rates in the 150 to 175 bpm range and above threshold zones at $\dot{V}O_2$max (180 to 190 bpm) and lactate production with maximum heart rate. The last week in the cycle is devoted to a short taper (rest period) followed by a major midseason competition.

The second macrocycle is also 12 weeks long. This cycle includes only 3 weeks of aerobic endurance training followed by full training in all training zones and energy systems. More emphasis is paid to $\dot{V}O_2$max (race pace) and lactate-production work. This period also includes the competitive dual-meet season with two to three dual meets per month.

The third macrocycle is the taper period that extends 3 to 4 weeks in preparation for the conference championship. Dryland workouts and weight exercises are reduced to maintenance levels (50 percent) and dropped completely in the last 10 days. Total training distance is gradually reduced from 60,000 meters or yards per week to 30,000 to 20,000 meters or yards per week out from the competition. Individual differences come into play for each swimmer's taper.

The fourth macrocycle is the period between the conference championships and the NCAA Championships. It is usually a four-week cycle that includes one week of aerobic endurance work (total of 60,000 meters or yards), 10 days of full training zones (40,000 to 50,000 meters or yards), and 10 days of taper period.

This weekly training plan can be broken into two three-day microcycles, each including five workouts. The microcycle includes a 40- to 60- minute Monday afternoon threshold workout of breaststroke; a Tuesday afternoon focus on descending sets/subjective individual medley and breaststroke combinations; and a Wednesday afternoon workout in the anaerobic zone, with breaststroke sets done at $\dot{V}O_2$max (race pace) for lactate-threshold development. The following section shows the details of sample workouts for one long-course microcycle shown in table 21.1.

Monday Morning

Warm-up. 2,000 meters of mixed aerobic skills and drills.

Preset. A set of 800 to 1,000 meters total designed to get heart rate up. Short-distance 25s, 50s, or 75s. Individual medley rotation work, short rest intervals.

Hypoxic pulling set. 800 to 1,200 meters of freestyle or intervals; 8 × 100 breaststroke pulling, 2 up/4 underwater, 30 to 40 seconds rest.

Endurance kick set. Breaststroke 4 × 200, 30 seconds rest.

— TABLE 21.1 —

University of Michigan Weekly Training Cycle— Midseason Breaststroke Group

	AM **Pool**	**Supplemental**	PM **Pool**
Mon.	Aerobic technique Pull/power Kick/endurance Hypoxic swimming Fin swimming 5,500 meters	Dryland Medicine ball	Main set: anaerobic threshold work 3,000-4,000 meters Energy system EN2 7,000 meters
Tues.	IM/breaststroke Recovery drills Skill work Off-stroke work Kick power Swim-specific power (buckets and stretch cords) Positive and negative work (speed assistance) 6,000 meters	Strength training Weight room	Main set: IM or breaststroke active rest Go by feel, subjective Easy/fast Energy systems EN1 and EN3 7,000 meters
Wed.	Off Makeups	Dryland Medicine ball	Main set: breaststroke $\dot{V}O_2$max and lactate work Test sets Energy systems EN3, SP1, SP2 5,000-6,000 meters
Thurs.	Aerobic recovery work Drills Hypoxic swimming Speed play (:06 to :12 per surge) Skills (starts and turns) 5,500 meters	Strength training Weight room	Main set: Anaerobic threshold breaststroke and IM Energy system EN2 7,000 meters
Fri.	Aerobic power speed Fins Buckets, stretch cords Negative and positive work (speed assistance) 6,000 meters	Dryland Medicine ball	Main set: breaststroke active rest Component training • kick • pull • swim Energy systems EN1, EN2, EN3 7,000 meters
Sat.	Main set: $\dot{V}O_2$max (race pace) Lactate production Test sets Energy systems EN3, SP1, SP2 5,000-6,000 meters	Strength training Weight room	Off
Sun.	Off Sleep in		Off

Total of 10 workouts equals 60,000 to 65,000 meters per week.

Monday Afternoon

Warm-up. 400 freestyle drills; 400 rimo (IM backwards); 6 × 150 (50 fly, 50 back, 50 breast) at 2:30.

Preset. 12 × 50 (1 fly, 1 free) at :45.

Main set. 4,000 meters threshold work, pulse 150 to 175 bpm. 1:00 rest between sets.

- 8 × 50 breaststroke at 1:00 descending 1 to 4 (:35). Work pull-outs and fast, lunging finish.
- 4 × 100 breaststroke at 1:50 (25 3 kicks per pull, 25 pull, 50 swim). Hold 1:16.
- 6 × 150 breaststroke at 2:40 (50 2 kicks per pull, 50 pull 2 up/2 down, 50 swim). Hold under 2:00.
- 3 × 300 breaststroke at 5:00 (100 2 kicks per pull, 100 pull, 100 swim). Hold under 4:00.
- 4 × 150 breaststroke at 2:40 (50 kick, 50 pull 4 up/2 down, 50 swim 4 up/4 down) descending 1 to 4.
- 4 × 100 breaststroke at 2:00. Best average swimmer can hold (1:12).
- 8 × 50 breaststroke at 1:00. Keep stroke count at 18 and hold at :33.

Swim down. 300 (50 free/50 back).

Tuesday Morning

Warm-up. 1,500 total, mixed strokes.

Off-stroke drills. 1,200 total, 300 of each stroke.

Power kick. 8 × 50 at 1:30 using five-gallon bucket attached to waist by belt and four-foot stretch cord.

Power pull. 8 × 50 at 1:30 using bucket.

Fin swimming recovery. 800 total, mixed freestyle and backstroke.

Breaststroke tethered swimming. Use stretch cords attached to waist.

- Negative work: 8 to 10 max stretched 25 to 40 meters. At the end of full stretch, continue swimming in place for :15 to :20 at 200-meter stroke rate. Rest for :10.
- Positive work: Swim back, speed assisted breaststroke.

Transition work. IM tethered swimming:

- 4 × max stretch butterfly going out (negative)/backstroke speed assist coming home (positive).

- 4 × max backstroke/breaststroke.
- 4 × max breaststroke/freestyle.

Tuesday Afternoon

Warm-up. 600 free plus 4 × 100 IM at 1:30; 400 IM (50 drill/50 swim); 6 × 100 freestyle at 1:20 descending 1 to 3.

Preset.

- 4 × 100 (50 fly/50 back) at 1:30 descending 1 to 4.
- 4 × 100 (50 back/50 breast) at 1:30 descending 1 to 4.
- 4 × 100 (50 breast/50 free) at 1:30 descending 1 to 4.

Main set A. Active rest (slow to fast swimming)

- 4 × (50 fly easy at :40 + 100 back at 1:30) descending 1 to 4 to 400 IM pace.
- 4 × (50 back easy at :40 + 100 breast at 1:30) descending 1 to 4 to 400 IM pace.
- 4 × (50 breast easy at :50 + 100 free at 1:30) descending 1 to 4 to 400 IM pace.

Fin recovery swim. 400 freestyle.

Main set B. Active rest breaststroke.

- 4 × (50 free easy at :50 + breaststroke at :50) descending to 200 race pace.
- 4 × (50 free easy at :50 + breaststroke at :50) at 200 pace + :01 per 50.
- 4 × (50 free easy at :50 + breaststroke at :50) at 200 race pace per 50.
- 4 × (50 free easy at :50 + breaststroke at :50) at 200 race pace - :01 per 50.

Swim down fins. 400 (100 free/100 back).

Wednesday Afternoon

Warm-up. 800 (400 free, 400 mixed); 600 (300 free, 300 IM [75s of each stroke]).

Preset. 6 × 75 fly-back-breast at 1:10 descending 1 to 3; 6 × 75 free at 1:00 descending 1 to 3.

Kick. 4 × 150 kick at 3:00 (50 3 kicks per pull, 50 2 kicks per pull, 50 regular).

Pull. 8 × 100 at 1:45; 2 × (25 chin up + 25 fast lunges)

Main set. $\dot{V}O_2$max (pulse 180 to 200 bpm range)—4 × 200 breaststroke at 8:00 sendoffs.

- 50 from dive, going out at 200 pace, controlled at 1:30.
- 100 from push off, mid 100 for 200 race pace at 2:30.
- 50 from dive, max speed coming home at 1:30.

Add up 200 time. Should be 4.0 seconds under your goal 200-yard time. Average = 1:50.0 (26.0, 58.0, 26.0).

Recovery swim with fins. 500 continuous lactate removal.

Dryland Training

Dryland training works to improve flexibility and strength in three specific areas: core, upper body, and lower body. The body's core strength needs to be established first. This strengthening can start as early as high school using a general strength-training program that targets the core muscles (abdominals, back, hamstrings, and quadriceps). Once the core strength is established, strength that is more specific to breaststroke can be developed.

The wave breaststroke requires powerful upper-body strength from the fingertips to fingertips across the chest and back muscles. One of the best methods for strength improvement in this area is using a medicine ball routine of 15 to 45 minutes in duration three times per week. Special emphasis must be paid to shoulder shrug flexibility for fast lunging.

To strengthen the lower body for breaststroke, work on strengthening the adductor muscles of the thigh (closing the legs together) and the knee extensors (quadriceps muscle). Strengthening the hamstring muscles is also important so that swimmers can bring the heels to the buttocks fast. Pay attention to ankle flexibility, especially dorsiflexion (toes toward shin bone), by stretching the Achilles tendon. Squat jumps on a flat surface or steps are an excellent way to strengthen the knee extensors. A good strengthening and stretching exercise is rising up from a kneeling-sitting position, starting with the insteps on the floor and the buttocks between the heels. This is a very good way to dorsiflex the ankles and to help the inward rotation of the knees. Use caution! Take time to gradually increase flexibility so that there is less risk of injury. Here are some other effective dryland exercises that simulate some of the movements specific to breaststroke.

The *Vasa trainer* can be used for the catch and pull phase of the breaststroke (outward and downward sweep in breaststroke). This device helps develop hand, wrist, and forearm strength. The Vasa trainer is also an excellent training device for freestyle and butterfly strokes. It allows elbow extension from 90 to180 degrees for triceps development. It also benefits acceleration through a full range of motion in freestyle and fly training.

Stretch cords (tubing) may be substituted for the Vasa trainer. Stretch tubing provides a better way to accurately simulate the breaststroke pull as it is done in the water.

Breaststroke bench (sled) may be used for breaststroke kick simulation. The Vasa trainer is anchored down two feet from a padded wall. Lying on the stomach on the Vasa trainer sled, the swimmer kicks against the wall, pushing off with the insteps to drive the body up on the sled. The goal is a soft landing on the padded wall with an explosive push off. The swimmer should do 12 to 20 repetitions following a good warm-up. Use caution, for this exercise is extremely stressful on the knees and ankles.

Swim bench. This device is not very specific for breaststroke training, but it can be used for improving specific power for other strokes. Interval sets of 4 × :45 at the #4 setting for freestyle and at the #2 or #3 settings for butterfly are beneficial.

Summary

- The wave breaststroke is driven by the lower arms; the flat breaststroke was driven by the legs.

- Lunging makes the new breaststroke more energy efficient.

- Breaststroke has the highest energy requirement of any stroke.

- The rhythm of the pull, lunge, and kick is important in setting up a breaststroke training program.

- Training drills for breaststroke include sculling, pulling variations, kicking, and swimming variations.

- Training sets for breaststroke are made up of combinations of training drills.

- The amount of breaststroke and breaststroke-related drills can be 50 percent or more of the total training load.

- Breaststroke threshold training speed is difficult to accurately establish. Heart rate is a better indicator of whether an athlete is training at his or her anaerobic threshold.

- Flexibility and strength training are essential for breaststroke success.

CHAPTER TWENTY-TWO

Individual Medley Training

Dick Shoulberg

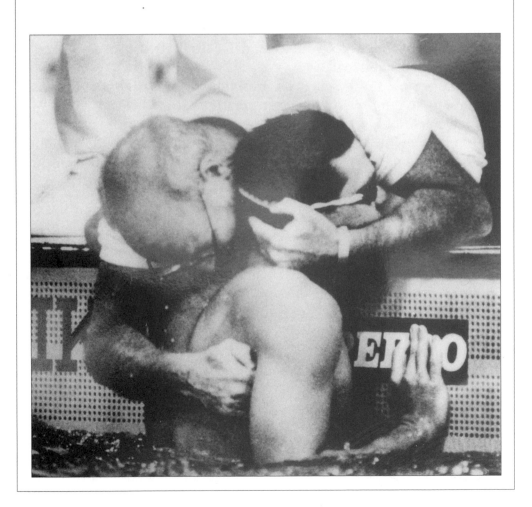

Before I get into the heart of the individual medley training, let me explain my coaching philosophy and why I do the things I do. I've had 13 years of experience coaching YWCA, YMCA, and summer club swim teams and am finishing my 31st year at Germantown Academy as the aquatics director and head swim coach of the school and club teams. I also teach five swimming classes a day, from pre-K through grade 12 including lifesaving.

My philosophy, as a grass-roots swim coach, is that it is important to expose athletes to all four competitive strokes and not to allow them to specialize in any one event or one stroke before the age of 12. Conditioning athletes with all four strokes creates a stronger team atmosphere, as all the athletes practice together, and most important, it is the best way to develop total body strength, coordination, and balance in the young or developmental swimmer. Working all four strokes each day combats the fatigue factor in training, and changing the stroke patterns builds more strength than doing only one pattern per day. If you keep accurate records—daily, weekly, monthly, and yearly—you will be able to analyze them and see for yourself the benefits of training well-rounded swimmers in all four strokes.

In my opinion, the IM incorporates everything a swimmer needs to know about swimming. It teaches proper pace, race strategy, conditioning, and transitional turns. The IM specialist may not be an athlete who is going to excel in one particular stroke, but he or she will be able to combine all four strokes very successfully. An accomplished all-around swimmer in the developmental stage may be the athlete college teams are most interested in recruiting.

Decreasing Freestyle Training

Every year from 1980 through 1992 an individual medley (IM) swimmer from our program represented the United States on the National A Team, and many years we sent more than one. During the 1970s, I focused more on total yardage than on the range of movement in swimmers' stroke patterns during training. But after studying the training patterns I decided to change them in the 1980s by increasing the percentage of butterfly, backstroke, and breaststroke in training and by decreasing our freestyle training (per day, week, month, and year) to about 42 percent of the total. This way, my flyers, backstrokers, and breaststrokers would increase the percentage of swimming their primary stroke each day (to about 25 percent), but would still work all four strokes every day.

One reason I love the IM is that it forces me to teach and train the athletes' less efficient strokes. Never tell athletes that they are lousy breaststrokers, backstrokers, or butterflyers. Rather, tell them which stroke is their least efficient stroke and dedicate time in their training to correcting flaws. In our program every Thursday morning is "less efficient stroke morning." During this time the athletes work on drills that teach them to be aware to the speed of the stroke that they need to work on.

Training IM Endurance and Speed

I prefer to train swimmers for the longest IM event, the 400 IM, or for the 12-and-unders, the 200 IM, rather than the 100 IM. The longer race incorporates all the elements they need—stroke mechanics, endurance, speed, starts, and turns—while the shorter event does not cover endurance as adequately.

For the 400 IM, I tell my athletes to focus on conserving energy in their primary stroke but not to be afraid to use their speed. I also emphasize the need to negative split the 100 leg of their least efficient stroke. Really, I want all four strokes to be negative split—this helps swimmers build up tolerance to swim hard in the second half of the stroke and push their threshold. With the fly that is sometimes hard to do, given the excitement of the race and the effect of the dive, but if swimmers train the center part of the IM, the back and breast, they will find it very easy to settle down and use proper pace.

I tell my IM swimmers to increase their speed in the last half of the breaststroke and to try to get into the freestyle leg before their opponents. If your athlete is swimming freestyle while the competition is finishing up swimming breaststroke, your swimmer will be tough to beat. If you don't train enough breaststroke, your athletes will spend too much energy trying to get ahead of their competitors before the freestyle leg and the resulting fatigue will cause them to be inefficient in the freestyle leg. Many great swimmers have speed in the fly and back, are decent in the breast, and are terrific individual freestylers, but can't seem to bring home the freestyle leg of the IM. I think this failure is caused by not training enough breaststroke, and more important, by not training enough combinations of back-breast, and breast-free. I think the combination of types of training—the mix of freestyle, other strokes, kicking, and pulling—is the key to effectively preparing for the IM.

Preparing IM Specialists for Success

Our program's first Olympian, Karen La Berge, made the 1980 Olympic trials. She qualified second in prelims to Tracy Caulkins in the 400 IM with a six-second improvement over her lifetime best and was preparing for the finals that evening. She warmed up with only fartlek training, a method we still use today that has the athlete count either strokes—18 strokes technique work, 12 strokes build up, and 6 strokes race pace—or distance—75 meters technique, 50 meters buildup, and 25 meters race. This warm-up helps the athlete change speeds and work on transitional turns, fast stroke patterns, and technical stroke patterns until he or she feels ready to race.

After her warm-up, I brought Karen a Popsicle, and we sat down and talked about the race. I think I was more nervous than she was! I told her to float the fly and be in eighth place, build the backstroke, build the breaststroke, and race the freestyle. She dropped another 1.5 seconds and in one day bettered her time over eight seconds—and made the team. It wasn't just the Popsicle that did it; the training prepared her for this breakthrough!

Two examples of sets we used to prepare Karen for the trials are a broken 7,000 yards in 70 minutes—8 × 100 on :59; 1 × 800 on 8:08; 7 × 100 on :59; and 1 × 700 on 7:07—and a 10 × 1,000 freestyle on 10:20. In the latter set, she failed at #8 and so rested an extra 30 seconds, then repeated #8, and #9 and #10 were her fastest. Her mental toughness, desire to compete every day, desire to maintain a high level of fitness, and willingness to take care of her body through proper conditioning, bed rest, nutrition, and hydration were exceptional.

Polly Winde Surhoff made the World Championships in 1982. She came out of Murray Steven's age-group program in north Baltimore. She was primarily a breaststroker, and she was a great one. Murray had done a great job of teaching strokes to her. That year she was second to Tracy Caulkins in the 400 IM short course and went on to make the World Championships, where she passed Sippy Woodhead, the former American record-holder, with 20 meters to go. I think the reason was that Sippy had to expend so much energy in her breaststroke that Polly was able to go past with easy speed and then race the freestyle. And, again, there is a fatigue factor in the IM for swimmers who do not train all four strokes on a regular basis. The following summer Polly made the Pan-Am Games in the 400 IM.

In the fall of 1983 Sue Heon took a leave of absence from the University of Pittsburgh, where she would have been a senior, and began her training at Germantown Academy. Sue was, in my opinion, a natural backstroker and a strong middle-distance and distance freestyler. To this day, I think my butterfly is better than hers, and mine was never good! Her breaststroke was good. Her intensive training, at the pool and away from the pool, over those 11 months was incredible. I will give you an example of one particular day that I will never forget.

We rent lanes from the old Philadelphia Aquatic Club, now called the Pennypacker Club (Germantown did not—and still doesn't—have a long-course pool). The Pennypacker Club pool is 55 yards (about 50.3 meters), eight lanes. I told the athletes two weeks in advance that the second Sunday in May was a mandatory meet at Pennypacker. There would be a 400 warm-up and then a 15,000 meters for time. I wanted Polly to do a lot of backstroke, so I changed the times for her; I wanted Karen to mix her strokes; and I wanted Sue to swim 7,500 freestyle (since it was so close to the trials—about five weeks out). Sue decided that she would go an even pace. Her first 100 meters was a 1:10. Her next 74 were all 1:10. She turned to do an additional 100 and one of my former assistant coaches, Chris Martin, went over to stop her. She swam another 100, then another 100, and I told Chris to let her go. She completed the 15,000, and every 100 was exactly 1:10.

That swim gave Sue so much confidence that at the Olympic trials, with a little more that 75 meters to go, she turned on the afterburners and came home in a 31.0 for the last 50 freestyle, bringing her best time from a 4:53.8 to 4:46.1. She made the Olympic team. In her mind, the May race put her on that team. In my mind, making the team was a culmination of all the different training she had done that year. That race taught me a lot about the value of having the mind ready the day of the meet. At the Olympic training camp she was told not to do that type of long training; at the Olympics she qualified second in the morning but ended up fourth at night. I think Sue should have been able to continue the type of training she was used to doing with our team all through the Olympic training camp. I also think that it helped for her to have kids around her, her teammates at Germantown—Erica Hansen, Kathy Hettche, Jeff Prior, Dave Wharton, Peter Boden, and Trina Radke—in May of 1984 who were also willing to do that kind of training. Erica Hansen, one of the greatest talents I ever trained, went on to make the 1988 and 1992 teams in the 400 IM.

Jeff Prior was my second great male IM swimmer (the first was Chuck Bauman, a graduate of Southern Methodist University). Jeff was the gold medalist in the 400 IM at the 1985 World University Games and at the Pan-Pacs. After Jeff came a young man named David Wharton, who was asked years later, "Who helped you the most in your training?" He said that it wasn't a coach; that it was Karen, Polly, and Sue who told him to stick with it, to listen to his coach and assistant coaches, and to train fast. He went on to break two world records and to represent the United States for six consecutive years at the highest level. He won gold at nationals and at the Pan-Pacifics, won seven NCAA titles for USC, and still holds the American record in the 200 IM. He is by far the most competitive male athlete I have ever coached.

I sat Dave down in the fall of 1985 and told him that I had learned a lot from Sue Heon's 15,000 race and that I wanted to see how mentally tough he was. I challenged him to a 16,000 IM for time ([250 fly, 250 back, 250 breast, 250 free] × 16) . After 9,000 meters, Dave swam 100 meters of backstroke and stuck his head out of the water and said that he had miscounted freestyle in the race. I knew then that I had one of the greatest and rarest male swimmers in the United States—a thinking swimmer! We used the same type of swim in preparation for the World Championship trials but pared down the distance each week: 13,000, then 10,000, 7,000, 4,000, and finally 1,000 just a few days out from the trials. At those trials Dave, a junior in high school, passed Jeff Kostoff in the last 25 meters (just as Polly Winde Surhoff had passed Sippy Woodhead in 1982) to establish a new American record in the 400 IM.

The next summer at the Pan-Pacific trials, our national championships, Dave set another new American record. We went to Brisbane for the Pan-Pac meet, and he qualified second in the prelims behind the great Alex Bauman, 1984 gold medalist and world-record holder. Dave was disappointed with his swim and informed me that he didn't know how to race well on foreign soil. I told him that either I could ask the FINA officials if the 400 IM in the fall could be swum in the United States or he could pick it up and swim fast in Brisbane! He responded by focusing on his technique and race strategy, breaking the world record by over two seconds. He did so by negative splitting each stroke's 100. His transitional turns were flawless; every time I show the videotape to my team, I get chills. The following night he dropped almost two seconds in the 200 IM and won. He received the "Outstanding Swimmer of the Meet" award.

One girl in our age-group program really started to shine in the summer of 1997. Maddy Crippen dropped seven seconds at the 1997 World Championship trials and went 4:40 in the 400 IM, second to Kristine Quance. I would have to say that Maddy is the toughest IM trainer and all-around natural athlete I have ever coached, holding personal bests of 2:11 in the 200-meter fly, 2:16 in the 200-meter back, 2:29 in the 200-

meter breast, 4:43 in the 500-yard freestyle, 4:40 in the 400-meter IM, and 2:15 in the 200-meter IM. She doesn't have innate speed except in breaststroke. What she has is the ability to combine the four strokes to achieve success. Tables 22.1 through 22.3 show some of the workouts Maddy used to train for the IM.

I am very fortunate that my former athletes not only swam fast but typically stayed on to receive postgraduate degrees and still give back to the sport today. As I have said again and again to my wife, Molly, I am the luckiest guy in the world because I get to coach kids.

I love it when coaches spend a day or two on our deck and interact with my athletes; I learn something every time they come. I will tell you a short story about one coach who came to visit. After observing three practices this coach pronounced our training methods "bull." He then took some of the sets back to his team, and they swam real fast! So apparently the bull didn't hurt his team.

TABLE 22.1

Sample Morning Workout

Set	Stroke	Pace
32:00 16 m hopblock, lunges	Dryland	
16 × 50 on :40, 25 rpm*	Backstroke	1:20
3 × 600 on 7:45 hipbelt** /paddles	Backstroke	1:18
1 × 2,000 on 25:15; 1,000 paddles, 1,000 fly	Butterfly	1:16
8 × 100 on 1:45 head-high waterbug	Breaststroke	1:45
18 × 25 on 1:30 power rack	Power rack	6:00
Total: 5,850 yards		
Stroke categories	**Yards**	**Percent**
Backstroke	2,600	44.44
Breaststroke	800	13.68
Butterfly	2,000	34.19
Power rack	450	7.69

rpm is a spin or turnover drill. I refer to it as "rpm" because the athletes sit high in the water, have a fast turnover and their legs are always driving the whole way.

**A hipbelt is a belt the athletes wear that helps with correct hip rotation. I used it every day for about 18 minutes with Maddy Crippen for 10 months prior to the Olympic Trials. We basically only use hipbelts for backstroke or freestyle.*

TABLE 22.2

Sample Afternoon Workout

Set	Stroke	Pace
16 × 75 on 1:05 2-stroke IM	Individual medley	1:27
3 × (3× 300 on 4:05) 1 = pull buoy, paddles/tube 2 = paddles/tube 3 = paddles/tube	100 Backstroke, 200 freestyle	1:22
3 × 400 on 6:05 fast kicking	Kicking	1:31
3 × (1 × 150 on 2:10; 50 race, 50 technique, 50 race)	Freestyle	1:27
3 × (1 × 150 on 1:55; 25 technique, 25 race)	Freestyle	1:17
3 × (1 × 150 on 1:35 race)	Freestyle	1:03
3 × 800 on 9:55	Backstroke	1:14
75:00 Dryland training		
Total: 8,850 yards		
Stroke categories	**Yards**	**Percent**
Freestyle	3,150	35.29
Backstroke	3,300	37.29
Individual medley	1,200	13.56
Kicking	1,200	13.56

TABLE 22.3

Sample Saturday Workout

Set	Stroke	Pace
12 × (1 × 30 on :30 turn) (1 × 25 on :20 turn) (1 × 20 on :25 race finish IM order)	Freestyle Freestyle Individual medley	1:40 1:20 2:05
3 × 300 on 4:30 hipbelt* or drill	Backstroke	1:30
4 × (1 × 600 on 7:15 free zoomers, must negative split) (1 × 300 on 5:15 zoomer paddles, 25 breast, kick, pull, race) (1 × 200 on 2:45; 25 rpm high, 50 stroke, 25 zoomers and paddles)	Freestyle Breaststroke Backstroke	1:13 1:45 1:23
6 × 500 on 7:55 1/2 mix IM 3 = 400 IM (race) 100 float	Individual medley	1:23
16 × 25 on :20 free	Freestyle	1:20
12 × 150 on 2:25 50 technique, drill, race	Freestyle	1:37
12 × 125 on 1:45 odd = rev IM; even = normal IM	Individual medley	1:24
Total: 12,900 yards		

Stroke categories	Yards	Percent
Freestyle	5,260	40.78
Backstroke	1,700	13.18
Breaststroke	1,200	9.30
Individual medley	4,740	36.74

A hipbelt is a belt the athletes wear that helps with correct hip rotation.

Summary

- Never allow athletes to specialize in one stroke at a young age.
- Working four strokes each day lessens the fatigue factor in training.
- Maintain training records from year to year and analyze them for possible changes.
- The IM teaches pace, race strategy, conditioning, and transitional turns.
- Train to the longest IM race available in your swim classification.
- Negative split the 100 leg of the last three strokes in the 400 IM and the fly if you can.
- Race to be out front going into the freestyle leg.
- You must pay the price of intensive training to be successful in the IM.

CHAPTER TWENTY-THREE

Relay Training

David Marsh

The most overlooked and arguably the most enjoyable racing events in the sport of swimming are the relays. My heart still jumps with excitement when I recall an NCAA Championship relay team made up of relative unknowns Michael Bartz, Adam Jerger, John Hargis, and Brett Hawke in lane two outtouching the 1997 medley relay field and recording the fastest time in history. More important than the record was the fact that this relay catapulted the Auburn Tigers to our first ever NCAA Team Championship.

Another all-time favorite memory of mine involves the relay team made up of Katie Ryan, Brook Monroe, Mimi Bowen, and Katie Taylor, none of whom had ever been on a USA National Team at any level. At the 1999 Southeastern Conference (SEC) Championships, this team broke the American record in the 200 medley relay. Their relay eclipsed a time that had been set by a Stanford relay team featuring three USA Olympians. In the television interview following the race, freestyler Katie Taylor was asked if they had been going for the record. She responded, "I had no idea or concern about any record; I just wanted to touch the wall before Georgia did!"

Throughout the recent history of swimming it seems that many of the most heroic performances have occurred when four swimmers combined to perform well beyond the expected limits of four individual swimmers. Perhaps the best example is from the 1976 Olympics when the USA 400 freestyle relay team made up of Kim Peyton, Wendy Boglioli, Jill Sterkel, and Shirley Babashoff dug down deep to end the swimming events with an enormous upset of the East German women's team, who were known to have achieved dominance in the sport through the use of performance-enhancing drugs.

In this chapter, I outline some of the key areas we focus on at Auburn University when we prepare for relay racing. I explain the strategies and methods we use to improve starting and finishing technique, then discuss the decisions coaches face in selecting relay participants and in determining the best relay order. The following takeoff and finishing recommendations apply to all relay events (all distances).

The Relay Finish

The most vital ingredient in consistent, successful relay exchanges is the proper finish of each leg. Swimmers can and must learn how to finish the final stroke with a full extension through the fingertips while maintaining a consistent rhythmic tempo. Short stroking or gliding into the finish will "hamstring" the relay swimmer on the blocks.

There are a couple of strategies we use to develop and improve the finish. While we use these drills specifically to prepare for relays, these are good drills for nonrelay swimmers as well.

1. Practice finishes at the midpool area where there is no wall to serve as a distraction. By doing midpool finishes, swimmers can focus on extension skills. Whatever the stroke swimmers come into the finish with, there should be no excessive up or down movements of the arms, hands, or body as they approach the wall. The focus should be on "that spot" three to six inches under the surface in the center of the touch pad (or wall) where the fingertips will touch.

2. Have swimmers learn to adjust their stroke length by slightly shortening or lengthening strokes on the last three cycles into the wall during practice. Make sure that athletes learn to adjust their strokes at a variety of speeds. As with most skills, they should try to perfect movement patterns at slower speeds, then increase to race speed. Have swimmers learn to adjust strokes using equipment such as fins and paddles.

The Start Off the Block

The best relay swimmers gain an advantage by using a whole-body surging movement off the block, one of the most athletic moves involved in the sport of swimming. The complex movement involved in the start encompasses explosive jumping, timing, acceleration, streamlining, body stabilization, and flexibility. At the age-group level the start can be performed with merely an accelerating arm swing. At the senior and elite levels, athletes should shift the whole body, including the feet, forward as they perform the full accelerating arm swing that is known as "the launch."

To help swimmers understand the advantage of using the type of momentum gained in a launch, have them practice vertical jumps. Find a tall brick wall and have them stand next to it. First, have the swimmers raise their hands over their heads and jump as high as possible. Mark the spot. Then, have them jump up and touch the wall using a full arm swing, and mark that spot. Finally have them approach with one or two steps on the block before they jump. This helps enhance the arm swing. The progression in vertical distance will be obvious. Now have the swimmers imagine gaining the three to twelve inches they acquired with the arm swing in a tightly contested race!

Here are several tips swimmers can use to maximize their block departure.

1. Swimmers can perfect the timing of the arm swing by standing on the deck first, then taking the arm swing from a vertical jump to a horizontal leap (into the water).

2. Have swimmers learn relay start skills solo at first rather than having a swimmer performing a finish to cue them.

3. Swimmers can practice vertical power progression jumps with arm swings off the blocks for maximum height, then go for horizontal distance.

   - Movement should include a streamlined, feet-first entry into the pool to show control.

   - Swimmers should increase the body lean on jumps and eventually perform controlled pike dives, entering the water with no splash.

   - Swimmers should increase the body lean to regular dive position. Ideally the hamstring and calf should be at approximately a 90-degree angle, and the body should be almost parallel to the water before the final explosive movement with the legs.

   - To add one or two step-ups to further develop a feel for exploding off the blocks, have swimmers start again with vertical leaps—jumping up as high as possible from the deck, and then from the block, and progressing to the "running launch."

Entry Through Breakout

As important as the explosive departure from the blocks is the proper alignment of the body on entry. A smooth "no-splash" entry that carries an unassisted streamlined glide as far as possible is a great starting point. Keep in mind that the speed at which a relay swimmer comes into contact with the water is the fastest a swimmer will ever travel in the water; therefore, maximizing the efficiency of the above to below the surface transition is critical.

After the entry, a smooth transition from below to on the surface should be accomplished with a subtle, whole-body shift rather than more dramatic hand, head, or arm shifts. Breaststroke and butterfly swimmers (and freestylers who use butterfly kickouts) will make this whole-body adjustment at the point where the feet submerge to establish optimal pullout or kickout position. Freestylers who do not use butterfly kickouts will make the subtle adjustment as the knees submerge.

The typical breakout time for a swimmer of a relay start should be .2 to .5 seconds slower than a flat start. This is because the running start takes the swimmer farther out than a flat start; thus the swimmer is underwater longer. The distance gained from using a relay start over a flat start should be between six inches and a full yard.

Timing the Exchange

Only after the start is developed should a swimmer be concerned with timing a relay start off an incoming swimmer. The following exchange strategy is one that legendary Auburn track coach Mel Rosen used in bringing together the 1992 USA Olympic track sprinters. He had the athletes practice the majority of relay starts at a 50 percent effort level, focusing on rhythm and timing. Only after several smooth exchanges at this speed would he have the runners attempt an explosive exchange.

Initially swimmers should practice "safe" relay takeoffs emphasizing the incoming swimmer's finish technique, then the starting swimmer's launch and breakout. A differential of .1 to .2 seconds from the time the finishing swimmer's fingertips touch to the time the starting athlete's foot leaves the block is good for developing safe but fast relay exchanges. If the swimmer on the block waits to begin the arm motion until the swimmer in the water has begun the last arm stroke, the start should be safe.

To reduce the differential between the finisher's touch and the starter's launch, the swimmer on the block needs to learn to read the finisher. If the swimmer in the water has a stroke with a high tempo, he or she will typically end somewhat choppy and short, whereas a swimmer with excellent distance per stroke will typically have a long extension. A swimmer's finishing style needs to be consistent to allow the team to gain the competitive advantage in a close relay race. The athlete on the block must be able to trust the swimmer in the water.

Here are some tips for improving relay start timing:

1. Have a relay swimmer stand above the lane while each swimmer finishes. The athlete can become familiar with a particular swimmer's finishing tendencies just by observing.

2. Use a video camera to record practice and meet exchanges. Viewing an exchange that is a jump on videotape in slow motion will make such an exchange more obvious when it occurs live at full speed.

3. A swimmer will develop a good feel for whether a fast, medium, or slow start is called for through trial and error. Obviously, the

swimmer cannot develop a feel if the coach does all the immediate evaluating. With practice, the swimmer should develop a sense of timing for a relay exchange.

Coaching Decisions

My first assignment as the head coach of a USA National team was in 1995 for the Pan-Pacific Team in the newly completed Georgia Tech Olympic Pool. This experience turned out to be a lesson in relay strategy for me. The meet's last event was the 400 freestyle relay, and expectations were high as Gary Hall Jr. was having a tremendous meet having split a sizzling 47.95 on the 400 medley relay. In our final team meeting I announced the relay order: Gary Hall, Joe Hudepohl, John Olsen, and David Fox. I was sure that this team would give us an insurmountable lead after the second leg and would ensure victory over the Australians in the final event of the meet. The veteran relay members respectfully approached me with an alternative relay order to consider. Their thoughts were that that David had traditionally been an excellent lead-off swimmer and that Gary, always at his best when the lights were brightest, should take the anchor leg. Their input proved to be 100 percent correct. The relay team went on to set the only world record of the competition; the key legs were David's leadoff and Gary's anchor.

On my teams, I have always tried to make relay participation an honor; great relay splits garner as much or more acknowledgement as individual swims. The first consideration in deciding who swims on a particular relay is the goal of the relay. Yes, the goal is usually to win, but by how much? The best relay entries may not always be the fastest four swimmers available. For example, to ensure a win in the final relay of the meet, it may be necessary to save the four fastest swimmers and to take a bit of a chance on winning the first relay by using some swimmers who are slightly slower but who could win anyway. On the other hand if the meet has already been won, it might make sense to use slower swimmers in the final relay so that more swimmers have a chance to excel. Why not offer other swimmers the chance to prove themselves in a relay position? The goal may not always be to win; it could be to reward some hardworking swimmers with the chance to compete or to increase the team depth on relays by providing relay experience to more swimmers.

When coaching age-group level swimmers, I have always tried to use as much objective data as possible (i.e., putting together the best times from individual events) in determining participants for a relay. At the more elite level, there are certain swimmers who seem to have an innate ability to consistently swim at phenomenal levels on relays, in season and throughout taper. A few of Auburn's such relay experts were Rowdy Gaines, Dave McCagg, Per Johansson, Greg Schmid, Yoav Bruck, Nick Shackell, Adam Jerger, Annie Lett, Sandy McIntyre, Keri Reynolds, Katie Taylor, Brett Hawke, and John Hargis. I can picture each one of these athletes running down or outtouching their competitors in relay situations, generally extending themselves well beyond their performance in their individual races.

As the saying goes, "When you're hot, you're hot!" Never in our sport is this phrase more true than in championship meets. My first inclination is to select the swimmer who seems to be "hottest"—swimming fastest—at that time. At the 2000 Women's NCAA Championships, junior Brook Monroe found herself on her first collegiate 400 freestyle relay while more experienced and historically much faster 100 freestylers watched from the bleachers. Brook was having a great meet; despite being a breaststroke specialist and despite having a two-beat freestyle kick, she was able to give us the 55.6 relay split that secured a top-five NCAA team finish. I also encourage my swimmers to express their desire to be on the relay. A simple "I am ready if you need me coach" is always appreciated.

Having determined the goal of the relay and which swimmers seem to be "on" or "up" for a particular relay, it's time to consider the relay order. The following factors should be taken into account:

1. Goal of the relay. A goal of performing the fastest time possible usually dictates a fastest to slowest order, to use the calm-water advantage.

2. Psychological makeup of relay team members. The first and fourth slots are for pressure performers.

3. Type of pool and type of competition. For example, if it's a slow pool, the team must be able to quickly get out front.

4. Types of competition. End of season, championship, and season meets call for different strategies.

5. Familiarity with relay exchanges. The bigger the meet, the more important it is that the swimmers be familiar with relay team members' tendencies.

If there is any question about whom to select for a relay spot, I consider who *wants* the pressure, who has historically performed well under similar conditions, and who has "easy speed." Finally, I pick someone I can trust to have a quality takeoff and finish.

The beauty of relays is evident when the TV cameras capture three swimmers gathered around the starting block using whatever air they can capture to cheer home their anchor leg swimmer, then embracing in celebration of the extra points earned toward a championship title or gold medal. Equally exciting and remarkably similar is the relay scene down at the neighborhood pool, in which the age-groupers vie for blue ribbons with stickers on the back noting the winning time. That shared enthusiasm is what relay racing is all about.

Summary

- Successful relay exchanges depend on a good finish by the swimmer of each leg.
- The start involves explosive jumping, timing, acceleration, streamlining, body stabilization, and flexibility.
- Swimmers should perfect the timing of the arm swing in the relay start by practicing on the deck first.
- Swimmers should practice vertical jumps with arm swings off the blocks for maximum height, then distance.
- Entry into the water must be streamlined and should produce little or no splash.
- Have swimmers practice "safe" relay exchanges with the focus on finish, launch, and breakout before emphasizing time.
- Have swimmers practice relay exchanges by watching the finish only at first—no launch.
- Use a video camera to help critique relay starts and finishes.
- Swimmers must develop their own feel and confidence for relay starts.
- Relay swimmers may have valuable input into the order of the relay.
- Knowing who wants the pressure is important in making relay decisions.

CHAPTER TWENTY-FOUR

Power Training

Randy Reese

Power is an important part of conditioning for swimmers of all strokes, but especially for those who swim breaststroke and butterfly sprint events. In those strokes there is a pull, executed by using both arms simultaneously, followed by a recovery period during which the hands are not in the water and the swimmer's forward motion relies on the pull from the previous stroke. This is in direct contrast to the freestyle and the backstroke, in which one hand is always in the water producing a pulling effect. The breaststroke and butterfly strokes also require the swimmer to pull up and out of the water to breathe; thus there is an even greater need for a powerful forward motion.

The textbook definition of power is strength times speed. It is relatively easy to increase strength in traditional dryland training by using a combination of weight training and exercises that use the swimmer's own body weight. Speed, on the other hand is more a matter of conditioning the nervous system to fire nerve impulses at a more rapid rate. Maximum speed cannot be achieved as long as there is muscular tension; tension in the muscles is like static in a telephone line that prevents clear reception. Muscle tension does not allow a clean signal for a rapid contraction of the muscle. Once swimmers have increased their muscular strength and improved their muscular relaxation to get maximum speed, theoretically they have gained power.

Most people think of strength work as something a swimmer does out of the pool. The problem with such training is how to take this power into the water and condition it into useable, specific speed for swimming. There is a surefire way to rapidly develop strength and muscular power endurance with swim-specific training, however, using a system of pulleys and baskets. The remainder of this chapter is devoted to a description of my own pulley and basket training.

The pulley system our athletes use is designed to maximize their strength and endurance as well as their stroke-specific feel for the water as they train. Swimmers are attached to the system by a belt worn around the waist. The belt is attached to ropes, which are fed through a pulley system and are attached to weights. The weights increase resistance in the swimmers' motion as they move through the water. The weights are placed in sturdy milk baskets or wire baskets that can be specifically made; alternatively the weights can be attached to a chain that runs through the hole in the middle of the circular weight and that is snapped to the pulley. The baskets are hung from the ropes, allowing for maximum use of the pulley system in each lane. Usually two swimmers per lane are attached to baskets. The simple construction of this device can be accomplished with some basic materials that are readily available at any hardware store (see figure 24.1, a and b).

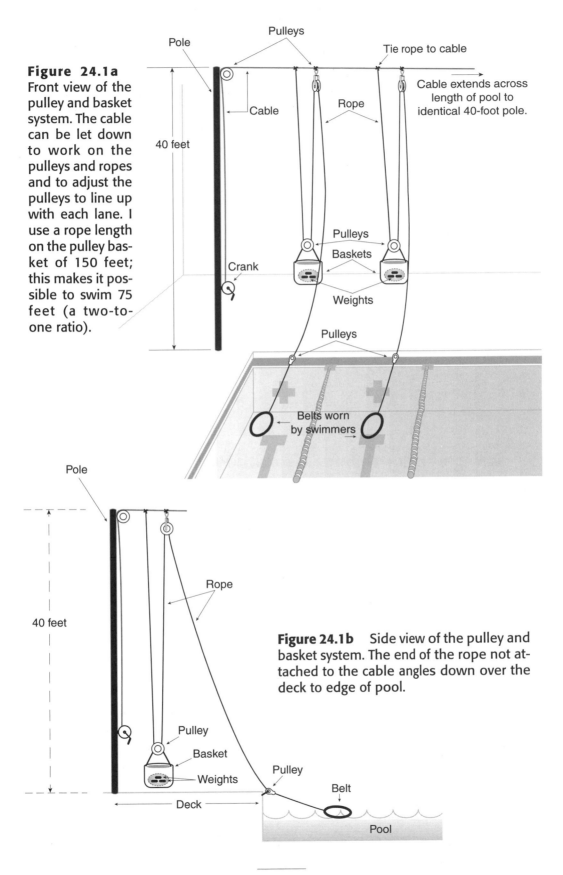

Figure 24.1a Front view of the pulley and basket system. The cable can be let down to work on the pulleys and ropes and to adjust the pulleys to line up with each lane. I use a rope length on the pulley basket of 150 feet; this makes it possible to swim 75 feet (a two-to-one ratio).

Pole

Pulleys

Tie rope to cable

Cable

40 feet

Cable extends across length of pool to identical 40-foot pole.

Rope

Crank

Pulleys

Baskets

Weights

Pulleys

Belts worn by swimmers

Pole

40 feet

Rope

Figure 24.1b Side view of the pulley and basket system. The end of the rope not attached to the cable angles down over the deck to edge of pool.

Pulley

Basket

Weights

Pulley

Belt

Deck

Pool

329

Using pulleys and baskets to aid in training swimmers has been done since the late 1970s. Although this technique has not been used extensively, it has produced significant improvement in both age-group and senior swimmers (see table 24.1). There is a certain novelty involved in being attached to a weight system in the water, and swimmers seem to like these workouts.

I have found that the greatest conditioning benefit for swimmers can be achieved by using the basket system on Monday, Wednesday, and Friday during the high yardage part of the season. It is beneficial, I believe, to give swimmers at least a day's rest between basket workouts to allow the body to recover. Most of my team, which includes age-group and senior swimmers, focuses on muscular endurance for two basket workouts a week (Monday and Friday), and focuses on strength development using the baskets once a week (Wednesday). Most sprint-specific swimmers, however, should switch the focus on Monday and Friday to strength development and on Wednesdays to muscular endurance.

— TABLE 24.1 —

Swimmer Improvements With Pulleys and Baskets

Swimmer	Age	Event (m)	Time training with pulleys	Previous best	Improved time	Improvement
Tommy Hannon	20	100 fly	4 months	54.9	52.8	3.8%
Nate Dursing	21	200 free	4 months	1:51.0	1:48.9	1.9%
Jamie Rousch	21	200 free	4 months	1:50.7	1:48.6	1.9%
Andrea Axtell	14	100 fly	11 months	1:06.0	1:01.3 (unshaved)	7.1%
Andrea Axtell	14	200 fly	11 months	2:28.0	2:15.1	8.7%
Lexi Spann	14	200 breast	11 months	2:49.0	2:37.7	6.7%

Building Muscular Endurance

Developing muscular endurance enhances the swimmer's ability to maintain a consistent rate of speed over a long period of time. To build this endurance with baskets, our athletes swim a total of 4,500 to 5,000 yards with short rest interval sets of 100s and up using light weights.

Swimmers who have used the basket training device for several weeks show the same muscular endurance conditioning level as individuals who have used regular pull, kick, and swim drills for two months. Swimmers notice much quicker improvements in the water with the pulley and basket system than with typical dryland weight training. I think the biggest reason for this is that swimmers must maintain good technique to pull the weight up in the water, whereas swimmers who are working on a swim bench or using surgical tubing to simulate strokes on dry land do not need to use exact stroke technique to move the resistance.

Some coaches have also tried building muscular endurance by taking surgical tubing and using it in the pool. Tubing can be used to partially simulate work done with baskets. However, the problem with using surgical tubing is that, in the beginning, the resistance provided is usually too easy for the swimmers. Because of this, the swimmers using surgical tubing take only a few strokes in which they exert the correct amount of pressure; after that the pressure becomes too great and the swimmers cannot continue moving forward. This completely changes the stroke technique; too much pressure alters technique in a negative way. If the swimmers use surgical tubing instead of baskets, I recommend that they stop and turn around as soon as their forward progress is stopped. This will prevent them from developing bad stroke technique.

Strength Building

Raw strength is necessary for explosive speed in sprinting. Strength building sets should use heavier weights in the baskets and should be shorter sets than those used for building muscular endurance. I help swimmers determine the proper weight through trial and error.

On strength days, we generally keep the total yardage of basket sets to under 3,000 yards, and sets consist of intervals of 100 yards and under. Using fins and paddles enables swimmers to increase resistance to make the set a more strength-producing exercise.

Pulley and Basket Workouts

During the drills that follow, regardless of the strokes being practiced, swimmers can swim back very fast with weights and create a towing effect. This is a good training method to enhance the swimmers' feel of going fast in the water and awareness of the magnification of resistance produced by nonstreamlined movements in the water. Another option is for swimmers to float back or swim easy to help them recover for the next resistance lap. Most swim sets are 400 or under for freestyle, backstroke, and breaststroke. Sets of 100 or under are more appropriate for butterfly unless the swimmers are using a triple or double kick. The reason for this is that it is very difficult to maintain good butterfly technique on longer swims. The following are drills that can be used with particular strokes, examples of strength workouts, and examples of muscular workouts.

Freestyle Basket Drills

Using fins and paddles with most of these drills is also an option.

- Touch and pull (catch up). The swimmer swims one-arm freestyle. The arm that is not used to pull is either held at the side or extended in front.
- Freestyle kick with board
- Kick with thumbs locked, head out

Backstroke Drills

- Single-arm pull with arm not being used held at the side
- Double-arm pull
- Spin drill
- Kicking on back with arms locked overhead
- Kicking on back with arms at sides

Breaststroke Drills

- Breaststroke pull with dolphin kick. One stroke up on surface of water, three strokes underwater (one stroke per kick).
- Head-out breaststroke pull with freestyle kick
- Breaststroke kick with arms at sides
- Breaststroke kick on back with arms at sides

- Breaststroke kick with a board
- Breaststroke pull with a pull buoy

Butterfly Drills
- Triple-kick butterfly
- Double-kick butterfly
- Kicking drills on side with bottom arm out in front and top arm at side
- Kicking butterfly on back with arms locked overhead
- Kicking butterfly on back with arms at sides
- Kicking with a board
- Butterfly pull with a pull buoy

Strength Workouts

4 × 100 pulley stroke drill on 2:00

6 × 50 pulley stroke drill on 1:15

1 × 200 pulley stroke drill on 3:30

3 × (1 × 100 pulley kick with fins on 2:15 and 2 × 50 pulley kick on 1:15)

4 × 50 stroke drill on 1:00

5 × 100 pulley swim on 2:00

1 × 200 stroke drill on 3:30

2 × (2 × 100 pulley swim with fins on 1:45 and 2 × 50 swim with fins on 1:15)

4 × 50 stroke drill on 1:00

10 × 50 pulley swim with fins and paddles on 1:30

Muscle Endurance Workouts

1 × 400 pulley stroke drill, 1:30 rest

2 × 200 pulley stroke drill, 1:00 rest

3 × 300 pulley swim, 1:00 rest

8 × 100 pulley kick with fins on 1:45

1 × 1,000 pulley swim with fins, 2:00 rest

2 × 400 pulley swim with fins and paddles, 1:30 rest

2 × 200 swim with fins and paddles, 1:00 rest

Summary

- Power is strength times speed.
- Dryland training is the main method of developing strength.
- Improve speed in the water by using resistance in the pool.
- The pulley and basket system rapidly develops muscular endurance.
- The weights inside the baskets in the pulley system increase the resistance and the challenge encountered in the training.
- The pulley system requires and encourages good technique.
- Surgical tubing swims can improve water power.
- Strength training should be done with heavy weights in the basket.
- Fins and paddles can be used to increase resistance in the power drills.

CHAPTER TWENTY-FIVE

Preparing to Excel in Competition

Don Gambril

Gambril

Swimming is, without a doubt, one of the most demanding sports in the world considering the number of years, hours per day, weeks, and months involved for coaches and athletes. Most of today's world-class swimmers have 10 or more years invested in training—and what training! Not many other sports require an athlete to train twice daily for a total of 10 to 12 sport-specific workouts per week and to endure extensive flexibility training and strength conditioning. Getting swimmers to get in the pool in and of itself can be a very stressful endeavor. Often the challenge for the coach is to get his or her swimmers in the pool to start practice without losing patience.

It only makes sense that the most important goal of the team is to swim the best possible times in competition and to get the very highest marks in the most important meets of the season. Perhaps the greatest measure of a coach's career is how well his or her athletes performed in the championship meets, when it counted. Many coaches, having been inducted into their respective sport's Hall of Fame, are still tortured by the fact that they never won the Super Bowl, the World Series, or the Stanley Cup.

How then does a swim coach approach this most important accomplishment? I will attempt to answer this based on the experience that I have had over 40 years of coaching swimmers. My experience has been acquired as coach of novice teams and age groupers in countywide competitions; of high school, junior college and Division I collegiate teams; and of national teams at the Pan-American Games, Pan-Pacific Games, World Championships, Goodwill Games, and other competitions, including five Olympic Games—once as head men's and women's coach and four times as an assistant. Just imagine having the experience of assisting George Haines, Peter Daland, and Doc Counsilman before becoming head coach of a US Olympic Team. Needless to say, having worked with them gave me a lot of confidence.

It isn't easy for an old coach reminiscing about his greatest moments and trying to decide exactly what was the reason for his success to draw a detailed conclusion. Perhaps, after reading this chapter, you will be able to draw your own conclusion. While it may not be possible to create one guaranteed, detailed list for success, I do have thoughts and feelings about what's important in preparing for success and excelling in competition. Let's see if I can list some of these for you. My list, I am sure, does not contain all of the elements of success, but a program built on this foundation would, with hard work, yield good results. Looking back over the five decades in which I have been involved in swim coaching, I find that the following items come to mind when I attempt to identify the elements of success in swim competition:

- Having confidence in oneself
- Making, believing in, and dedicatedly following a plan but not being afraid to adjust as needed
- Being a motivator
- Setting the example and being consistent

The final cornerstone for success is putting in the necessary hard work and evaluating that work honestly.

Having Self-Confidence

The most important element of success, probably, is confidence in oneself and in the program you are delivering. Forbes Carlile, the famous Australian swimming coach, has a sign at his Ryde Swim School that says something like, "We strive to develop an environment from which champions evolve." This statement really says it all. The level of competition in practice, the talent in the pool, the work ethic in the group, the belief in the program, and the coach define the level the team can reach. The workout that the coach delivers in the daily practice is only as important as the confidence the coach shows in his or her program and in the swimmers' abilities as well as the way the coach motivates the team to do the workout. The end result will be directly proportional to the effort the swimmers put out. Therefore the successful coach must get the swimmer to put forth the effort required.

In my first 15 years of coaching our teams won 13 league championships. As I look back, I can see that our attitude from the beginning was that we were going to win. There are lots of things that allowed us to have that attitude along the way. Perhaps by giving you the following examples I can convey the importance of both the athlete and the coach having confidence. Keep in mind that hard work must be the foundation of this confidence. Without that basic component, all the confidence in the world will not deliver the results for which a team strives.

I believe the fact that we were among the first, if not the first, high school program to shave our athletes for competition gave us a huge advantage. Back in 1960, I did my master's thesis on improving swim times by shaving. While we were reaping the benefit of shaved performances, others scoffed. It wasn't long, however, before everyone was shaving and enjoying that same advantage. Confidence was a big part of our success. We expected to have huge improvements in the championships and in big dual meets, and we did. Having established confidence in our program, our swimmers took it for granted.

In the 1963 long-course Nationals, the water temperature in the pool was in the high 80s (F). This had a much stronger effect on the distance swimmers than on those who swam the shorter events. The women in the 1500-meter event were about 20 seconds over their entry times across the board. We had a young 12-year-old on our team, Patty Caretto, who actually improved her entry time in this event by 20 seconds, from 20:20 to 20:00. I give you this information just as a reference.

The next year we were in Pittsburgh for the indoor National meet, in a brand new, state of the art pool. We had several very strong distance swimmers on our team. In the team meeting the night before the meet began, I talked to our girls and told them that we could be in first place at the end of the first event if they all did their jobs and swam the races they were capable of swimming. I spoke to each of our girls by name and gave them a time to shoot for—this was in front of the entire team—and then turned to Patty, and said, "Patty, if you improve your time the way you did last summer, you may score too." The next day Patty dropped her best time from 19:48 to 18:47! The other girls did well too, and we were first place, ahead of the great Santa Clara team, be it only for one event.

After the first day's final, I asked Patty to come downstairs with me to get some ice cream. When we sat down I told her, "I did say we had a chance to get second in the 1,500, but I didn't expect it to be you." She replied, with fire in her eyes, "That's what made me so mad!" I came right back and said, "Well, you know what you should be thinking of now, don't you?" "No, what?" she asked. I said, "The world record for long course is only 18:42, and you are much better long course than you are short course." To put all this in proper perspective Patty was 13 at the time, stood five-foot-one, and weighed 100 pounds.

That summer in the first day of a four-day meet, I entered Patty in the 1,500 (the only race of the day) with the American record holder, Carolyn House; the indoor national champion and record holder, Sharon Finneran; and the defending national champion, Ginny Dunkel. Patty went out in 4:47, her best 400 time, on the way to breaking the world record for the 800 meters by :05, on the way to breaking the world record for the 1,500 meters by almost :15! She swam a time around 18:30, almost two minutes faster than the summer before.

Looking back, it now seems like a daring challenge to give a 13-year-old. Over the years I have issued several such challenges that at the time, viewed realistically, seemed unlikely to be achieved. However, several of these challenges were accepted by different swimmers and yielded world-record accomplishments. These challenges became goals.

What part these challenges played in breaking world records cannot be determined. There is just no way of knowing. But my philosophy is and has always been *If you don't believe you can, you probably won't.*

After that strong first day performance, our team advanced, led by 16-year-old Sharon Stouder, who won both the 100- and 200-meter butterfly events with new world records. We had won our team's first individual national title that spring at Pittsburgh, where Sharon had won the 100-yard freestyle. Later that year, at the Olympic trials, Sharon and Jeanie Hallock took first and third, respectively, in the 100 freestyle to become my first US Olympic team members. We had a third young lady, Sandra Nitta, who made it in the 200 breaststroke later in the trials. Sharon also qualified first in the 100 butterfly, breaking the world record. I might point out that I never attended a national championship myself until 1961. Three years later, three of our athletes were going to the Olympic Games in Tokyo, Japan.

Sharon went on to win three gold medals in Tokyo, breaking the world record again in the 100 fly (no 200 fly for women in those Olympics) and taking second in the 100 free with a 59.9. Sharon, just 16, became the first American and the only woman at that time besides Australian Dawn Frasier to have broken the 1:00 mark.

We had set a team goal the year before to be second in the nationals in 1964 and to win our first team title in 1965. We accomplished both goals. None of the many champions, world-record holders, and Olympic medalists I've coached since that time have brought me more satisfaction or meant more to me than this group of young women.

Why I do I relate these war stories? I hope that they will awaken in some of you young coaches the thought that you can accomplish the same thing through hard work and confidence. Far too many coaches fail to see themselves as being able to accomplish great things. As one moves further up the ladder of success, there is generally more access to top talent. Confidence and hard work will take you as far you want to go.

Making and Sticking to a Plan

Where do we go from here? Looking back over the many teams I have coached and thinking about the great swimmers who swam on those teams as well as those who competed against us, it is clear that confidence was an extremely important element in their success. "One cannot achieve what one does not believe!" as the T-shirt slogan goes (Jack Nelson's team wore T-shirts with this slogan). There are, of course, such things as overconfidence and false confidence, but teams who work hard to create and follow a plan are not likely to experience them. The way to ensure that your belief becomes reality is to make a plan and see it through. A good plan will address mental strategy, specific training and preparation, and even how to handle time away from the pool.

I remember my first head-coaching assignment in 1966. I was selected to take the US Swim Team to Moscow for a meet. Olive Mucha of the Multnomah Athletic Club was my assistant, and Bill Lippman was the head manager. Our team was loaded with Olympians from the 1964 team as well as some young up-and-coming swimmers: Don Schollander, Greg Buckingham, Dick Roth, Ken Merten, John Nelson, Steve Rerych, Bill Utley, Ross Wales, Charlie Hickcox, Sharon Finneran, Judy Hombarger, Cynthia Goyette, Pam Kruse, Sue Pitt, and Martha Randall. We went into the meet as underdogs. Truth be known, we would not have been invited if the Russians didn't think they could handle us!

I won't go into details of the races here, but I will discuss the way we approached the competition. There have been many coaches who have influenced my own coaching; two are swim coach Peter Daland and football coach Paul "Bear" Bryant. They had one thing in common. They always approached a competition by trying to get the underdog role; their philosophy was *Never go into competition talking about what your team can do.* Peter successfully used this philosophy with the 1972 US Olympic team. Coach Bryant would speak at length with the press every year about why his talented and successful team should not be favored in a given contest or season. I will always remember the first football game I attended after arriving on the Alabama campus as a swim coach. The game was against Cal-Berkeley, and Coach Bryant did nothing but praise Mike White and the California passing offense. He continued right up to game time, bemoaning the bad scheduling. Would you believe we won the game 66-0?

Now you must understand that when you use this technique, you must make your own athletes understand that what they read in the papers and hear on TV is not reality, and that what is shared in your own locker room must stay there. This was our plan from the time we got to Moscow: to convince our opponents that we were out of shape and not prepared to compete with the likes of Simon Blitzgimon, Propopinko, llichev, and the other great swimmers we would face. The girls especially loved the game and talked to each other about it in the teenage language that they knew so well—pig Latin.

The Russians loved to follow Don Schollander around with a movie camera and film everything he did from the time he got into the pool each day. Therefore Don probably swam more backstroke and breaststroke in warm-up than in his entire life. He hoped to give them lots of film to study!

Can you imagine my position as coach to all these veterans? These great Olympic champions, world-record holders, and national champion swimmers had joined the squad and left their home coaches such as George Haines, Doc Counsilman, and Peter Daland. Who was I to lead them in such an important venture? The first thing I did, though, was to make the athletes believe that I was in charge and that I had no doubt about how to prepare them for their events. Olive went along with me on this and if she, as a veteran coach, had any doubts, I never saw them.

The challenge was to prepare these great athletes for their individual races. It was important that they have confidence in whatever they were asked to do. In those days, there were no instructions sent by home coaches to guide us. We planned to swim the complete Olympic schedule, except relays. That meant everything from the 100-meter events to the 1,500 (not all strokes were competed at the 100 and 200 distances at that time). We went to Poland for a few days and swam a shakedown meet in Warsaw. Things went well and the lack of competition there made the experience a good outing and a confidence builder.

We took Aeroflot, the Russian National plane, to Moscow. The meal was interesting, to say the least: hot dogs with no buns, caviar, and beer! When we arrived in Moscow, it was late at night. We went on to the hotel Younis, a bare-bones hotel with very small rooms. We all imagined that our rooms were bugged. I'll never forget waking up the next morning and looking out the window at a big building on a hill with a huge red star on top; yes, we realized, we were in Russia.

Most of our training there consisted of a warm-up with broken swims—these were designed to instill confidence in the swimmer's own readiness. There were no pace clocks in those days, at least not in Russia; they had just begun to be used back home. This meant that Olive and I had to give the swimmers their sendoffs on respective broken swims. I was working a stopwatch with each hand, the kind with sweep hands. I was terrified that I would mess up someone's sendoff. This didn't happen, fortunately.

Don Schollander hurt his shoulder just sitting down on his bed. He reached out behind him to catch himself and wrenched it. I was able to get some rubbing alcohol—vodka?—which I mixed with olive oil and wintergreen. The oil and wintergreen was George Haines's magic rubdown formula. I massaged Don until the skin was about worn through, assuring him that I would have his shoulder ready to go. (Yes, I was scared to death.) He recovered and easily won his events, as did most everyone on the team.

The trip was a great success. The US swimmers gave a great account of themselves. In fact, they did so well that the results were not printed in the Russian newspapers. I have always wondered what people must think when they read about a big meet coming up, as the Russian citizens did in this case, and then never see any results. The only success the Russian swimmers had was in the breaststroke event that they dominated in those days.

I have further reason to remember the trip fondly, as my son Greg was born just four hours after my arrival home. My wife, Teddy, had sent me on this all-important trip knowing that it would be touch and go as to whether or not I would be back before the baby was born. (Our oldest child, Kim, was born while I was on a destroyer in the Formosa Straight in 1957 on plane guard during the shelling of Qumoi.) This is the kind of sacrifice that a coach's spouse and family are routinely faced with. This trip was no doubt a large factor in my being selected at a young age as assistant coach to George Haines for the 1968 Olympics.

The 1968 and 1972 Olympic Games were great learning experiences in themselves. I could write chapters on each highlighting the ways George and Peter differ in their approach to preparing for the Games. It is the similarities, though, that I think are significant. These include approaching the Games with confidence but also with sound preparation in the pool. We had a great but lengthy training camp—a full month in Colorado Springs—before the Olympics in 1968. The feeling, probably correct, was that the team (swimmers of the longer events, in particular) needed that much time to prepare for the mile-high altitude in Mexico City. Our slogan from the start was that it was not altitude that our success depended on, but *attitude*!

A lot of planning also went into the off-time activities during the month-long camp to prevent team members from being bored and homesick, and to keep them focused on the task ahead. We scheduled everything from mountain climbs to golf to a mixed (men's and women's teams) evening of dancing and having a good time at the Junction.

Before the 1972 games, we set up the training camp at West Point. Once again the Olympic training was left to only two coaches, Peter Daland and me. The swimmers were completely cut off from outside distractions. We did go into New York City for a Sunday tour conducted by long-time AAU supporter Jack Abramson. The team had dinner at Mama Leoni's restaurant, then went on to Rockefeller Center to see Goldie Hawn in *Butterflies Are Free*. I was very impressed with Rick DeMont deciding, at the age of 16, not to go with us because it was a work day. He would not think of altering his grueling schedule for the outing! Peter stayed with him.

The team trained very diligently. Peter stressed in every team meeting the need to keep a strong "party line"—meaning that we should be overly cautious with the press in all interviews and should continue to play up the strengths of our competitors.

When we arrived in Munich for the Games it was 11:00 PM. Peter and I had discussed our arrival plan. In those days, we had no athlete's code of behavior and had to rely on our own tactics to try to get the swimmers to take care of themselves. We decided to check into the village and to take the team at once to the Olympic pool for a short loosening down workout. This was Peter's idea and was a product of his being a very experienced college coach. We knew that if we took the swimmers to their rooms at 11:00 PM the more adventurous members of the team would be off to town, maybe even to the famous beer gardens, that night. By going to the pool, then back to the village, the swimmers would get to their rooms close to the usual college bedtime of after midnight! There was some grumbling, but as far as we know, the plan worked as intended.

The main complaint was from Steve Genter, who talked of his chest hurting. We weren't concerned at first, nor even over the next couple of days as he continued to talk of pain in his chest. When he finally went to the team doctor, they found that one of his lungs was 20 percent collapsed. What causes a lung to deflate is air gets outside the lung, in the chest cavity, thereby depressing the lung. The assumption was that the flight and altitude had in some way caused the problem. The treatment is to make a small incision into the intercostal area and insert a little tube that lets the air out as the lung inflates. Steve was in the hospital for a couple of days. He came back to practice the night before he was to swim his first event, the 800 freestyle relay. A thoracic surgeon was assigned to be poolside whenever Steve was to swim. To keep the story short, Steve swam on the winning 800-meter freestyle relay, and later in the meet swam the 200 and 400 free events, winning a silver and a bronze. Imagine the courage it took for Steve to finish what he had set out to do in the Olympic Games.

Being a Motivator

This brings me to the 1976 Olympic team. We were up to three coaches, but still way below the current allotment of eight men's and eight women's coaches for the US Olympic team. Doc Counsilman was the head coach, and George Haines and myself were the assistants. What a great position for me to be in! It was my third successive Olympic endeavor, and I had had nothing but admiration and the deepest respect for my coaching cohorts since the beginning of my coaching career. My swimmers had successfully competed against teams they had coached, though, and I considered myself equal to them as far as preparing swimmers for top competition. That's not to say everyone else held me in high esteem, but I believed I could do the job, having just been involved with the two teams that had dominated the Mexico City (1968) and Munich (1972) Olympics, and having helped my own club teams win four national championships. One has to have confidence when training top-level competitors. It is also important to know the swimmers' times and to have knowledge of their respective competitors

The 1976 Men's United States Olympic swim team is the most successful team ever to represent this nation. The United States has the most medals won and the most gold medals collected in Olympic history.

From the first team meeting, head coach Doc Counsilman set the goal for the team: to be the best in history. He challenged those athletes to win every gold medal, to break as many world records as possible, and to sweep as many events as they could. At that time, each country was allowed three entries in each individual event.

From the start of training camp that year, things went well. Doc divided the team among us. I was assigned the distance swimmers, the sprint butterflyers, the sprinters, and Mike Bruner, a 200 butterflyer who was famous for his 100 × 100-yard repeats, leaving on 1:00. There have been other and yes, faster, sets but none that can truly be said to be faster relative to the times being swum at that time. George Haines had the stroke swimmers in his group settling mostly around the 200-meter distance. No one up to that time had had more success at that distance with their swimmers than George. Now get this—Doc took the weakest, on paper, members of the group. This included mostly individual medley swimmers and breaststrokers. No one could argue with the success Doc had had with breaststrokers and IM swimmers (not to imply that he hadn't had success with all distances and strokes), but he gave up Jim Montgomery, his own swimmer and an odds-on favorite to win three or more gold medals, to my group, and put swimmers in George's and my groups who had broken world records in the trials held in Long Beach three to four weeks earlier. Doc was clearly interested in total team success. In most cases, the athletes in the same events were put in the same groups and pitted against each other in training.

We had a great training camp in Canton, Ohio. Doc allowed each practice to be open. The stands were packed for almost every workout. Lots of age-group coaches in the area took advantage of the team's training to motivate their own swimmers. John Nabor held court with the young swimmers every day at every practice. He must have been on extended taper! It seemed that he was in the stands signing autographs long before my distance-oriented group was out of the pool!

I must tell you that Jim Montgomery did so little in training that I went to Doc about it. He asked me about the training Jim had done. I showed the records to him, and he said, "That looks about right." He was right, the training seemed to work; Jim had outstanding success, winning the 100-meter and becoming the first in history to break 50 seconds. He placed third in the 200, behind John Nabor and the winner, Bruce Furness. Matt Vogel's unorthodox training, doing untold amount of dryland preparation on deck, also prepared him well for his upset win in the 100 butterfly. Both cases were object lessons to me, illustrating the fact that there is more than one way to prepare and train for a race. Things had changed since 1968 when George Haines and I had trained the entire men's team in isolation in Colorado Springs for nearly one month before going to Mexico City. At that time, we split the team and trained them almost the entire time and had little contact with the home coach. In the training camp prior to the 1976 games we Olympic coaches were on the phone often with the home coaches to go over the training we were giving the swimmers.

It would be fun to tell all the details of the training camp if space permitted. Some of the highlights concern "Rocket Man," otherwise known as Olympic breaststroke champion John Henken, who built a rocket for each team member and coach to set off at the big barbecue the town held for us on the Fourth of July. It was a fireworks extravaganza, with John's homemade rockets a big part of the show. Evidently John was taking classes on rockets at Stanford. He made up a three-stage rocket to set off as we left Canton. It almost went well! The problem was that as he set it off in the parking lot, just as the bus was to depart, it began to lean slightly. As it went into the launch, it shot off across the interstate. Fortunately it didn't hit any cars or cause an accident and came to rest in an electrical yard, without hitting any equipment. No harm done.

When we arrived in Montreal the security was a shock. Whenever we loaded a bus to go to a satellite pool for training, two armed guards with automatic weapons went with us. They unloaded first, and one would run to the rear of the bus while the other secured the front as we unloaded. It must have seemed like overkill, or at least overprotection, except to those of us who had been in Munich. Sitting in the Olympic Village in Munich, looking out the window at the terrorists in the next building holding the Israeli hostages is an experience we will never forget.

The confidence that Doc had continually drilled into the team at training camp prevailed, and the team delivered. They took all the gold medals but one, the 200 breaststroke won by David Wilkie of Great Britain. They were awarded 12 of 13 gold medals, 10 of 11 silver medals (two relays were conducted; having won the gold, the silver was not available to them), and a bronze. The 400 free relay would have been a lock, had it been held. The squad broke eight world records and swept five events, while placing second in five other events.

Setting an Example

Being a coach means leading the team. A coach's decisions and actions set an example for swimmers to believe in and to follow. The following story is a case in point. Our most successful team at Alabama placed second in the 1977 NCAA meet to a great University of Southern California team. At our first team meeting in September, when we were discussing the upcoming 1977 season, I asked the team what they thought was the highest place we could reach in the NCAA championships. After some careful consideration of the top teams in the country, we decided to go for second place, bowing to the powerhouse Trojan team. Looking ahead to the NCAAs, we did not shave seven individuals for the SEC meet and lost by around 70 points to Tennessee. We won nine events, but lost on depth. This was a tough decision, seeing as how Alabama had never won the conference meet and likely could have that year (certainly if we could place second at the NCAAs to USC, we could win the conference meet). But we were focusing on the bigger goal.

When our time came at NCAAs, we did achieve our goal. When captains Jonty Skinner and Monty Daily picked up our second-place trophy, we knew that we had had our ultimate season. Having freshman Casey Converse upset Steve Shaw in the 1,650 and become the first to go under 15:00 added a great deal to the team's sense of accomplishment.

All programs are limited only by the imagination of the coach, the level of talent on the team, and the squad's motivation and confidence. There are other things that sometimes make success easier: adequate funds, good facilities, strong support, and so forth. None of these, in my mind, will have much effect without a dedicated, confident, motivated, and visionary coach.

Summary

- Swimming is an exceptionally demanding sport in terms of the time involved in both swim and dryland training.
- The most important goal for swimmers is to swim their fastest in the most important meets of the season.
- The greatest measure of a coach is how well his or her athletes perform in championship competition.
- Success comes from confidence in oneself and in the program.
- The training program is only as important as the motivation provided by the coach.
- Confidence is essential for success, but hard work must be the foundation of that confidence.
- Be specific in establishing goals and believe that you and your team can accomplish them.
- Take the "underdog" approach when going into competition.
- Communicate and sell the team plan to athletes preparing for competition.
- Commitment can help swimmers rise above even major adversity.
- Set the example and be consistent.
- Evaluate your plan at the end of the season and use it as a basis for a future plan.

ABOUT THE EDITORS

Dick Hannula is one of the winningest high school and club coaches in the history of swimming. While serving as the boys' swimming coach at Wilson High School in Tacoma, Washington, from 1959 to 1983, Hannula racked up the longest high school undefeated streak on record, winning 323 consecutive meets without a loss including 24 consecutive boys' Washington state high school swimming championships.

Hannula is a former multiple-term president of the American Swimming Coaches Association and currently a vice president of the World Swim Coaches Association. He has been inducted into the International Swimming Hall of Fame. Hannula is the author of another Human Kinetics book, *Coaching Swimming Successfully*. He resides in Tacoma, Washington.

Nort Thornton is the head men's swimming coach at the University of California at Berkeley. Thornton's Cal teams have consistently finished in the top 10 in the nation over the past 30 years. Thornton has coached Cal to two NCAA Championships and was named the NCAA Coach of the Year in 1979 and 1980. An inductee into the International Swimming Hall of Fame, he has coached the US national team at the Olympics and Pan-American Games. He has also served the swimming community as the president of the American Swimming Coaches Association.

ABOUT THE CONTRIBUTORS

Jack Bauerle has been women's coach at Georgia since 1979 and men's coach since 1983 and is the SEC's all-time winningest swim coach with 302 dual meet victories. He has led the Lady Bulldogs to three consecutive NCAA championships (1999 through 2001), and he has elevated the Bulldogs men to a perennial top 10 team. During his tenure, Bauerle has coached 130 All-Americans, 17 NCAA individual champions and three relays champions, and 11 US  Olympic swimmers. Of his swimmers, 33 have been awarded Academic All-America status and 14 awarded NCAA postgraduate scholarships. Bauerle is a three-time NCAA Coach of the Year and a nine-time Southeastern Conference Coach of the Year. He also served as the head US women's coach for 1997 World University Games and assistant women's coach at the 2000 Olympics. As a swimmer, he was a four-year letter winner at Georgia (1970-1974), a team co-captain, and a three-time school record holder.

Michael Bottom is the co-head swim coach at the University of California at Berkeley and is regarded as one of the world's top sprint coaches, having coached three of the top five sprint performers in 2000—Anthony Ervin and Gary Hall Jr. of the United States and Bart Kizierowski of Poland. All three swimmers made the finals at the 2000 games and for the first time in Olympic history, two men—Ervin and Hall—tied for the gold medal. In all, Michael's sprinters won  six Olympic medals at the 2000 games, more than any other US men's Olympic coach. In January 2001, another of Michael's swimmers, Gordon Kozulj from Croatia, broke the world record in the short-course 200-meter backstroke. Bottom graduated with the Scholar-Athlete award and a bachelor's degree in psychology from the University of Southern California. He earned a master's degree in counseling at Auburn. As a swimmer, Michael was a member of the 1980 Olympic team, a member of a world record-setting 4 × 100 freestyle relay, and part of three NCAA Championship teams at USC.

Peter Daland was the head coach at the University of Southern California from 1958 to 1992, where he led his team to nine NCAA Team Championships (the second most in NCAA history), 12 second-place NCAA team finishes, and 93 NCAA individual and relay titles. He also won 17 national AAU titles (15 men's titles at USC and 2 women's titles at the L.A. Athletic Club). His dual meet record was unparalleled: 318-31-1 (.917) in 35 seasons. USC went undefeated in dual meets in 20 seasons, including 1990-91 and 1989-90, and his 1977 team might have been the finest collegiate swim team ever. Among the world-class swimmers he coached are John Naber, winner of 4 Olympic gold medals and 10 NCAA titles; American-record holders Dave Wharton and Mike O'Brien; and Olympic stars Roy Saari, Murray Rose, Jeff Float, Joe and Mike Bottom, and Bruce and Steve Furniss. He was appointed women's US Olympic head coach in 1964 and men's US Olympic head coach in 1972. In 1977 he was inducted into the International Swimming Hall of Fame. A cofounder and editor of *Swimming World* and founder, editor, and publisher of *Junior Swimmer*, Daland also served as president of the American Swim Coaches Association from 1993 to 1994 and vice president of the World Swim Coaches Association President from 1968 to 1970 and again from 1994 to 1998. Now retired, Daland is working on several books chronicling the history of swimming, and he coaches the masters swim team at the Daland Swim School.

University of Arizona associate coach **Rick DeMont** specializes in coaching sprint training. Since joining the UA program in 1988, he has coached several USS and NCAA individual and relay national champions. A two-year and eight-time All-American at UA, DeMont swam for the Wildcats from 1977 to 1979. He is a former world-record holder in the 1500-meter and 400-meter freestyle events and the 4 × 100 free relay. He has collected numerous titles, including national, Pan American, world, and Olympic champion. He was the first man in history to swim the 400-meter freestyle in less than four minutes and is credited with pioneering negative split swimming. DeMont has been inducted into the University of Arizona Athletic Hall of Fame and the International Swimming Hall of Fame. He is also an artist and has had his paintings shown in local and national galleries.

Since 1973 **Jean Freeman** has built a competitive swimming and diving program at the University of Minnesota, placing at the NCAA championships in each year since 1986. A three-time Big Ten Coach of the Year, Freeman has coached 60 swimmers to All-American status 169 times. More than 100 swimmers have garnered All-Big Ten honors, and 92 Minnesota Gophers have received academic All-Big Ten honors with 13 student athletes named academic All-Americans.  Freeman's coaching philosophy centers on a total person concept, in which academics are emphasized as much as athletics. For the last decade, the Gophers have been involved with community service programs and the squad has works with the younger swimmers of the local age-group USS teams. A graduate of the University of Minnesota, Freeman was a member of the swimming and diving team from 1968 to 1972. She has been named to Team Speedo—an advisory board for swimming and diving—and to the board of the College Swim Coaches Association (CSCA). She also received an award from the CSCA in recognition of over 15 years of excellence in college coaching and service to the coaching association. She has been inducted into the Minnesota Swim Coaches Association Hall of Fame.

Doug Frost is the coach of Ian Thorpe, world-record holder in the 200-meter, 400-meter, and 800-meter freestyles. Frost has been bestowed the honor of life member of the Australian Swim Coaches Association (New South Wales) and the Padstow Swim Club, where he served as head coach from 1978 to 1997. He has coached on the Australian national teams at the 1995, 1997, and 1999 Pan-Pacific Games; 1998 World Championships team and Commonwealth Games team  and the Sydney 2000 Olympic team. He has served as director of the Australian Swim Coaches Association since 1989 and the Doug Frost Swim School since 1978. He is currently the elite coach responsible for the national team at Sutherland Leisure Center on the south side of Sydney, Australia.

Five-time US Olympic swim coach **Don Gambril** has long been recognized as one of the nation's finest, coaching such swimmers as Mark Spitz, Jon Olsen, John Naber, Matt Biondi, Nancy Hogshead, and Mary T. Meagher. In all, his own team swimmers have held more than 20 world records and 14 Olympic gold medals and his teams garnered a 351-58 overall combined career mark. During his time as head coach of the University of Alabama (17 years with the men's team and 11 with the women's team), 15 of his men's teams and 5 of his women's teams finished in the top 10 nationally with 114 of his swimmers receiving All-American honors. A three-time Southeastern Conference Men's Coach of the Year, Gambril was inducted into the International Swimming Hall of Fame and given the United States Swimming Award in 1983. He is in nine swimming halls of fame. He was also named ASCA Coach of the Year before retiring after the 1990 season and handing the torch to his first NCAA champion, Jonty Skinner.

Shane Gould held every women's freestyle world record from the 100 to the 1500 meters, as well as in the 200-meter individual medley, in September 1972. At the Munich Olympics that year she won five individual Olympic swimming medals—three gold, one silver, and one bronze. Throughout her swimming career she has held 11 world records, 21 Australian records, and 13 Australian national titles. In 2000 she set five masters records. Shane hosts a coaching information Web site at **www.swimmingcoachonline.com** as well as a personal Web site at **www.shanegould.com.au**.

Dick Jochums has been head coach at Santa Clara Swim Club since 1996. A veteran coach at the collegiate, swim school, and USS club levels, he has held assistant coaching positions at the University of Washington and University of California at Berkeley, and head coaching positions at Cal State Hayward, Concord Swim Club (today the Terrapin Swim Club), Long Beach State, and the University of Arizona. In his 20-year collegiate coaching career, his teams earned 12 top-10 NCAA finishes. His club programs have won 5 national titles and were always in the top 10 with 18 top-5 finishes. At Santa Clara, he has coached the club to three summer long-course men's national championship titles from 1996 through 1998. He has trained a number of Olympians, 12 Olympic medalists, 25 world-record holders, 60 American-record holders, and 7

NCAA-record holders. Dick holds a doctorate of education from the University of California at Berkeley.

As head coach of Stanford University men's swimming since 1979, **Skip Kenney** has led the Cardinal team to seven NCAA titles and has been named NCAA Coach of the Year six times. His team's 1998 NCAA performance ranks as one of the finest in the history of the meet with Stanford having a representative in every individual and relay event championship final. His Stanford athletes have won 60 individual NCAA titles, including 11 by Pablo Morales. Kenney has guided the Cardinal team to 20 consecutive Pac-10 conference titles, breaking John Wooden's record for consecutive Pac-10 championships in any sport. Kenney has been named Pac-10 Coach of the Year 13 times in the last 17 years. He has served as head coach of the United States Olympic men's swimming team (1996) and was an assistant coach at both the 1984 and 1988 Summer Olympics. He has also served as US national team coach at countless other World Championships, Pan-American Games, and Pan-Pacific Championships.

John Leonard has been executive director of American Swim Coaches Association (ASCA) since January 1985. In this position he has overseen the creation of the certification program for coaches, the development of the SwimAmerica Learn to Swim program, the implementation of the first-ever coaches code of ethics, and a membership growth from 1,100 to over 5,200. He serves on the Olympic International Operations Committee and the International Relations Committee at USA Swimming among other ad hoc committees. He is a founding officer of the World Swimming Coaches Association (WSCA) and continues on the board of directors with the WSCA. He travels extensively to swim clinics and meets around the world on behalf of ASCA and is actively involved in reform of Olympic governance and anti-doping activities of both ASCA and WSCA. In 1996 he was given the Athletes Appreciation award from USA Swimming's Athletes Committee for his work in anti-doping. Before assuming the ASCA post in 1985, he was regarded as one of the most successful club coaches in the United States. He has coached more than 120 high school and collegiate All-American swimmers, 2 NCAA Championship divers, dominant state championship teams in New York and Illinois, more than 70 Senior National qualifiers and place winners, 18 USA Olympic Trials qualifiers, and 1 Olympian. He has worked in every Olympic Games since 1984. Leonard has consulted with more than 390 American swimming clubs ranging from national championship teams to developmental teams. He currently owns a club of more than 250 swimmers and 6 coaches in Fort Lauderdale, Florida. In August 2001 he will lead the USA Universiade team into Beijing, China.

Since he became head coach in 1990, **David Marsh** has reestablished the Auburn University swim program as one of the top programs in the country. His men's program has garnered two national titles, five Southeastern Conference titles, and six top-10 NCAA finishes. His women's program has had seven runner-up SEC finishes and twice has finished in the top 10 nationally. Marsh's teams have earned 596 All-America honors by 83 swimmers, along with 42 NCAA individual titles and 127 SEC individual titles. He has coached five Olympic medalists, including gold medalists Scott Tucker and John Hargis. In 42 events, 23 Auburn swimmers have won medals internationally. Marsh is a three-time NCAA Men's Coach of the Year and a multiple SEC Coach of the Year. He served as an assistant coach of the 1996 and 2000 US Olympic and 1999 Pan Pacific teams. A five-time All-American backstroker at Auburn, Marsh was ranked sixth in the world in 1980.

Originally trained as a physical education teacher, **Bruce R. Mason** also holds a degree in mathematics from the University of Sydney and completed his PhD in biomechanics from the University of Oregon in 1980. He served several years as a lecturer in biomechanics at the University of Wollongong before being appointed the head of the biomechanics department at the Australian Institute of Sport in 1982. Since 1994, Bruce has concentrated his professional efforts in providing a biomechanical service to elite swimmers in Australia and has published and presented extensively on the subject of the biomechanics of swimming. He is a director in the International Society of Biomechanics in Sports (ISBS) and at the ISBS 2000 Conference was named the Geoffrey Dyson Memorial Lecturer in recognition of his service of applying biomechanics to performance in elite swimming.

Pablo Morales, 1992 Olympic gold medalist and two-time former world record holder in the 100-meter butterfly, is one of the most highly acclaimed swimmers of the 1980s and 1990s. At the 1984 Olympic games, he earned gold in the 4 × 100 medley relay and two silvers in the 100 meter fly and 200 meter IM. At Stanford University, Morales was the most prolific male swimmer in collegiate history, winning 11 NCAA titles and leading the Cardinals to three straight NCAA

championships. A Stanford Academic All-American in his senior year, Morales holds a law degree from Cornell. He returned to swimming as assistant men's coach at Stanford for the 1997-98 season, was women's head coach at San Jose State University from 1998-2001, and is now women's head coach at University of Nebraska. Morales is a 1998 International Swimming Hall of Fame inductee, was named Swimmer of the Year in 1984, USOC Male Athlete of the Year and Sullivan Award finalist in 1992, and was inducted into the International Swimming Hall of Fame in 1998.

Richard Quick is head women's swim coach at Stanford University and has served as a coach of the US Olympic team for the past five Olympiads. At the 2000 Olympics, Quick led the women's team to 16 medals, seven of which were gold. In his 24 years as a collegiate head coach, Quick has compiled an overall dual meet record of 178-33 (.844), capturing 12 of the last 17 NCAA titles and 17 conference crowns. Since 1988, Quick has guided Stanford to seven NCAA

championships—and 11 of 12 Pac-10 Conference crowns. In the five years under Quick's coaching in which Stanford has not claimed the national title, the Cardinals have recorded either second- or third-place finishes. He has lost only four dual meets while at Stanford, sporting an 89-4 dual record mark (.957) while coaching 73 All-Americans to 611 All-America honors. In addition, Quick has helped develop 35 NCAA champions at Stanford who have captured 50 NCAA individual and 25 relay titles. Along the way, he has picked up five NCAA Coach of the Year honors and three Pac-10 Coach of the Year awards. Quick has continued to coach 1995 Stanford graduate Jenny Thompson, the most decorated female swimmer in the history of the Olympics, who brought home a total of eight gold medals throughout her career. He also coached Dara Torres, who at 34 came out of a seven-year retirement to swim in her record fourth US Olympic team in 2000 and won three individual bronze medals and two relay gold medals.

Former US Olympic coach and ASCA National Coach of the Year **Eddie Reese** has coached at the University of Texas since 1979. Reese's Longhorns captured the 2001 NCAA Championship title—their eighth under Reese's tenure—and have won 7 of the last 13 NCAA Championships and an incredible 22 consecutive conference titles. Reese had five of his swimmers (Ian Crocker, Nate Dusing, Scott Goldblatt, Tommy Hannan, and Jamie Rauch) as well as three former
Longhorns (Josh Davis, Gary Hall Jr., and Neil Walker) swim for the United States at the 2000 Sydney Olympics—accounting for one-fourth of the entire USA swim team. Since his initial campaign at Texas in 1979 when the Longhorns finished second in the Southwest Conference (SWC) and 21st nationally, Reese's teams have won every conference title (22) and have never finished lower than fifth at the national meet. Reese has coached 31 NCAA individual champions, 29 national champion relays, 124 All-Americans, and 18 Olympians, 6 of whom have claimed 18 gold medals in five Olympiads. Reese's ability to technically train his athletes has been a big part of his success, but his unique approach to swimming and training may be his best attribute. As a swimmer in his native Florida, Reese won two state championships in the 200-meter IM. He was also a standout swimmer at the University of Florida where he helped lead the Gators to three SEC titles.

Randy Reese coaches at Circle C Swim Club in Austin, Texas, where he attracts swimmers from all over the world, including 2000 US Olympian Josh Davis. Before coaching at Circle C, Reese was the head coach at the University of Florida for 14 years, where he was known for his innovative theories on training and nutrition as well as his winning record. Under Reese's direction, the men's team at Florida captured 2 NCAA titles, 7 SEC titles, and 51 All-
Americans with almost 200 All-American honors. The women's team earned an NCAA and an AIAW title, 8 SEC titles, and held a 95 percent win record. While at Florida, Reese earned NCAA Women's Coach of the Year twice (1982 and 1988) and NCAA Men's NCAA Coach of the Year twice (1984 and 1985). He also was selected as assistant coach of the 1980, 1984, and 1988 US Olympic teams. Overall, Reese has produced more than 40 Olympic swimmers, including 34 medal winners with 18 gold, 7 silver, and 9 bronze medals among them. Reese serves as chairman of the board of Systems Go International, which markets the sport drink GO!

Bill Rose has coached the Mission Viejo Nadadores Club in California since 1992. A former coach of the Canadian Dolphin Team of Vancouver and women's team at Arizona State University, Rose has served as US national team coach in international competition and as head coach of the Canadian Pan-American women's team, the Canadian World Championship team, and the Canadian Commonwealth team. After a successful 10-year stint as vice president with  Dean Witter and Prudential Bache, Rose returned to his first love, coaching, joining the Nadadores and leading them to seven Junior National Championships. Rose served as head coach for the US team at the 1999 World University Games and the Mexican team at the 2000 Olympics and coached six international 2000 Olympic qualifiers including silver medalist Chad Carvin.

Since becoming head coach at Irvine Nova Swim Club in California in 1990, **David Salo** has seen his team win countless age group, junior national team, and US National Championships. Salo has also coached several individual swimmers to the US national team. He coached 1996 Olympic medalist Amanda Beard and four swimmers to the 2000 Games as well—Aaron Peirsol, Jason Lezak, Gabrielle Rose, and Staciana Stitts—who together brought home five medals. Salo served as assistant coach for the US women's team in the 1999 Pan American Games as well as the 2000 Olympic Games and was recently appointed by USA Swimming to head the men's team at the Goodwill Games in 2001. Salo holds a PhD from the University of Southern California, where he also served as an assistant coach to the legendary Peter Daland in the 1980s.

Dick Shoulberg has been aquatic director and head coach of Germantown Academy, a private instructional day school in the Philadelphia area, since 1969. A self-described grassroots coach, he trains his team primarily in a 6-lane, 25-yard pool. Shoulberg has coached a 400-meter IM swimmer to a berth on the US Olympic team in five of the last six Olympics and has had athletes make the US Olympic team in the 100-meter back-  stroke, 200-meter IM, and the 200-, 400-, and 1500-meter freestyle events. He has coached a high schooler to 20.01 in the 50-meter freestyle and his girls' 400-meter freestyle relay held the national prep record for 11 years. His boys' 400-meter freestyle relay held the national age group record for 17- to 18-year-olds. A high school and prep school swimmer himself, Shoulberg has also coached at the Norristown YWCA, Roxborough YMCA, and the Mermaid Swim Club in Blue Bell, Pennsylvania. He and his wife, Molly, live near Valley Forge, Pennsylvania, and have four children.

Deryk Snelling served as Canadian Olympic coach from 1972 to 1996 and founded the first National Centre for Swimming in Canada. He has coached 60 swimmers to nine Olympic Games from 1964 to 1996. Of these swimmers, 21 have earned Olympic medals, including Mark Tewksbury, who won an Olympic gold medal in the 100-meter backstroke in 1992. Snelling has coached 10 athletes to World Championship medals and 7 to world-record performances. From 1996 to 2000 Snelling served as the first national performance director of swimming for the Amateur Swimming Federation of Great Britain. During his tenure there, Great Britain became known as the fastest-improving swimming nation in the world. At the developmental level Snelling has been an innovator of many Canadian national policies on coaching and has been instrumental in developing the Canadian Coaching Certification Program. He has been a member of the Canadian Swim Coaches Association for more than 20 years.

Four-time Olympic star **Jill Sterkel** has served as head women's coach at the University of Texas since 1991, where she has directed the Longhorns to three top-3 team finishes at the NCAA Championships and four others in the top-10, six conference titles, and two runner-up conference finishes. Sterkel has coached two Olympians, three NCAA individual champions, and numerous All-Americans and has twice been named Big 12 Conference Women's Swimming Coach of the Year. An inductee of the National High School Sports Hall of Fame and Texas Women's Athletics Hall of Honor, Sterkel made her own Olympic swimming debut at the age of 15 at the 1976 Olympic Games and claimed her first gold as a member of the US 4 × 100-meter relay team. Her second gold came in that same event at the 1984 Olympics. The three-time Olympic team captain capped off her incredible career by winning two bronze medals (in the 50-meter free and 4 × 100-meter free relay) at the 1988 Olympics. As a collegiate swimmer, she claimed 16 individual national titles. She was recognized as the nation's College Female Athlete of the Year in 1981 and twice earned honors as the National Women's Swimmer of the Year. Her school record of 53.10 in the 100-yard butterfly, set in 1981, still stands as the best in University of Texas history.

Bill Sweetenham has led the Australian swim team at four Olympic Games and five Commonwealth Games appearances. As the head swimming coach at the Australian Institute of Sport from the late 1980s to 1994, he coached 15 Olympians, with 63 of his swimmers earning spots on the national open team. As the National Youth Coach for Australian Swimming from 1995 to 2000, Sweetenham coached up-and-coming swimmers in preparation for the 2000 Games. Since December 2000 he has served as the national performance director of Great Britain. Through the course of his career he has worked with nine world-record holders in long-course and short-course events. He considers his best coaching effort to date placing nine swimmers on the 1989 Pan-Pacific team with a 100 percent strike rate for improved heats to final performances and 100 percent personal best times. Sweetenham continues to lecture, publish, and conduct clinics worldwide on a variety of coaching and swimming subjects.

John Trembley's accomplishments as coach at the University of Tennessee have included a winning record of 90 percent including an 89 percent victory rate in the tough Southeastern Conference (SEC). His team has secured 11 top-10 national finishes and two SEC team championships, and his entire team has earned Academic All-American status 5 times. He has coached swimmers to 45 SEC individual championships, no less than 77 school records, three American records, and 51 of his swimmers have earned 206 All-American honors. He has coached 14 Olympians, who between them have set a total of six world records and brought home seven Olympic golds. Trembley has been honored for his success as a swimming coach with the prestigious NCAA Silver Anniversary Award, honoring former student-athletes who have distinguished themselves in their chosen fields 25 years after their graduation from college. During his own All-American career at Tennessee, he was a member of nine NCAA championship efforts and set American records in the 50 freestyle and 200 and 400 freestyle relays. He was the first swimmer in the history of the NCAA to win five gold medals at one championship. Trembley was inducted into the Tennessee Swimming Hall of Fame in 1985. He is the founder and president of United Swimming Clinics, a summer swim program that has helped more than 13,000 young athletes worldwide.

Jon Urbanchek has been at the helm of the University of Michigan men's swimming program since 1982 and led the team to an NCAA Championship in 1995. It was Michigan's 11th such title, tying them with Ohio State for the national record. Urbanchek has coached 9 relay NCAA champions and 6 NCAA individual champions, and 25 of his swimmers have made Olympic teams. Urbanchek has been honored as NCAA Coach of the Year, has been twice named Coach of the Year by the American Swim Coaches Association, and has been named Big Ten Coach of the year six times. He has served as head coach for World Championship teams in 1994 and 1998 and as assistant US Olympic coach in 1988, 1992, 1996, and 2000. Jon coaches world-record holders Mike Barrowman (200-meter breaststroke), Tom Dolan (400-meter IM) and Tom Malchow (200-meter butterfly) as well as several world-ranked 200-meter breaststroke swimmers—Eric Wunderlich, Steve West, Scott Werner, and Eric Namesnik. From a 16th-place NCAA finish in 1982, Urbanchek led Michigan to four straight NCAA top-3 finishes from 1993 to '96, the only team to accomplish such a feat in that time span. A member of the team from 1958 to '62, he contributed to three NCAA champion teams and placed second in the 1500-meter freestyle at the 1959 NCAA meet.